Culture and Environment in the Pacific West

## Other Titles in the
## CULTURE AND ENVIRONMENT SERIES

*Series Editor: William L. Lang*

*The Great Northwest: The Search for Regional Identity*, edited by
William G. Robbins
*Planning a New West: The Columbia River Gorge National Scenic Area,* by
Carl Abbott, Sy Adler, and Margery Post Abbott
*The Tillamook: A Created Forest Comes of Age* (second edition), by
Gail Wells

# EMPTY NETS

Indians, Dams, and the Columbia River

Roberta Ulrich

Oregon State University Press
Corvallis

This book is dedicated to the People of the River. They endure.

Front cover photo: U.S. Army Corps of Engineers collection.

The paper in this book meets the guidelines for permanence and durability of the Committee on Production Guidelines for Book Longevity of the Council on Library Resources and the minimum requirements of the American National Standard for Permanence of Paper for Printed Library Materials Z39.48-1984.

**The first edition of this book was cataloged by the Library of Congress as follows:**

Ulrich, Roberta.

Empty nets : Indians, dams, and the Columbia River / Roberta Ulrich.

  p  cm. — (Culture and environment in the Pacific West)

Includes bibliographical references and index.

ISBN 0-87071-469-4 (alk. paper)

1. Indians of North America—Fishing—Law and legislation—Oregon—History. 2. Indians of North America—Fishing—Law and legislation—Washington (State)—History. 3. Indians of North America—Fishing—Oregon—History. 4. Indians of North America—Fishing—Washington (State)—History. 5. Pacific salmon fisheries—Columbia River—History. I. Title. II. Series.

KF8210.N37U45  1999

333.95'656'09797—dc21        99-39467

CIP

**Oregon State University Press**

500 Kerr Administration

Corvallis OR 97331

541-737-3166 •fax 541-737-3170

http://osu.orst.edu/dept/press

# CONTENTS

# SERIES EDITOR'S PREFACE

In this compelling story of the struggle for justice in Native fisheries on the Columbia River, Roberta Ulrich introduces readers to a man who has lived most of his adult life in the shadow of an unfulfilled promise. Federal government officials made the promise during the 1930s, guaranteeing Native fishers access to fishing places—so-called "in-lieu" fishing sites—as partial compensation for those lost to dam construction and inundation by reservoir waters. Nelson Wallulatum stands literally and figuratively as the personification of this powerful Columbia River story. The story starts with the federal government's decision to build behemoth, multi-purpose dams on the river, and it stretches to yesterday's headlines about that unfulfilled promise and the lives it has affected.

A man's tenure on earth is short by any measure of culture in the Pacific Northwest, which reaches back more than ten millennia, but Nelson Wallulatum's life and his quest for fulfillment of the government's promise are emblematic of a history that is larger and longer than his own. It is a history that includes his people's earliest days on the Columbia, when salmon runs dominated the rhythm of life, and that also includes federal court decisions in the 1960s and 1970s that have reaffirmed Indian sovereignty and fishing rights on the river. Treaties written out in 1855 between Native nations and the United States provide the basis for fishing rights, but the story of the in-lieu sites reveals a much more important historical dynamic. As Ulrich's text explains in humanistic detail, bureaucratic inertia and political resistance explain why Indian fishers have "empty nets," why they have been forced to battle again and again for their rights, and why they have endured in their pursuit of acceptable in-lieu fishing sites.

The struggle that Columbia River Indians have waged for legitimate and promised access to fishing sites is about equity, justice, cultural tradition, and environmental policy. *Empty Nets* is as much about human will and faith as it is about politics and environment. Roberta Ulrich personalizes this history to underscore how legal, institutional, and even abstract elements of the fishing-site disputes are inherently embedded in the lives of Indian people on the Columbia. For centuries, they focused their lives on the river and the fish that came home up the Columbia each year. To abandon the river and fishing amounted to an abandonment of tradition and cultural meaning. "We thought that was our country," Ulrich quotes Myra Sohappy about their family's traditional fishing site on the river. Sohappy's sentiment reflected disillusionment about the government's appreciation of their place and legitimate access to the river and about the government's mercurial and disingenuous policies dealing with in-lieu sites. Ulrich documents the reasons for complaint and disbelief that the Sohappy family and many others expressed, and the indefatigable struggle they have waged to regain legitimate rights. "They didn't give up," Nelson Wallulatum said, summing up his family's posture.

The history told in this remarkable book is about an intersection of environmental values and cultural values in the Pacific West. Books in this series dwell on these historical intersections, because they often include very revealing developments, changes in culture, and new directions in history. The complex of events Ulrich describes on the Columbia are fascinating, in part, because they underscore the importance of human advocacy and action. The story of the struggle for justice on the Columbia River for Indian fishers reminds us that changes to the environment usually mean changes in human culture and that the consequences have repercussions well beyond the limits set by political institutions and officials. Nelson Wallulatum's viewpoint, as Ulrich makes clear, stands as an antidote to late twentieth-century cynicism about the ability of people to defend their environment, while it is also a cautionary tale about the detrimental effects of government intransigence. There are many messages in this book, but surely one of the most powerful conveys the strength, commitment, and passion Native people have for their place and rights on the Columbia River.

*William L. Lang*

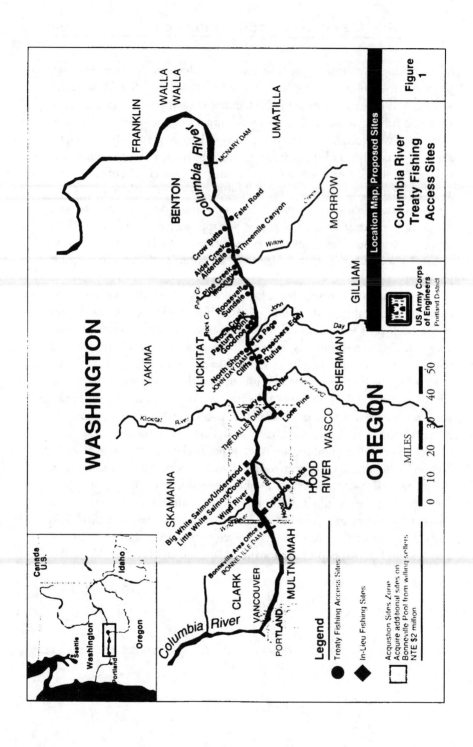

Legend

Treaty Fishing Access Sites:

In-Lieu Fishing Sites:

Acquistion Sites Zone
Acquire additional sites on
Bonneville Pool from willing sellers,
NTE $2 million

Location Map, Proposed Sites

Columbia River
Treaty Fishing
Access Sites

US Army Corps
of Engineers
Portland District

Figure
1

# INTRODUCTION

*Justice delayed is justice denied.*

—Attributed to British Prime Minister
William Ewart Gladstone

The issue of the in-lieu sites first caught my attention sometime in the 1970s. At the time, the Bureau of Indian Affairs was making one of its periodic threats to remove a few Indians living on sites fifty and ninety miles east of Portland. These sites were tiny pieces of land on the shore of the Columbia River. The Indians in question had taken up full-time residence on the scraggly land bits. BIA officials argued that the sites were supposed to be used only for fishing and the Indians could camp there only during very limited fishing seasons. The Indians argued that their treaties with the United States protected their right to fish for family food at any time, and that right carried with it the right to stay at the places where they fished and processed their catch.

In the course of writing about the eviction efforts for United Press International, I learned that the government had promised the sites to the Indians to replace more than two dozen traditional sites flooded when Bonneville Dam was built. Bonneville was built in the 1930s. The government, in the form of the Army Corps of Engineers, made its promise of six sites totaling four hundred acres in 1939. At the time I stumbled across the matter, nearly forty years had gone by. The Corps then had furnished five sites totaling just over forty acres—one-tenth the promised area—and apparently had no intention of doing anything more. I was appalled that the federal government would take so long to fulfill what appeared to be a fairly straightforward promise.

*Chief Nelson Wallulatum of the Wasco, one of the three Confederated Tribes of the Warm Springs Reservation. He is the only known person who was there when the dam started and remains involved in the in-lieu sites. Photo by John R. Lynch.*

Over the next almost twenty years, as I moved from UPI to newspapers, I occasionally encountered the issue of the replacement—or in-lieu—sites. In 1988 Congress passed legislation to provide the Indians more sites up to the promised four hundred acres. But by the time I retired in 1996 only one of the new sites was close to being usable. Sixty years had passed since the original sites disappeared into the dam pool and nearly that many since the government promised to make restitution. The issue haunted me.

In my last years as a reporter I wrote about Native American issues and came to know people of families dispossessed from those fishing sites. They had lost much, been promised moderate recompense and had received little. Yet I found them more determined than bitter, holding to their traditions and beliefs and possessed of remarkable humor. I also traveled the Columbia Gorge and saw the federal and state parks, the launching sites for sports fishing boats, the inlets landscaped for sailboarders. The unfairness of a promise unfulfilled while the land went to other uses is on display every day.

How could a nation that claims to be honorable ignore so long an acknowledged promise? The sites became a metaphor for this country's treatment of its native people. The delay in replacing the sites carries all the elements of cultural arrogance, hostility and, at bottom, indifference that has marked so much of white Americans' dealings with those who were here first. This then is a story about a promise and why it was not fulfilled. It is a story of shifting federal policies about Indians. It is a story of white society's urge to develop resources no matter the cost. It is a story of prejudice and politics. Above all, it is a story of a people's persistence.

Two notes about the text: The treaty of 1855 between the United States and fourteen tribes and bands in Eastern Washington, was with the Yakama Nation. The spelling soon changed to Yakima, and the settlers attached that spelling to a river, city and county. In 1992, the Yakama Nation decided to return to the original spelling. I have adopted that use throughout, except for direct quotation of documents that use the "i" spelling. The federal agency most responsible for dealing with Indian tribes has had a number of titles in the past century. For clarity, I have used the current title, Bureau of Indian Affairs.

# 1

## THE DAM

*For I say to you that our health is from the fish; our
strength is from the fish; our very life is from the fish.*

—Yakama Indian fisherman George Meninock to
Washington State Supreme Court 1921

Nelson Wallulatum was there at the beginning of the struggle. The year was 1934, and Nelson was eight years old, a lively child already learning his tribe's centuries-old fishing ways. His grandmother took him to the bank of the Columbia River near the family's south shore fishing camp, and pointed across to the north shore, another traditional fishing site. White men were working there. They were building a dam, his grandmother said. It would stop the flow of the Columbia and maybe the salmon too. For the people of Nelson's Wasco Indian Tribe that was a threat to their livelihood and their way of life. Even an eight-year-old could sense the danger.

Nelson lived with his grandmother, Susan Palmer, moving with the seasons from the Warm Springs Indian Reservation in Central Oregon to the shore of the Columbia River and back again. Already he was joining the men as they dipped their nets into the swirling Columbia and pulled out salmon weighing up to a hundred pounds apiece. To Nelson, learning to fish was like learning to speak his tribe's Wasco language. It was second nature. He learned to make nets and to mend nets, how to bend wood from river-bank trees into a strong wooden hoop to hold his net. As soon as a boy could understand the safety rules he was allowed to go with the men, who stood on rocks or wooden platforms jutting over the turbulent river, waiting for fish fighting their way upstream. He learned to imitate the way the men held their long-handled dip nets and the way they pulled them quickly from the water and flipped the shimmering fish onto the rocks.

If he caught a salmon, Nelson might carry it up the bank to his grandmother. She and the other women hung the fish to dry or pounded them into a meal to be mixed with berries and dried deer or elk meat for winter food. More often, like the men, he left the hauling to the women and girls. That was women's work. The men needed to stay on the platforms, catching as many fish as they could to make sure their families did not go hungry through the long winters on the cold, dry reservation. Winter was always on their minds. The Wasco men caught more salmon than their families could eat, then traded the surplus for other foods that also made up their traditional diet—elk and deer meat, roots and berries. They traded for other things too, clothing and baskets. By the time Nelson was growing up, in the 1930s, they also sold a few fish for money to buy things they had adopted from white men's society—sugar, coffee, salt, wood to build their traditional plank houses. Indian children had little time to play during fishing season, except perhaps a few foot races at the end of a long day. Winter, back at Warm Springs, was the time for stories and dancing and play.

There was little thought then that the fishermen would catch too many Columbia River salmon. Indians had fed themselves for centuries without depleting the fish runs. When white men first arrived on the Columbia River, they described salmon so numerous a person could walk across the river on their wriggling backs. In the 1930s, after decades of whites' use of fish wheels, fish traps, gill nets and ocean purse seines, the number of salmon in the Columbia had dropped. But there still seemed to be plenty for everyone. Some Indians lived along the river and fished all year around. Others, like Nelson's Wasco family, spent winters at Warm Springs or on the Yakama Reservation in Washington state. In the spring, the Warm Springs Wasco took a circuitous one hundred-mile route from the reservation's dry high prairie to the forested banks of the Columbia. Traveling in a caravan of cars, they went by way of Estacada, Oregon, on the western foothills of the Cascades, stopped two or three weeks to fish along the Willamette River, then moved up the Columbia. Nelson Wallulatum's family built its summer base at Eagle Creek, near the present site of Bonneville Dam. They stayed on the river, following the various runs upstream into the fall until the fish had passed or they had enough to last until the next April's first salmon ceremony.

Salmon were the center of life for the Wasco tribe and for the other Indians along the river. More than food, the fish were vital to the Indians' religion, nourishment for the spirit as well as the body. So important were the fish that in three 1855 treaties tribes gave up an area larger than Tennessee in exchange for a guarantee that they could forever fish, hunt, and gather roots and berries in their usual and accustomed places. They were about to lose more than two dozen of those usual and accustomed fishing places as Bonneville Dam rose across the narrow tumultuous Cascades of the Columbia forty miles east of Portland, Oregon. The Army Corps of Engineers, builder of the dam, agreed that the Indians were entitled to compensation for the lost sites. It said it would replace them with six new sites totaling four hundred acres along the lake behind the dam. That was in 1939.

Nelson Wallulatum is a tribal elder now, for forty years the elected chief of the Wasco Tribe. He stands erect, an imposing figure in fringed and beaded buckskin and an eagle feather headdress that sweeps to the floor. Dignity adds inches to his 5-feet-6 height. His gray/black hair falls straight to his shoulders. His stern visage seems chiseled from Columbia Gorge basalt. Away from solemn ceremonies, his deeply-lined face lights with a charming smile. His hazel eyes twinkle. As fisherman, tribal councilman and chief, he has spent much of his adult life trying to push the Army into fulfilling its 1939 promise. He hopes now to see it done by 2004—seventy years after his first view of the men at work.

Chief Wallulatum is only one among countless tribal leaders and fishing people from the river and from the Umatilla, Warm Springs and Yakama reservations who have spent six decades prodding the government to make good on its word. Fifty years after the promise was made, the Army had supplied five sites totaling forty acres, one-tenth the promised land. Ten years later the Army had added a few more small sites but was still working on its reduced goal of something over three hundred acres. To the Indians, the issue always has been simple: The government destroyed their fishing sites. It owed them replacements. To the government, there was always something else: War. Appropriations. Disputes over locations. Procedures. Changing federal policies. More pressing issues, such as recreational parks.

Through all the years, the Indians had other battles to fight as well, both in court and on the river. Oregon, Washington, and sometimes the federal government tried continuously to restrict Indian fishing. Railroads and other property owners barred them from reaching their treaty-guaranteed fishing grounds. White fishermen, barges and, later, sailboarders, destroyed or tangled their fishing gear. To many Indians, the delay in providing the fishing sites is part of a 150-year effort to get them off the river and leave the salmon to white fishermen. If the government has not broken the 1855 treaties, it has bent them severely. Thousands of Indian people stretching over four generations saw their lives disrupted by the government's failure to keep its promise. So long has the struggle continued that only the elders remember its beginning, and they only dimly from their childhoods. But they carried on the battle their parents began, and their children and grandchildren persist. This is their story.

When the Indians tell their history, they begin, "From time immemorial . . . " It is a fitting phrase. Archaeologists have found evidence of riverbank settlements along the Columbia River dating back 10,000 years or more. Then, as now, fish were central to the peoples' lives. And the Columbia, that mightiest of Western rivers, was their lifeline. The Indians who live along the river call themselves the "People of the Salmon." Salmon are anadromous fish: that is, they hatch in the upper reaches of streams, swim to the ocean, spend several years there, then swim back to their birthplace to spawn and die.

Abundant and nutritious, salmon provided the Indians with a comfortable livelihood, as food and as a commodity to sell or trade. Although their diet included deer, elk, sometimes bear and other animal meats along with roots and berries, salmon was part of every day's fare—fresh, smoked, dried or pounded into a mixture with meat and berries called pemmican. Some middle-aged Indians remember when they ate salmon at every meal, and say they never grew tired of it. Even now, the Yakama, Warm Springs, Umatilla and Nez Perce people eat nine times as much fish as the national average. More important, salmon are a key element of the native religion, the food given by the Creator to sustain the people. They honor the fish as they take them from the river, and as they consume them. For traditional people, religion and life cannot be separated; religion is the thread that weaves through every activity. The Salmon People regulated their lives to the upstream migration of the various species. Their year began with a "first salmon ceremony" welcoming the fish's return and thanking the Creator for sending him. Salmon were an integral part of every religious ceremony, from announcing a baby's name to bidding the dead farewell. Few lives are regulated by the salmon runs now, but the ceremonies and the salmon remain a vital part of tribal life. First salmon ceremonies still mark the spring chinook's return. Continuing their tradition of hospitality, the Indian people of Celilo still invite the public to share their fish, although sometimes in recent years the fishermen have been hard pressed to catch enough to go around. Salmon feasts still accompany name-givings, weekly Washat religious services, funerals and ceremonies marking special events. The fishing people's struggle for the in-lieu sites was, and remains, a battle for their culture and dignity more than a battle for food and livelihood. For them the separation from the activity of fishing, as well as from the fish, was a major disruption of their lives. They have found the indifference of bureaucracy incomprehensible.

The Columbia, scene of the Indians' six-decade struggle, makes a westward turn twenty miles south of its junction with the Snake River, then forms three hundred miles of Oregon-Washington border to the Pacific Ocean. Before dams turned it into a series of lakes, the Columbia was a quarter-mile to half-mile-wide stream as it cut through layers of volcanic flows in the dry grasslands of Eastern Oregon and Washington. As the river flowed westward, the terrain on either side, ever rugged, changed from dry brush-covered cliffs a few hundred feet high to gray basalt escarpments towering five thousand feet above the river into dense forests. The river's battle to cut its way through the mountains to the sea can be read in the cliffs' rock layers. At Celilo, The Dalles and the Cascades the rock forced the river into a channel a third its size elsewhere, creating falls and rapids that challenged explorers, traders and settlers. Before the white man came, the river and its banks provided nearly everything the Indians needed— fish, game, edible and medicinal plants, and wood for their plank houses.

When explorers Lewis and Clark floated down the river through the breach in the Cascade range in 1805, they found the narrow shelves of land along the shore dotted with settlements. The people were hospitable fishers and traders, although the captains complained they were inclined to filch small items from the visitors. The two U.S. Army captains and their party were the first whites through the Columbia Gorge, but articles of their culture had preceded them. In Indian villages they noted brass teakettles, a sailor's jacket, a British musket, an imposing sword, and quantities of glass beads. The river people had obtained the items in trade with coastal tribes, who had dealt with vessels along the coast. Another aspect of European/American civilization also had preceded the Corps of Discovery: disease. A smallpox epidemic wiped out a large portion of the tribes around the mouth of the Columbia in the late 1700s. The effects filtered up the river, although inland there were fewer deaths.

After Lewis and Clark, the fur traders were not long in coming. The traders and later settlers gave the river Indians something of a bad reputation. Whites resented the Cascade people's control of the portage around the rapids. The Cascades were one of the Indians' major fishing grounds, and a barrier to river transportation between Fort Vancouver and inland trading posts. The Indians by all accounts did just what the later white controllers of the portage did. They protected their monopoly on the paths around the rapids and charged hefty fees to use them.

In the early 1830s, just as white settlers began venturing into the Oregon country, another epidemic, probably malaria, swept up the river as far east as present-day The Dalles, Oregon. Tribes between present-day Longview, Washington, and the Cascades lost as many as 90 percent of their people. Tribes farther up river, including the Wasco and Klickitats, were less affected, but still debilitated by four years of outbreaks.

The newcomers, whom the Indians soon called "the greedy ones," found the river people— except at the Cascades—generally helpful and friendly. Not until the 1850s, when whites began trying to push the Indians away from their beloved river, were there more than minor hostilities. By then, General Isaac I. Stevens had arrived in the Northwest as governor of the new Washington Territory, superintendent of Indian affairs for the territory, and mapper of a transcontinental railroad route. His major mission was to compress the Indians onto as little land as possible, preferably in areas not coveted by whites, to open the way for settlement. In the summer of 1855, he and Gen. Joel Palmer, Superintendent of Indian Affairs for the Oregon Territory, signed three treaties with tribes east of Fort Vancouver—the Yakama; the Walla Walla, Cayuse etc.; and the Nez Perce. Palmer negotiated a fourth treaty with the Tribes of Middle Oregon. In making the treaties, the agents lumped together people of varied tribes and bands who had ranged over vast territories from the Cascades to the foothills of the Rockies. Most of those forced to share new, limited areas on reservations had previously been independent of one another; some had been downright hostile. This was especially true of the Yakama, which included fourteen named tribes and bands with dozens of semi-autonomous family units. The Indian agents split other tribes, such as the Wasco, assigning some members to Yakama, some to Warm Springs. Palmer reported that one group of families who lived sometimes on the north bank and sometimes on the south bank between present day Hood River and the Cascades refused to budge from the river. Palmer called on the chief of the band, Mal-La-Chein, personally but "he declined signing the treaty, alleging as a reason that his people could not subsist away from the Columbia River." Palmer described their riverside territory as valueless and predicted Mal-La-Chein's people eventually would ask to be included in the treaty.

When the rest of the Indians moved to the reservations far from the Columbia, many of the river people, like Mal-La-Chein's, remained. Late in the century, there was still some land the whites had not wanted. The government opened it to Indians through the Indian Homestead Act and, mostly, by issuing allotments of up to 160 acres to tribal members. In the last decade of the 1800s and first decade of the 1900s more than two hundred Indians obtained land allotments or homesteads within six miles of the river. Most lay between Vancouver and what is now Tri-Cities on the Washington side, and between Cascade Locks and the John Day River on the Oregon side.

Beginning in 1840 the natives had competition for the fishery from the Hudson's Bay Company, which sent its fishermen to the Cascades—Chief Wallulatum's family fishing ground. By 1870, commercial fishing and canning the catch were major industries. The growing white population in the region saw the Columbia River as its major highway and the Cascades as a major obstacle. White entrepreneurs built portage roads around the rapids in the 1850s and took over the disease-devastated Cascade Indians' role as toll takers and transporters. The Army built a military road in 1855. The Corps of Engineers made its first permanent alteration of the Columbia in 1868, blasting out rocks that impeded navigation near the mouth of the John Day River 115 miles east of Portland. The government began work on a canal around the Cascades in 1877 and finally finished it in 1896. By that time, the Union Pacific's link to the transcontinental railroad was roaring along the south bank to Portland. The Spokane, Portland and Seattle finished laying tracks along the north bank in 1908. Despite the railroads, the government completed The Dalles-Celilo Canal around the upriver rapids in 1915. By then Oregon was building the Columbia Gorge Scenic Highway, and within a few years paved roads paralleled the river along both banks. Each piece of construction changed the shore. Blasting and digging and moving earth covered fishing rocks, filled little bays, and altered currents. The railroads alone destroyed a hundred fishing sites, most of them on the

Washington side, according to William Yallup Sr., the Yakama tribal chairman, who comes from a river family. The Indians adapted and went on fishing.

In the 1930s, when the federal government embarked on its Columbia River dam building program, many river people were still following their ancient patterns of life based on the migrations of the fish and eels and the ripening of berries. Some were in villages where Lewis and Clark had sighted their ancestors—Celilo, Spearfish, Sk'in and Alderdale, and the mouths of the Wind, White Salmon and Little White Salmon rivers. Others had homes among the whites in the small towns on both sides of the river. Some retained their families' land allotments. Still others spent winters in tepees or wooden houses in sheltered spots near the river or returned to the reservations. Dorothy Simtustus, a granddaughter of Celilo Chief Tommy Thompson, now lives on the Warm Springs Reservation. She remembers the way her family combined traditional tule mats with canvas to construct a winter tepee when she was a small child in the 1930s. "It was made of tule mats, a layer of canvas between layers of tule mats, then wet mud, then another canvas over that to hold it all together, then over that tule mats. It was cold outside but that kept us warm."

From spring to fall, hundreds of people camped on the river bank to fish and made seasonal excursions into the hills to gather roots and huckleberries. Sale of a few fish brought small amounts of cash to buy what they could not get by trading. Both the river people and the tribes on the reservations retained their traditional organizations, small groups led by headmen, larger groups led by chiefs, and decisions made by consensus. Many spoke no English. Although Indians formally became U.S. citizens in 1924, the Bureau of Indian Affairs still considered them its wards and purported to speak for them in most dealings with non-Indian society. No formal tribal governments existed until the mid-1930s after Congress passed the Indian Reorganization Act. The three tribes of the Warm Springs Reservation quickly took advantage of the act, creating a tribal council to manage reservation affairs. The Yakama tribes had a tribal council then, but it dealt only with cultural issues such as pow wows and ceremonies, not business or government. Those tribes did not organize a formal government until 1944. The Umatilla tribes continued their chiefs and headman system until creating a business committee also in the 1940s. Even then, tribes had little or no money, no attorneys of their own, and no experts outside the government to advise them. But they had, in at least five lawsuits from

1888 to 1942, asserted the power of their treaties to assure their right to fish and their right of access to fishing grounds.

During the 1930s—and later—the government, in its efforts to strip away Indian culture, was still abruptly taking Indian children from their families and sending them to Indian boarding schools. Their long hair was cut, their traditional clothing and ornaments were taken from them and they were beaten for speaking their native language. Nathan Jim Sr. of Warm Springs, born in 1937, remembers vividly the day two Indian policemen tossed him and three friends onto the back of a fish truck at Celilo Village. The boys had never been more than a quarter of a mile from the village. "We thought we were going for a ride." Instead "We wound up at Warm Springs boarding school." A terrified five-year-old, he spoke no English and had no idea what was happening to him.

> I saw all my relations there wearing gray and blue coveralls, their hair cut. I had braids and overalls.
>
> They gave me a shower, took off my clothes and moccasins and threw them away. They gave me some round-toed shoes with paper soles. I couldn't wear them. They were teaching us to march. We couldn't figure out why. We'd march outside, salute the flag. I was punished for turning my hand over—a five-year-old. I'd end up kneeling on the hard floor for an hour.

Jim demonstrated the conventional flag salute with the palm held upward; the Indians' traditional arm-extended gesture is with palm down.

Jim spent a lot of time on his knees.

> The way we were raised we spoke no English. Every time I spoke I ended up in the hallway on my knees. Every time I spoke in class I got hit with a ruler—"bad Indian!" Imagine a five-year-old there with those people. I'd give them hell in Indian. They'd make me kneel on the floor with my head against the wall. I don't understand the rules and regulations. Every time I'm myself—an Indian—I got punished—slapped hands, march. We had to go to white man's church three times on Sunday.

Jim tells his story with ironic humor. But there is a tinge of bitterness as he describes his school days.

> We were prisoners of war. The Warm Springs tribe helped the U.S. government against the Snake River Indians. They helped get rid of

Paulina and captured Captain Jack [two of the last Indian leaders resisting white encroachment in Oregon]. But we were treated like prisoners. They say you can control the parents if you take the kids away. Save the man—kill the Indian. Make them forget their culture. Save the devils, the heathens. Teach them Christianity . . . . I did not learn a darn thing about my own people. Indians were a bad thing.

The teacher was Mrs. Strauss. She reminded me of a great horned owl, made me feel like a mouse . . . . I had a helluva time learning English. They started using the edge of the ruler. That hurt. I quit talking. They punished me for that too.

The result was that "now I hardly speak my language. I have that feeling in my hand" when I try.

He survived the boarding school, graduated from high school in nearby Madras and learned the printing trade. He worked for years on a weekly newspaper. As a member of his tribes' fish committee, he has long been involved in prodding the Corps of Engineers to get on with the fishing sites. Jim also is the Warm Springs' premier master of ceremonies, noted for his humor and way with words as he presides over powwows and dances.

Nathan Jim's memory is a common one among Northwest Indians fifty and older. Russell Jim, now program manager for environmental and waste management for the Yakama Nation, was sent off to Chemawa Indian School at Salem, Oregon, when he was five. When he returned to Central Washington for the summer, he spilled out his anguish to an aunt. The aunt told his father the boy was staying home—if the father did not agree, the aunt would take Russell into the hills to live. Jim's father relented, but enrolling him in public school in nearby Toppenish was not easy. Jim's explanation: "They didn't want Indians." His father was a World War I veteran, however, and got help from the American Legion and Veterans of Foreign Wars to get Russell enrolled. He considers himself lucky because he remained close to home, where he could go to the longhouse, the center of tribal religion, and learn the Yakama language from his aunt and grandparents. In his view, that is exactly what the government was trying to avoid by removing children from the reservations. "We were sent to boarding school to break our cultural lifeline. It was a successful program." But not totally. Like many of his generation who survived the boarding school experience, Jim made the effort to learn his language and keep tribal customs alive. Suave, and given to quoting social critic Noam Chomsky, Jim is considered a hero by many neighboring non-Indians, as well as tribal members, for leading a successful battle against dumping the nation's nuclear waste at nearby Hanford.

Russell Jim's sister, Mamie Smith, was not rescued from Chemawa. She recalls a matron with "hands like baseball mitts" who used them to "beat the language out of me." When that failed, Mamie was sent to the office, where she got five hits with a paddle for saying "good morning" in Indian. She recalls making pacts with fellow students not to cry because they knew their stoicism angered the matron. Smith volunteers at the Yakama Nation Museum helping to preserve the heritage the matron tried—and failed—to beat out of her.

By the 1930s the Columbia had been a river of contention for decades. A multimillion dollar commercial fishing industry extended 190 miles from the river's mouth to the Deschutes River, and Indians fished for their livelihood from Portland suburbs to the Canadian border. The states, commercial fishers, and private property owners continually tried to limit the Indians' fishing. But tribal fishers persisted.

In the early years of the twentieth century, a man named Winans fenced the Indians off his property, which contained one of their usual and accustomed fishing places on the river's Washington bank. The Yakama pushed the government to sue on their behalf. In 1905, the U.S. Supreme Court ruled that Winans could not bar the Indians from their traditional fishing grounds although Winans claimed exclusive fishing rights for the fish wheel he had erected in the water just offshore from his land. Justice Joseph McKenna wrote in the court's majority opinion, "[T]he treaty was not a grant of rights to the Indians, but a grant of rights from them—a reservation of those not granted." The treaty made before Washington became a state remained binding on the state and its citizens. United States treaties with Indian tribes, like those with foreign nations, are part of the "supreme law of the land" along with the Constitution and the Supreme Court's interpretations. The treaties supersede state law. The Supreme Court recognizes tribes and tribal governments as limited self-governing sovereign entities, in many respects like states. Through diligent recourse to the courts, tribes have used their treaties to retain their identity and enforce the rights the federal government guaranteed in exchange for millions of acres of land. A few years after the Winans ruling, in 1918, the litigious Yakama were back before the Supreme Court, again with the government suing on their behalf and arguing the same issue on the Oregon side of the Columbia.

This time, the Seufert Brothers Co., the major upriver fish packing firm, tried to keep the Yakama off the river bank by claiming they had no rights on the south shore. Justice John H. Clarke, noting that Indians from all the tribes had fished on both sides of the river when the treaties were signed, wrote that the Winans decision applied. The Indians went back to their fishing sites.

Into this world where Indian lives were regulated by the seasons and by customs that extend beyond memory came Bonneville Dam. It disrupted life on the lower river as Grand Coulee Dam did for other tribes on the upper river at the same time. Bonneville was the second to be finished of the dams that turned the Columbia into a series of lakes. The Chelan County Public Utility District finished its run-of-the-river Rock Island Dam in 1933 as work was getting under way on the far more massive Bonneville. Behind Bonneville the river would rise sixty feet to spread over the narrow strip of lowland shrubs and basalt between the old river bank and the high cliffs of the Columbia Gorge. The dam would change the Columbia into a mile-wide stream flowing sluggishly, giving little hint of those eddies, rapids and whirlpools where Indian fishermen had caught their family's food since time immemorial.

Franklin D. Roosevelt ordered work started on Bonneville just weeks after he was inaugurated as President in March 1933. The dam was part of the new President's effort to fight the Depression, and most non-Indian Northwesterners cheered it as a provider of jobs and a spur to industrialize the sparsely populated region. Only the Indians, commercial fishermen, and the Oregon Fish Commission were skeptical. The commission demanded expanded provisions for fish passage through the dam. Three months after preliminary work began, Chief Tommy Thompson of the fishing village of Celilo called on U.S. Attorney Carl C. Donaugh in Portland to complain that the dam would submerge the Indians' long-established fishing grounds and interfere with the salmon migration. Thompson was right, although not immediately. It was two decades later that another dam drowned Thompson's fishing site at Celilo Falls ten miles upriver from the eastern end of the Bonneville pool. It was more than three decades before salmon numbers plunged low enough to threaten an end to fishing. Other Indians also voiced their objections to the dam in the beginning. Delbert Frank Sr., a longtime Warm Springs fish committee member who grew up on the river, remembers that Indians were concerned about the dam from the first day they heard of it. That was in 1930 when Frank had just started school and the dam was still just an idea. "Four or five carloads of old people went down" to the Bonneville site. "There were an old Model T and an Oakland pickup." Frank went along—his father was part of the group. "There was nothing there. There was swift water. They met with some people not knowing what the engineers had in mind . . . . My people were immediately opposed to such an idea." The Indians carried their objections to Congress a couple of times to no avail. Indians on the Washington side of the river also fought against the dam until the last minute. Frederick Ike Sr., a Yakama tribal councilman who grew up along the river, is too young to remember construction of the dam, but he is well versed in family and tribal history of the battle. "Due to the power of Congress to condemn land it was kind of hopeless. The only thing they could fight for was compensation and recognition of their rights." Ike is a substantial man whose coal-black hair and unlined face belie his sixty-three years. Hereditary chief of the Klickitats, one of the river tribes, he carries on the fight that began when he was a toddler.

The Corps of Engineers, with a strong nudge from Congress, heeded the Fish Commission's plea, and made plans to install fish ladders and elevators that eventually cost nearly $7 million. But it ignored the Indian fishing sites until 1937. One Bureau of Indian Affairs official, Frank B. Lenzie, the range supervisor in Spokane, Washington, wrote to the Indian Commissioner in April of 1934 urging him to look out for the Indians' interest. But Lenzie's concern was that the dam would cut off the salmon runs—and the Indians' income. The commercial fishing interests, including both riverbank canneries and fishermen, stirred up what Lenzie called "considerable agitation because of the apparently well-grounded fear that their industry is in a fair way to be pretty well wiped out." Contrary to their usual conflict, Lenzie said the Indians and the commercial fishermen in this case had identical interests. Loss of the fish runs would hurt Indians along the entire length of the stream. However, Lenzie's letter discussed only the fishing rights at Celilo and made no mention of the potential loss of sites on the Bonneville pool.

Before they could address the site issue, the Indians had to deal with another loss. The north anchor of Bonneville Dam had been the village of Chief Banaha until some white settlers filed a claim on it while the Indians were away visiting. Opposite the village was Bradford Island, an ancient Indian burial ground that became the dam's central anchor. Excavation for the dam turned up hundreds of bones. The Corps of Engineers gathered them, along with the baskets, jewelry and other burial items. In a ceremony arranged by the Corps May 28, 1936, the remains dug from the island were re-buried in a single grave in a cemetery on the north shore five miles east of the dam. Seventy-nine-year-old Isabella Underwood, a granddaughter of Chief Banaha and sister-in-law of the white founder of the town of Underwood, unveiled a monument inscribed: Ankutty Tillikum Musem— Here Sleep the Ancient People. Richard J. Grace, a civilian engineer for the Army who arranged the ceremony, reported to his boss, Lt. Col. C. F. Williams, that the day went very well despite an awkward start. Grace and the Army's resident engineer at Bonneville, Capt. Joseph Gorlinski, finished their speeches before they discovered that most of the older Indians hadn't understood a word. After that, an interpreter translated the English speakers for the Indians and the Indian speakers for the whites in the crowd of three hundred. Grace said the Indian speeches were "friendly and appreciative of the honor done their dead, except for occasional references to intrusion on the reservations and a few of apprehension as to what was going to happen to the Columbia River."

The site issue did not come up for another year, little more than six months before the water was to begin rising behind the dam. On April 19, 1937, Maj. Omar L. Babcock, the superintendent of the Umatilla Indian Agency, wrote a letter to the commissioner of Indian affairs pointing out that closing the gates on Bonneville Dam would flood many of the Indians' fishing places guaranteed in their treaties. He suggested the Indians might have a claim to compensation. The Corps had dealt with compensation for some property losses. It purchased "flowage easements" over land where the pool would rise. The easements, cheaper than buying the land, did not give the Army title to the submerged property but provided the right to cover it with water. When property owners did not agree to the easements, the Army resorted to condemnation and made court-determined payments. The Corps also moved a Washington state highway and a railroad on each side of the river to higher ground at a cost of $5 million. That work was done in two years. The Corps took that long just to agree to replace some of the flooded Indian fishing sites. At that point, the fishing sites involved no money.

Babcock's letter probably was prompted by tribal members who fished in what would become the Bonneville pool. Although the Umatilla Reservation—home to the Walla Walla, Cayuse and Umatilla tribes—is 175 miles east of the dam, tribal members fished as far downstream as

Cascade Locks five miles above the damsite. Tribal members remember Babcock most for his passion for golf and practicing chip shots on the agency lawn. He showed little interest in fishing issues, but gave tribal members strong support for their hunting rights. Elders recalled him as a by-the-book administrator who would have responded to violation of the tribes' treaty. Whatever prompted Babcock's letter, it created a stir in the Washington bureaucracy.

The Interior Department's acting solicitor, Frederic L. Kirgis, turned out a legal analysis of the problem in the bureaucratically rapid time of less than two months. He hedged his report to Commissioner John Collier with a lengthy legal discussion touching on fishing as a property right, whether navigation trumps treaties and whether the Indians' fishing rights would apply at new, still dry places. His conclusion: "... the Indians have a possible claim for compensation for the destruction of fishing places by the Bonneville Dam." Ordinarily, he said, the government would not have to compensate the Indians because the dam was being built to aid navigation. But the Supreme Court had ruled that Indians' treaty rights were "on a different plane from other private property rights." Kirgis advised the Commissioner there was "sufficient reasonable ground for a claim as to make it imperative to protect the interests of the Indians in all possible ways." He suggested that the Indian bureau negotiate a settlement with the Public Works Administration and the Corps. PWA, an agency of Roosevelt's New Deal, was the source of initial funding for construction of Bonneville Dam. The Corps was then completing the construction under appropriations specifically directed to the dam. Kirgis offered two conditions for any settlement: Compensation should go to the tribes, not individual fishermen, and "There is no possibility of transferring by any action of the Federal Government the special fishing privileges of the Indians from the existing places covered by the treaty to new areas." Only the states could now grant new fishing rights. He accurately considered it unlikely either Oregon or Washington would be interested in granting fishing privileges to Indians. However, he suggested that the Indians might find fishing spots elsewhere on the river and that should be a factor in determining damages from the loss of the traditional sites. Although Kirgis referred consistently to the Indians' fishing rights as a "privilege," he also quoted the Supreme Court's 1905 Winans ruling directly contradicting that view. Fishing was not a right granted by the government, the court said, but an aboriginal right, which the Indians specifically retained in their treaties. The treaties were like land owners' sale of property while retaining the right to develop minerals, such as oil, found on the property. The distinction has been vital in the evolving legal interpretation of Indian treaty rights.

Kirgis said his opinion, although written to respond to the query on behalf of the Umatilla Reservation Indians, also might apply to the Yakama and Nez Perce. (The Nez Perce, located far to the east on the Clearwater River at Lapwai, Idaho, never made a claim for loss of Bonneville pool sites, but twenty years later shared in compensation for loss of the river's major fishery, Celilo Falls.) Kirgis did not include the Indians assigned to the Warm Springs Reservation. In explaining the omission, he referred to an issue that has haunted the Warm Springs people through this and a dozen other issues—one of the most blatant frauds perpetrated upon Indian people in the Northwest.

As Kirgis noted, the United States in 1865 paid the Warm Springs $3,500 to relinquish their fishing rights. But almost as soon as it had done so, the government itself recognized that the treaty, even if legal, was an obvious fraud. Agencies regularly ignored the document, according to Owen M. Panner, who was the Warm Springs' attorney for twenty-five years before becoming a federal District Court judge in 1980. Panner describes how an unscrupulous agent named J. Perit Huntington defrauded both the Indians and the government: Huntington was the Bureau of Indian Affairs superintendent at the Warm Springs Reservation. Like most Indian agents of the time, he was annoyed because so many of his charges left for months at a time to fish instead of tending to crops on their barely-arable land. He told the chiefs that it would be wise if each Indian leaving the reservation got a pass signed by the agent. It would tell whites, who frequently challenged Indians' right to be off the reservation, that the Indian was legitimately at the river. It also would let the Army, which was still chasing hostile non-treaty Indians, know that these were friendly treaty Indians. To the chiefs, who could neither read nor speak English, Huntington's proposal sounded reasonable. They made their marks on the paper. Huntington inserted the clause about relinquishing fishing rights and sent the "treaty" off to Congress, which ratified it in 1867. Huntington later "borrowed" the $3,500 worth of goods that the government sent the tribes to pay for the fishing rights. He headed for California, where he disappeared. Nobody knows what happened to him.

As early as 1888 Indian Commissioner J.D.C. Atkins tried to get Congress to buy a piece of river bank for the Warm Springs on grounds that the 1865 treaty was a fraud. Atkins said every official who had looked into the matter considered the Indians' version of events to be true. Among other reasons, he said the tribes would hardly have relinquished valuable fishing rights for about $3.50 per member. Panner says correspondence later showed neither Indians nor the government intended to keep the tribal fishermen from their usual and accustomed fishing places. Nevertheless, attorneys digging for precedents and politicians opposed to Indian fishing occasionally still trot out the Huntington Treaty, and other tribes sometimes refer to it to gain an edge over the Warm Springs on management of fisheries and fishing sites.

Kirgis's haste in making his recommendation was prompted by Babcock, who urged immediate action because the Bonneville gates would close December 1, 1937. For the fish and fishermen, closure of the spillway gates was the key event in the final steps of construction although the dam would not be officially opened until July 1938. Closing the gates stopped the flow of the river, just as Susan Palmer told her grandson it would, and the water deepened into a lake with only a trickle allowed through the spillway. Fall 1937 would be the last fishing season before the water rose behind the dam and made it impossible to gather information on sites lost. The assistant commissioner of Indian affairs, William Zimmerman Jr., equaled Kirgis's haste. A week after the lawyer's report, Zimmerman ordered Kenneth R.L. Simmons, a Bureau of Indian Affairs attorney in Billings, Montana, to begin surveying the sites "at your early convenience"—do it now, in the language of bureaucracy. He told Simmons to confer with Babcock and the superintendents of the Yakama and Warm Springs agencies, the BIA's regional forester in Spokane, Washington, and the Federal Bureau of Fisheries. He suggested the forester might supply some staff members to help assemble information, and the regional fisheries director could supply information on the fishing industry on the Columbia.

Babcock did not wait for a response from Washington, D.C. He went to Underwood, Washington, the site of an Indian fishing village at the mouth of the White Salmon River, on June 24 to meet with the Cascade Indians. The Cascades, nominally a part of the Yakama treaty, had not gone to the reservation. Many had land allotments on or near the river. At the time, formal enrollment in a tribe was not much of an issue. The Indians kept no formal list of members, and the Bureau of Indian Affairs was more concerned with individual allotments than with keeping formal membership lists. Enrollment has since become formalized and some of the Cascades are engaged in a dispute with the Yakama Indian Nation's tribal government over their right to enroll there. Throughout the first twenty years of fishing site discussions the government dealt with the river people as entities along with the reservation tribes. So the committee of twelve formed to list and describe the fishing sites about to be destroyed included representatives of the Cascades. It included the Warm Springs too, along with the Yakama and Umatilla.

Babcock also took the issue directly to the Corps of Engineers, traveling to Portland to discuss the potential damage with Colonel Thomas Robins, who commanded Corps operations in the Northwest states. Robins did not concede any liability, but offered to provide a power boat to take the Indian committee to visit the sites. Simmons arrived on the river in time to make the boat trip July 24, 1937, with Nelson Wallulatum's grandmother, Susan Palmer, and a dozen other tribal elders. Mrs. Palmer took her grandson, then an eleven-year-old always eager to learn. Sixty years later, Chief Wallulatum recalled, "My grandmother went along because she could name the fishing sites. For example: 'Here is the dipping hole of the chipmunk.'" The boat traveled from The Dalles—eighty-five miles east of Portland—forty-five miles downstream to the rising dam. As Mrs. Palmer and the others named each site, the meticulous Simmons marked it on a map. A photographer hired by the BIA took a picture. In addition, Simmons recorded the position from which each photo was taken so the photographer could return to the same spot the following year to record changes in the terrain after the gates of the dam closed. The two sets of pictures would serve as the basis for an Indian claim.

The ride was memorable for Nelson. Indians had only canoes. A trip on an Army motor launch was an adventure. More important, he was part of an adult mission, a matter of pride for a boy from a family of chiefs. The Columbia was a different river then. At the Cascades, where Nelson Wallulatum's family spent its summers, the stream poured between the rock cliffs of the Columbia Gorge in a torrent 150 yards wide, dropping forty feet in two miles. Above the Cascades, the rushing water created eddies and whirlpools where Indians caught their year's supply of food. Wherever a rock point jutted into the rushing stream was an Indian fishing site.

The Indians pointed out twenty-seven sites—some with room for three or more fishermen. After the Army closed the gates on Bonneville December 1, 1937, the water rose to cover them all. By the summer of 1938 when the second set of pictures was taken, there was nothing to photograph but an expanse of calm water.

# 2

# THE PROMISE

*Your chiefs are good. Perhaps you have spoken straight, that*
*your children will do what is right. Let them do as they*
*have promised. That is all I have to say.*

—Yakama Chief Kamiaken. Treaty Council, 1855

President Franklin D. Roosevelt pushed the button starting Bonneville Dam's
first power unit September 28, 1937. Both Roosevelt and the cheering throng
on the Columbia River's south shore saw the nearly completed dam as the
centerpiece of a bright future. The cheers that sunny fall day were for the
dam as much as for the president. Roosevelt, to the approval of press and
public, outlined a plan for ever-expanding development and more dams
along the Columbia. Unnoticed among the crowd—at least by reporters at
the scene—were a few people who had no reason to cheer the dam or
Roosevelt's vision of the future.

Walter Speedis took his grandfather, Martin Speedis, and Thomas Yallup,
Yallup's father and a younger man, Jimmy George, to the ceremony. The
Ike family was there too. The Speedis, Yallup, George, and Ike families of
the Yakama Nation all fished on the Columbia River. Within months after
Roosevelt's jaunty speech, many of their fishing places would be under water.
Martin Speedis and the two Yallups would spend the rest of their lives
trying to get replacement sites. Walter Speedis, at nearly 80, worked in the
Yakama Nation's cultural resources department, and continued his
grandfather's efforts. He remembered the ceremony. "All we got" from the
president's speech "was a promise that he would keep us out of war. Then
we got in a war and everyone got drafted. I was one of them." At the time

the dam was built, the tribal fishermen recognized "we were in a pickle" because the dominant culture could and would go ahead with its projects regardless of the price to the area's original inhabitants.

The price for many river people was their homes. Reginald Winishut was a child when the river backed up behind the dam and covered his family's riverbank home east of the town of Cascade Locks, Oregon. Like some others flooded from their homes, the Winishuts moved to Celilo Falls ten miles east of The Dalles. Beside the falls was an Indian village that had existed probably for centuries. A few dozen people lived in the village year-round. Hundreds moved in for the fishing seasons. Winishut's memory remains vivid. Losing their homes "was worse than terrible" for the dam-displaced families. He believes his family received no compensation for their house, the shed where they dried eels and salmon, or their fishing places just west of The Dalles and on an island. Had the Army offered compensation, it probably would have been very little. The government was acquiring "flowage easements"—permission to flood the land—not title to riverside property. Newspaper articles record a $676 jury award for six acres of flooded land and a $300 award for five acres near the Winishut home. The land was largely shrub-covered and gravelly, at the time considered useless. Land owners built dikes to keep the rising water off the few fertile shelves, such as the fruit and vegetable gardens at Bingen, Washington.

As downriver families moved in, the Celilo Falls village became crowded. So did the fishing sites upstream from the Bonneville pool. As more fishermen used fewer sites, conflicts erupted over ownership and rights, but most disputes were settled peaceably. Eventually, with no certain sites and fewer fish, Reginald Winishut's father, Linton, was forced to leave the river to find work. The family moved to the Warm Springs Reservation, where Linton Winishut was first a dairyman, then a laundry operator. But he went to the river every year to fish, and later for many years so did his son. Reginald Winishut says with obvious regret, "There is nothing for me to do between salmon runs if I lived there today. I can't make a living there." He lives at Warm Springs and works operating heavy construction equipment.

In the last week of August and first week of September 1937, just before President Roosevelt came to Oregon to extol the virtues of Bonneville Dam, the Bureau of Indian Affairs was documenting its potential damage. Patrick Gray of the BIA took affidavits from thirty river people to determine the

*This is believed to be one of the photographs taken on the July 1937 boat trip to identify fishing sites. The white-haired man standing in the center, wearing a suit, is attorney Kenneth R.L. Simmons. From the files of Gary Berne.*

importance of the salmon and the lost fishing sites. By then, Gray had the photographs from the July boat trip to show the fishermen. As they gave their affidavits, the fishermen identified the pictures, providing additional confirmation that they fished at each site. The photos and affidavits would be used to support the Indians' claim against the Army Corps of Engineers, builder of Bonneville, for compensation for loss of the sites.

The affidavits carried a common theme: These places are where we make our living. We have no other. John Polk figured the value of the fish he caught to feed his family of six was $300 per year. He also sold and traded about $900 worth of fish for whatever else his family needed. His only other source of income was odd jobs. Polk was fifty-three, a Wasco and Spearfish Indian who lived part of the year on the Warm Springs Reservation and the rest at Celilo. He fished from Celilo to Cascades, a distance of fifty miles, mostly in the spring and fall. Meager as Polk's income sounds—even by Depression era standards—he and the other river people considered that the river provided a good living before Bonneville Dam was built. In addition to the fish directly from the river, the shores provided game, medicinal herbs and other plants. With the abundance of fish the Wasco built up trade to provide a comfortable life. Chief Wallulatum remembers "we were fairly well off."

Compared to non-Indian fishermen, Polk apparently was doing well. U.S. Census Bureau figures for 1939 (the closest year available) show that fewer than 150 of the 1,041 fishermen and oystermen in Oregon made as much or more than Polk. The state's fourteen thousand male manufacturing workers did better. The greatest number of them earned $1,000 to $2,000. But of 337,000 male workers in the state 83,500 earned less than $100 during the year.

James Jim, a Cascade Indian who lived near Hood River, supported his family of six by fishing, supplemented by cutting and selling firewood. He fretted that he did not know where he would fish once the dam was completed. Nor did any of the others. Elijah Miller, a Wasco, was eighty-six when he provided the affidavit to the BIA. He said the Indians made a good living before they were forced onto the reservation, but had hard times there. He still went to the river each year to catch a subsistence amount of fish for his family of five and "considerable" amounts to give to other Indians. Most older river people note in any account of their fishing that tribal fishing people always have made sure that elders, widows, the handicapped and others unable to fish had enough salmon to see them through the winter. The ethic prevails today.

All but a handful of the thirty Indians who provided the affidavits were Wasco and Cascade. BIA attorney Kenneth R.L. Simmons noted in his later report that the Yakama and Umatilla people fished mostly at Celilo and further upstream. Despite seeming to eliminate those two tribes from eligibility for damages, Simmons stayed after the July boat trip and met with leaders of both before he returned to his office in Billings. Both tribal groups voted unanimously to ask the government to buy new fishing sites instead of paying money. Simmons appeared to approve. In his report, he explained to his superiors that a money payment would go to the entire tribe to be shared by all members although only about ten percent of them fished. The fishermen, of course, kept whatever money they got for selling some of their catch. Simmons did not submit his thirteen-page report until November 23 after Gray finished collecting affidavits. He sent all thirty statements along for the authorities in Washington to ponder, and devoted much of his report to quotations from various historic accounts about Indian fishing along the river. He devoted another major portion to questioning the validity of claims by nearly all the Indian groups, although he exhibited some confusion as to who was who. For instance, he said the affidavits came largely from Wasco (correct) and Middle Oregon (instead of Mid-Columbia). He said the Yakama and Umatilla fished too far upstream to be affected, and the other tribes had no treaties and had never been granted fishing rights. But he ignored the fact that several Mid-Columbia chiefs were among the signers of the Yakama treaty, and that the Wasco were specifically listed in the Middle Oregon (Warm Springs) treaty. Warm Springs had no claim because of the Huntington Treaty, Simmons said, although the tribe had a suit pending in federal court contending the document was obtained by fraud. Yet the affidavits he bundled off to Washington included three from Yakama tribal members and one from a Nez Perce. Others of the affidavits described Yakama and Umatilla tribal members using the downriver sites, often in exchange for allowing Cascade and Wasco people to use sites upriver.

The affidavits were poignant and informative. The mapping of the fishing sites was precise. But some Indians say now the information Simmons collected understated the problem. The chairman of the Yakama Tribal Council, William Yallup Sr., who grew up on the river, says the government agents talked to too few people. "They only got certain places. There were countless numbers of sites along the river." Because the undammed Columbia fluctuated widely in width, the location of fishing sites changed with the season. In the spring, when water was high, Celilo and other sites were covered. "In July there'd be a hundred sites, in September a thousand. In those days we fished three hundred days a year."

Simmons told the commissioner it was impossible to estimate the ultimate damage to the sites or the fish runs. Expert opinion was about equally divided about whether the fish could get over the dam. If they did, some experts feared that the loss of river current in the pool behind the dam would keep the salmon in the new lake and they would starve rather than continue to their spawning grounds. The War Department scoffed at both fears, Simmons said. No one would know until the following spring when the first post-dam run of Chinook came up the river. Despite his doubts, Simmons made meticulous plans to maintain his chain of evidence for an Indian claim. He would get photos in 1938 from the same spots as the July 1937 pictures. He ordered the superintendents of the Umatilla and Yakama reservations to interview all the tribal fishermen during the winter to find out their annual take of fish, the value of their catch, and where the fish were caught. They would make similar records for 1938 after the dam began operation.

Simmons was looking ahead. The Army had assured him that Bonneville would not affect Celilo, the major fishing ground for all the tribes. But he said if navigation were to be extended upriver from the Bonneville pool it would destroy the Celilo sites. That, of course, is what happened twenty years later. And many years after that, The Dalles Dam that flooded Celilo and an even newer dam, John Day, would become involved in the battle over replacement fishing sites. But, for the time being in 1937, it was wait and see for the Indians. The gates of the dam closed December 1, on schedule. The water rose and covered seventy square miles of former shoreline, including the Indians' fishing sites, along forty miles on both sides of the river. Fish did manage to cross the dam in 1938, although in uncertain numbers, and fisheries experts realized that it would be several years before damage to the runs could be fully assessed. Spawning fish are mostly four to five years old; so any effect on a run is not evident until its progeny return to the river four to five years later.

The Indian fishermen faced a dilemma. Fish were there in the 1938 season, but the falls and fast water where Indians caught them were not. Some fishermen, like the Winishuts, moved their activities upriver to Celilo, to other spots on the still free-running stream, and to falls on the Klickitat and Deschutes rivers, tributaries to the Columbia. Fred Colfax, whose fishing memories stretch back to World War I when he was a child, fished on the Klickitat River, which flows into the Columbia at Lyle, Washington, on the Bonneville pool. His family moved from Sk'in on the flooded north bank to Celilo. He explains, "There was no place else to go." Colfax, who fished for forty-eight years while also working full time for the SP&S Railway, lives now in an apartment in the Yakama Nation Senior Center. Some river people went to the reservations. But most remained and, in Chief Wallulatum's words, "floundered until they realized they had to move or do something else." That was when the Indians themselves began pushing the government to find replacement fishing sites.

The U.S. commissioner of Indian affairs, John Collier, dispatched his personal representative, Floyd La Rouche, to the Northwest in July 1938 to make the second boat trip upriver with tribal delegates and Bureau of Indian Affairs officials to look at the flooded sites. Until then, all the discussion, except for Simmmons' 1937 meeting with the two tribes, had been between government officials. By November of 1938 the BIA in Washington, D.C., had decided what would be best for the Indians and was thinking about bringing them into the talks. John Herrick, assistant to Collier, wrote the

Corps' division engineer in Portland, Col. John C. H. Lee, that the BIA would recommend that the Army buy land and "construct the improvements necessary for an Indian settlement, and construct improvements at Indian fishing stations." He said the Indian bureau felt that in exchange the Indians should be willing to give the Army a release from any damage to their flooded sites. Herrick said the agency lawyer, Simmons, would meet with Lee in Portland in December to discuss such a settlement, bringing along the superintendents of the Yakama, Umatilla and Warm Springs agencies. "Later, of course, it will be necessary to bring representatives of the Indian tribes involved into the discussion," Herrick wrote. "During your talks, you can decide at what point the representatives of the Indians should be brought into the picture." Herrick made no comment about including the Warm Springs superintendent in the discussions, but the Warm Springs soon became involved and have remained so.

Simmons, the superintendents and Lenzie, the BIA's regional forester, met with Lee and other Corps officials December 7. Unlike the more patronizing BIA, Lee insisted that the War Department would take no action until the tribes submitted a claim in writing. Even then, the claim was to come through the agency superintendents, but only with the tribes' approval. Lee said he would concede that the flooded sites were usual and accustomed fishing places under the treaties. The Army and Indian bureau agreed the claim would place no monetary value on the damage and should include a request for a conference between the Army and the Indians, with the agency superintendents included, of course.

Delegates from the tribes met five days before Christmas at Underwood, Washington, one of the most severely damaged villages. Henry Charley of the Cascades reported that many camp buildings and drying sheds also were destroyed at the mouth of Wind River ten miles downstream from Underwood. He reported that "loss of fish and loss of property are extensive." While the engineers had moved railroads and a highway before any other work was done, Indian property was left on the banks to be destroyed.

Johnny Jackson lived at Underwood at the mouth of the White Salmon River during the fishing season when he was a small boy. Now chief of the Cascade Band, he lives on higher ground where the Corps built one of the sites it acquired in meeting part of its 1939 promise. During his boyhood, "This used to be a village here. There were a lot of people lived here, buildings from where the road is now . . ." He waves an arm at Washington Highway 14 where cars whiz by on an embankment twenty feet above the asphalt pavement of the fishing site parking lot, and just a few feet from the Bonneville pool shore. "There was no road there then. Drying sheds were down this way. My two grandmothers had drying sheds and my mother would be here in summer until way late in the fall. Then we'd move home . . . I was seven, eight, nine years old. I remember going down to the water. The river used to run the other side of the bank, When I was a kid I used to stand over there and throw rocks at the fish."

Jackson was too young to remember any of the Indians' negotiations with the Army, but he remembers what his parents told him. "What I've learned from my mother, my aunts and some of my elders was that when Bonneville was being completed and they were going to flood these sites . . . the Army told the people they'd be flooded and they'd have to get out. They promised other sites on high ground and said they would relocate them—replace the housing and drying sheds. That never happened." A wiry sixty-eight-year-old constantly on the move despite triple heart bypass surgery, Jackson lives in a house he built of weathered boards perched against a hillside at the edge of the asphalted in-lieu site. When the Bureau of Indian Affairs tried to evict Jackson in the 1980s, he won the right to stay after a celebrated court case and congressional intervention. But that is a later chapter in the long fishing site story.

Back in January 1939, the Indians submitted their claim for damages, listing twenty-three locations, each including at least several fishing sites. The claim was addressed to Colonel Theron D. Weaver, the Army officer in charge of Bonneville Dam construction. "We have duly considered these losses at our tribal meetings," the delegates wrote, "and it is the opinion of our people that an effort should be made to have the United States Government, through your department, take steps to provide us with additional fishing sites and facilities." As always, the Indians omitted damage to the fish. They consistently specified that the fish runs were a separate issue to be dealt with when the dam's full effects were known. But they did include replacement of homes and other buildings as a part of the replacement of the sites. The Indian claim said their feelings were pretty well summed up at the December meeting by Frank Winishut (Reginald's grandfather), who signed as one of four Warm Springs delegates. The Indians' petition quoted the minutes of the meeting:

> . . . (Winishut) urged all of the Indians to stand together in this matter and stated that the Indians did not want money for their fishing sites because the Indian did not know how to handle

money. These fishing sites represented food and a means of living for the Indian. They wanted only similar sites or facilities for getting this food in exchange for the ones that had been lost. He stated they had confidence in the good will of the War Department to deal fairly with the Indians. He pointed out that in many times of trouble the Indians had gladly assisted the War Department and the Army of this country. They had even shed their blood and died when their country needed them. Now when the Indians' means of living and food supply was threatened he felt sure that this same War Department would work with them in a cooperative and understanding way in an attempt to restore these losses.

Winishut, sixty-three years old, listed himself as a Celilo Indian living at Warm Springs when he provided one of Simmons's affidavits in the fall of 1937. He said then he sold $250 worth of fish a year, dried 500-1,200 pounds, and salted 53-146 gallons. Jerry Bruneau and Robert Smith, both Wasco Indians who also signed the claim on behalf of the Warm Springs, also had given affidavits. Smith, who was eighty years old, described bundling fish into one hundred-pound packages for trading. Bruneau, then sixty-one, the first in several generations of Bruneau leaders at Warm Springs, fished mostly at the upriver end of the flooded area, but went to the Cascades a few miles east of Bonneville Dam for sturgeon every fall.

Bruneau's affidavit also included an incident that made many of the Indians less confident than Winishut about the Army's willingness to keep promises. An Indian known as Old Smykes had a shack where the Army wanted to build The Dalles-Celilo Canal in 1903. "The Army tore down Old Man Smykes' smokehouse, with the understanding that they were to rebuild it, but never did," Bruneau told Patrick Gray, who recorded the affidavits. Smykes's story—his smokehouse growing to an entire village—came up several times during discussions of the Bonneville sites. It faded away as the efforts to replace the fishing sites stretched far longer than Smykes's battle to get a new smokehouse.

The Yakama petition signers included Alex Saluskin, the tribal interpreter who later served twenty-two years on the tribal council, eight as chairman. Also signing was Thomas Yallup, father of the current Yakama chairman. Allan Patawa, who signed for the Umatilla, was a chief of the Walla Walla tribe and longtime leader in a reservation Christian Church. Patawa died the following year. His grandson, Antone Minthorn, now chairman of the Umatilla Board of Trustees, remembers him as a big man, over six feet tall with long hair, "a gentle, fine man" with a flair for dressing well. Of the eleven Indian signers only George Redhawk of Umatilla signed with a thumbprint; the rest signed their names.

M.A. Johnson, the Yakama Agency superintendent, sent the claim to the Army January 28, 1939. That was just two days after Oscar L. Chapman, the assistant secretary of the Interior, told attorney Simmons to continue negotiations with an eye to getting the Army to provide some replacement sites. Chapman's letter told Simmons the importance of the issue: It had been the subject of a conference in Washington, D.C., involving the Interior, Justice and War departments. Bureaucrats in the field took the hint. The Army set about trying to figure out the potential cost of replacing fishing platforms and other structures on the flooded sites. It scheduled a meeting with the Indians for February 28, 1939, at The Dalles, Oregon. That meeting, which lasted from 10:30 a.m. to 5 p.m., was amicable but made little progress toward an agreement. It did, however, highlight the cultural differences that were to plague the issue into current times. Indians of the inland Northwest traditionally made tribal decisions by consensus. Neither a binding decision by majority vote nor a command from the top was within their experience. Corps officers, bound to the Army's strict military command structure, could not comprehend the Indians' way. Particularly galling to the military was the Indians' belief that an issue must be understood in context, and that context begins with "from time immemorial . . . ." The differences in decision-making were equally evident in meetings half a century later. Several days after the February 1939 session between the Indians and the Corps, an obviously frustrated Weaver made his report to Division Engineer Lee. He suggested a shortcut to an agreement "due to the extremely slow progress possible at Indian 'Pow Wows' where large numbers of individual Indians must be permitted to present their arguments in the characteristic Indian manner, including reminiscences of the early days prior to 1855 . . ." Although Weaver had no patience with Indian decision making, he did understand one circumstance that nineteenth-century Army officers and treaty makers had not: The tribes had so intermarried that there were few people of pure descent from any tribe, and most had relatives within the other tribes. Despite the treaty makers' arbitrary assignment of families and bands to larger tribes, the tribes were never the static, closed entities that non-Indian government pictured. Intertribal couples sometimes chose to live with the wife's tribe, sometimes with the husband's. Today it is not unusual for members of the same immediate family to belong to different tribes. So Weaver suggested that any settlement apply to all Indians, and their descendants, who have fished within the Bonneville pool "from time immemorial." He was catching on.

Weaver had asked the Indians to supply details of damage and assigned a civilian from the Corps, G.W. Shoemaker, to hear their complaints. Fishermen responded in the February 28 meeting with a litany of their losses. Alex Saluskin, the Yakama leader, and Henry Charley of the Cascades painted the bleakest picture. Charley said Indians on the north side of the river had been unable to catch enough fish for their own food in the past two seasons. Saluskin said he caught 1,500 pounds of fish a day in 1926. In 1938, he fished for three days and caught nothing. John Polk said some places near Lone Pine, at the upper edge of the pool near The Dalles, could be used, but the rising water had done considerable damage. Further downstream, the sites were gone, he said. The entire mouth of Rock Creek, now flooded, had been a fishing site where forty or fifty people had speared, gaffed and trapped enough fish in the fall to feed their families for a year. It was the same at Herman and Lindsey creeks and Hood River on the Oregon side, and Wind River on the Washington side. Charley said a hundred and fifty to two hundred Indians camped each fall in the area around Underwood to fish. The Indians read a list of twenty-two people at Underwood who had lost their fishing shacks—in reality, their seasonal homes—to the rising pool.

Discussion of the fishing site losses was interrupted by another issue, something that was to happen time and time again over the next half-century. The delegates received word that the Oregon Legislature was working on a bill that would curtail their fishing rights. They halted work on the fishing sites to compose a telegram to State Senator James A. Best, a Republican from Pendleton near the Umatilla Reservation, urging him to block the action. The immediate threat taken care of, they returned to the replacement sites, telling Shoemaker they wanted the Army to build camp sites near fishing spots, and they would furnish their own fishing facilities. By facilities, they obviously meant fishing platforms. They always considered replacement homes and usually drying sheds to be the Corps' part of the deal. The Warm Springs submitted a specific list of sites they wanted developed—the four tributaries Polk had described, plus the Columbia shoreline from the partly usable Lone Pine area at The Dalles several miles upstream along running water. Shoemaker made no proposal from the Army. Weaver, in his report to Lee, however, suggested seven sites to serve as replacements for

*Directly in front of the flagpole, in the black hat, is Chief Tommy Thompson, the legendary Celilo chief. To his right is Alex Saluskin, Yakama leader. The other two men are unidentified. From the files of Gary Berne.*

the list of lost places submitted by the Indians. He included three Washington sites at the mouths of rivers where Indian villages had been drowned—the Big and Little White Salmon and Wind rivers. On the Oregon side he proposed the mouth of Herman Creek and a spot between Rock Creek and Cascade Rapids, also in Hood River County, and North Pine Island near The Dalles. He also suggested sites on both sides of the Columbia near Five Mile Rapids above the Bonneville pool. He suggested that, if the Indians agreed on the general sites, negotiations would continue to determine the area needed and the cost of improvements.

Before talks began, however, they ran into complications that stalled proceedings. The Corps had gone to federal court in Tacoma, Washington, to condemn land owned by the Northwest Electric Co. that was flooded by the Bonneville pool. Forty Yakama Indians had intervened in the case, claiming damages to their land, largely fishing sites. The federal judge hearing the case had ordered a sixty-day delay to allow the Justice Department to sort out the status of individual Indians' claims, or for the Army to reach an agreement with them. The Army decided it would wait out the Justice Department's decision. When Weaver made his proposal, the judge's deadline was fifteen days away and nothing had been heard from the Justice Department. Nothing happened immediately in the lawsuit; in fact, it was not resolved until several years later through a negotiated settlement that gave the Indians a piece of the company land and the company its money.

Negotiations between the Army and Indians finally got under way later in the spring. On May 23, delegations from the three tribal organizations and the Mid-Columbia people visited the sites Weaver proposed. Their reaction was mostly favorable. However, the Warm Springs said a site on North Pine Island was too far from desirable fishing grounds and "is not a suitable location for the drying of fish." Both the Warm Springs and Yakama suggested sites at Old Smykes's former home and nearby Tenino to replace North Pine Island. Both tribes also disapproved of a site farther downstream on the Oregon side between Rock Creek and Cascade Rapids. The Yakama had other objections: the Big Eddy site should include some adjacent land owned by the Seufert Brothers cannery and include a road to Spearfish village; the Big White Salmon site was not large enough. Both tribes emphasized that the sites would compensate only for the loss of their original sites; the tribes would not accept them as compensation for dam-caused damage to the fish runs. Throughout the decades of negotiations, the tribes have steadfastly kept separate the issues of abundance of fish and places to catch fish. During the initial negotiations in 1938 and 1939 no one, including fisheries experts and the Corps, knew what effect the dam would have on the fish runs. The Indians reserved their right to seek compensation later if, as they feared, the dam diminished the number of fish available to catch. Neither the Umatilla nor the Mid-Columbia people responded to Weaver's proposal until a June 7 meeting of the Celilo Fish Committee. That committee had been formed in 1936 with representatives from the three tribes and the river people to deal with fishing issues. From this time until it disappeared in the 1960s, it also served as a venue for Indian discussion of what soon became known as "the in-lieu sites."

The Umatilla joined the other two tribes in suggesting the Tenino and Old Smykes's place instead of North Pine Island. Chief Tommy Thompson of the Wy'am, patriarch of the river, and Sallie Ann Joyce of the Cascades had more ambitious proposals. Thompson wanted much of the river shore from his home at Celilo to The Dalles—about ten miles—turned into exclusive Indian fishing sites. Both Thompson's Celilo Falls and the land he wanted were on the still free-running river above the lake created by Bonneville. Joyce asked for five miles of river bank on each side of the Columbia below Bonneville Dam. If given the land, she said, "then we Cascade Indians will agree to preserve these grounds as long as we live under the sun, to remain as during the time of our forefathers who once owned them, with lasting peace and harmony." Joyce did not get her wish,

and harmony was the last thing to be found on the Columbia from her
time to this.

Thompson's and Joyce's proposals got support from nine other fishermen
at the meeting but no serious consideration from the Army. But they did
get sympathetic support from a surprising source. C.G. Davis had been
recently assigned as an Indian bureau field aide at The Dalles, largely to
deal with fisheries issues and Indian allotments. Little is known about him,
but his official correspondence shows an understanding of the Indians and,
unlike most of the government agents, a willingness to let them pursue
their own kind of life. However, most Indians who remember him considered
him arrogant and opposed to their interests. Nevertheless, Davis wrote
Johnson, who was his supervisor, explaining some river chiefs' apprehensions
about the new sites. "I personally see their point of view," Davis said.

> Their pride, or something doesn't permit them to be moved around
> by the white man and they feel that some tribes of River Indians
> will, therefore, have more privileges than others. They feel that
> residents of the river country haven't properly been represented in
> dealings with the War Department—that the Yakamas, the Warm
> Springs and the Umatillas have been allowed to send reports in to
> the War Department as to what those people want, but that the
> Indians from Rock Creek, Celilo, Wishram, Spearfish, Hood River,
> Underwood etc. have had no chance to voice their wishes in the
> matter. They feel that those districts that are not accorded legal
> ownership of grounds will be discriminated against, possibly
> evicted, by the white people because the whites cannot do anything
> to them at the seven owned spots and will take it out on them
> where they can.

Davis urged Johnson to consider their requests "as I sincerely believe
their contention has high merit." He explained: "After all, these River Indians
only desire what we all contend to be their real rights. They are fisher folk,
depending principally on catch of fish for their food and the money received
from the sale of fish for their living expenses other than food. They want to
be allowed to live in their own peaceful way and not be harassed by malicious
whites and breeds. They are peaceful, genial and as a rule honest. They
dislike to have outsiders come in and deprive them of their happiness and
food supply. They believe the Reservation Indians should not crowd them
out because the Reservation lands they own bring them an income and the
River dwellers have no such income."

Davis's letter touched a chord that still resonates along the river. Although both the Celilo Fish Committee and early in-lieu site negotiations included representatives of the river people, the government, then as now, otherwise dealt almost exclusively with the tribes that it had formally recognized. It did not consider the river tribes separate entities. Much of the problem boiled down to the Indians' and government's different views of organization. The tension still exists today although nearly all the Indians are enrolled in one or another of the reservation tribes.

Weaver made his formal proposal to Johnson, the Yakama superintendent, on July 12. It included only six sites, four in Washington and two in Oregon, instead of the seven he originally listed, but he included several of the Indians' suggestions. The six sites, totaling about four hundred acres, were:

Tenino, on the Oregon shore east of The Dalles. "An irregularly shaped parcel of land lying between the Columbia River Highway and the Celilo Canal, situated partly on government land and land owned by Seufert Bros. in the vicinity of the Five Mile Lock of The Dalles-Celilo Canal." Water for domestic purposes was available from an existing system on the government land.

Big Eddy on Washington state land across from Tenino. The government would buy all the state land within a section in Klickitat County, Washington. Water was available from a spring.

Big White Salmon at Underwood, Washington, at the mouth of the White Salmon River. The site was on the west bank of the river between a state highway and the Columbia, and the Corps would include all the houses there. The site was to be included in the condemnation proceedings against Northwest Electric Co., which owned the land. Water probably would come from a well.

Little White Salmon five miles west of Underwood on Drano Lake at the mouth of the Little White Salmon River. The government expected to get the land through condemnation and Weaver said that would result in a larger site than the tract the Indians had visited. The government would develop a water supply.

Wind River, about ten miles farther downstream and five miles east of Stevenson, Washington. The government would get land along the power transmission line between Bonneville and Grand Coulee dams. A spring would supply water.

Herman Creek just east of the town of Cascade Locks, Oregon. Weaver said the location on state fish hatchery property and a tract beside the Oregon-Washington Railroad and Navigation Co. tracks was more accessible than the original site he proposed nearby. Water would be available from a spring or well.

Weaver said the Corps would build an incinerator and sanitary facilities at each of the sites except Herman Creek, where the sanitary facilities already existed. He asked Johnson to submit the proposal to the three tribes for approval so the Army could ask its higher headquarters for permission to obtain the sites. Within a month the three tribes had adopted resolutions approving. Both the tribes and Johnson emphasized again, however, that the sites were compensation only for lost fishing places, not for the fish if the runs later appeared to be damaged by the dam. By the end of August the Corps was appraising the land it needed to acquire. As soon as that was done, the matter would be submitted to the Army's Chief of Engineers for approval, wrote Don E. Meldrum, the Corps' land officer in Portland.

At the same time the Indians were negotiating to maintain their access to the Columbia River salmon, they also were involved in their perpetual battle to maintain their right to fish. Getting in their last seasons of fishing before the Bonneville pool rose, Yakama tribal members Phillip and Kennedy Charley were arrested in May 1937 for failing to obtain a commercial license from the state of Washington. Several similar arrests followed in both states. In July, Assistant Indian Commissioner William Zimmerman Jr. told U.S. Senator Lewis B. Schwellenbach of Washington his agency would not defend Indians who refused to obtain the state licenses. Leaders of the river people complained to state authorities, U.S. Attorney Carl C. Donaugh in Portland and the Indian bureau, contending their treaty rights were violated and their livelihood threatened. Donaugh agreed to meet with them along with his Eastern Washington counterpart, Sam M. Driver from Spokane. The two federal attorneys and T. Leland Brown, the Wasco County, Oregon, district attorney, met October 7, 1938, with two dozen tribal leaders from the Warm Springs, Yakama and Umatilla reservations and from the Columbia River. Superintendents of the three reservations also attended the meeting in The Dalles, Oregon. The *Oregon Journal,* a Portland newspaper, reporting on the several-hour session, found it noteworthy that the officials "heard the Indians speak for themselves." In the 1930s, the BIA more often spoke for the Indians. Reporter Joe D. Thompson added, "The matter of Indian fishing rights has at last received recognition from the United States department of justice, and the federal attorneys were instructed to investigate and report back to the attorney general." He quoted Driver as saying federal courts might "within the next few weeks" take steps to order the states to quit enforcing licensing laws against Indians. Omar L. Babcock, the Umatilla superintendent who initially raised the fishing site issue, told the newspaper the superintendents were urging the Indians to be patient and not take their case to court. But he said he had difficulty persuading the tribes to follow his advice. "The Indians have been victimized so often by insincere white promoters and white attorneys that they hold everybody in suspicion," Babcock said. He added, "What we need is that the government, itself, appoint well-equipped legal talent, men who are sincere and who will approach their problems with a sympathetic viewpoint."

The fishing people finally did win at least part of the ruling they sought, but it was a longer and more complicated struggle than Driver intimated it would be. Instead of a federal injunction ordering the states to rescind their license requirement, the legal path began with the arrest of a fisherman, Sampson Tulee, a member of the Yakama Nation. Tulee was convicted in Klickitat County, Washington, Superior Court of catching salmon with a net without first getting a $5 state license. The Washington State Supreme Court upheld his conviction and he appealed to the federal courts. The U.S. Supreme Court overturned the conviction March 30, 1942. In doing so, Justice Hugo L. Black wrote that, from reading the record of treaty negotiations, he was impressed "by the strong desire the Indians had to retain the right to hunt and fish in accordance with the immemorial customs of their tribes." He added, "It is our responsibility to see that the terms of the treaty are carried out, so far as possible, in accordance with the meaning they were understood to have by the tribal representatives at the council, and in a spirit which generously recognizes the full obligation of this nation to protect the interests of a dependent people." The state could not charge Indians the license fee, he said, but it could continue to regulate tribal fishing in the interests of conservation.

Other issues also weaved around the site negotiations. At the direction of his superiors, Davis, the Indian agent at The Dalles, was keeping an eye on the Northwest Electric Co. condemnation suit that had temporarily stalled the site negotiations early in 1939. In August that year, he attended a hearing in the continuing litigation at White Salmon, Washington. Davis reported that the government attorneys argued that the Indians' fishing had been destroyed by the power company's dam and a state fish hatchery before Bonneville Dam was built. The company argued that Bonneville Dam had damaged the Indians' fishing. So, while the Army was working toward compensating the Indians for damage to their fishing resulting from Bonneville's construction, the Justice Department was arguing in a federal court that Bonneville had done no damage to Indian fishing.

Meanwhile, Davis was fending off a man named J.M. Jessup of Cook, Washington, who was more than eager to sell the government a fishing site for the Indians. Jessup wanted Davis to persuade the Corps to buy all his land at the mouth of the Little White Salmon River instead of just a portion of it. "He seemed to want to TALK more than anything else," Davis wrote his boss, Johnson, after Jessup had spent two hours haranguing the agent in Davis's office. "He is rather advanced in years and his mind seems to be wandering a bit." Later, Jessup tried to reinforce his efforts to sell the land by blocking the Indians from crossing it to reach the river. Davis wrote him a stern note requesting that he "refrain from further molestation of Indians who have a right to travel over a definitely marked road to these grounds."

Despite contradictions in agency policies and minor irritations, everything in late 1939 seemed to be going well toward creating new fishing sites for the Indians. Then another federal agency tossed in a potential obstacle. On December 19, Fred J. Foster, the regional director of the Bureau of Fisheries at Seattle, wrote to Meldrum, who was negotiating land purchases. If Meldrum's potential land purchases "are in any way related to the taking of fish" the Army should get approval from the acting commissioner of fisheries in Washington, D.C., Foster said. Meldrum ducked the issue with delay. He said he would direct Foster's request to the chief of engineers when he asked formal approval to begin acquiring sites under the agreement with the Indians. That would come later.

By the end of 1939, it had been two years since the Indian fishing sites disappeared under the waters of the Bonneville pool. This was just the beginning.

# 3

# MONEY AND WAR

*We were content to let things remain as the Great Spirit
made them. They were not, and would change the rivers if
they did not suit them.*

—Young Chief Joseph, quoted by Chuck Williams in
*Bridge of the Gods, Mountains of Fire*

Everything looked so simple at the beginning of 1940. The government
had agreed, with a minimum of fuss, to provide replacement fishing sites.
A Corps of Engineers civilian was looking at land to buy. The Corps
expanded its planned purchase at the Little White Salmon River mouth to
160 acres, bringing the total for the six sites to 408 acres. Since December
1937, the fishing people had been making do with inadequate fishing sites,
too little room to camp during fishing seasons, and not enough fish. Both
Corps and Indians hoped the new sites would be available for the upcoming
fishing seasons. Instead, one thing after another kept the Corps from getting
the land it had promised: its own bureaucratic procedures; a court case;
money; and finally, war.

World War II, of course, caused a four-year delay. It put almost everything
else in the country on hold too. But from the Indians' point of view the
sites should have been theirs months before bombs dropped on Pearl Harbor
December 7, 1941. By then their original sites had been under water for
four fishing seasons. In the time between the 1939 agreement and the 1941
Pearl Harbor attack the Corps followed its rigid land acquisition processes
with all the speed of the Columbia's dam-slowed current.

The Indians meanwhile struggled to survive. Some, like Susan Palmer, gave up and faded back to their reservations because they had no place to fish, at least in the traditional way, Some tried to adjust their fishing to the "new" river. Indian dip net, gaff hook and spear fishing depended on the swift shallow water of rapids and falls. After Bonneville Dam was built there were no mainstream rapids or falls west of The Dalles. Some tribal people gathered meager numbers of fish at points of land where the water moved a little more rapidly. Some tried using set nets anchored on the river bank. Although Indians historically had used set nets and gill nets, neither had proven as effective on the Columbia as the combination of hand held nets and swift water. At the time, Indians lacked the motor boats that enabled non-Indian commercial fishermen to use deadly effective gill nets. Others of the Columbia River fishers concentrated their efforts on the Klickitat and Deschutes rivers, where falls had long provided good fishing and continue to do so. But these tributaries were not as productive as the Columbia had been. Still other fishers crowded to Celilo.

For many fishing families, cut off from their usual resources, the main source of salmon became state and federal fish hatcheries. There, government workers gave them dead fish that had been stripped of eggs to breed replacements for dwindling wild runs. The Fish and Wildlife Service took the fish by boat to Underwood, on the river's north bank above a flooded village twenty-three miles east of Bonneville Dam. In exchange, the agency exhorted the Indians to refrain from spearing salmon below the hatchery traps. The hatchery salmon filled a hole in the Indians' diet left by losing the fish. But losing the fishing left a larger hole in their cultural fabric. Salmon were—and are—not just something for dinner. Catching, preparing, and eating them was an integral part of the people's lives and religion.

In December 1939 and January 1940, Indian agents met with some fishermen to discuss their lack of fishing and camping places and the states' continuing efforts to keep them from fishing. Yakama Agency Superintendent Johnson told them the Interior Department was making a serious effort to improve conditions. But nothing changed. At the end of the year, William Yallup, chief of the Rock Creek band and a fisherman himself, made two pleas to the Corps. One was for "fair and impartial treatment" of Indians seeking fish carcasses at the nearby hatcheries. Yallup complained, through Indian Agent Davis, that as long as any white people were around, the hatchery staff refused to let the Indians have any fish. Yallup's other appeal to the Corps was for more room for the families to

*Chief Johnny Jackson has identified this as a photo of the Underwood in-lieu site soon after the water backed up behind the dam, before the water was raised again, and before the highway cut across between the houses and the river. This is one of the photographs that won the eviction case in the 1980s by showing that the Indians had historically had permanent homes on the sites. From the files of Gary Berne.*

camp at Underwood at the mouth of the White Salmon River and at Cook's Landing a few miles downstream on the Columbia. Underwood remained the subject of the long-running Northwest Electric Co. condemnation suit in which the Corps of Engineers planned to acquire land for an in-lieu site. Cook's, not yet chosen as an in-lieu site, was the unflooded remnant of a traditional fishing place. Fishing families were using both sites, but Yallup said there was room at each place for only one or two families to camp while they tried to adapt to the changed river. There was no room to dry the few salmon that they caught and the carcasses they obtained from the fish hatcheries. Yallup asked the Corps to provide space for tents and drying racks for at least twenty families at each site. In forwarding Yallup's plea, Davis commented, "The above requests all seem reasonable to me." He suggested to Johnson that the Indian bureau provide some temporary facilities.

By that time, the end of 1940, Indian patience was wearing thin. Both Indians and Indian agents began asking when the fishermen would have their new sites. The Corps was encouraging—in a way. Don E. Meldrum, head of the land section in Portland, gave a typical bureaucratic reply to an immediate human problem. He said preliminary work had been done toward getting title to the promised lands. However, he said, he didn't expect any money to be available to buy the sites until the next session of Congress, scheduled to begin a month after his December 5 letter. That meant it would be at least July 1941 before the Corps could begin buying land. The agency expected it would have to go through condemnation proceedings, which would not be finished in time to make the purchases before the fall fishing. Another season gone.

There was one exception, Meldrum said. The Corps expected to get the Underwood site soon in settling the condemnation action against Northwest Electric Co. The case, which had been in the courts for several years, was scheduled for hearing on January 7, 1941. Meldrum was over-optimistic. The litigation was still going on in August 1941 when it halted with a three-way standoff. U.S. District Court Judge Lloyd L. Black in Tacoma, Washington, heard evidence for a week, then said he probably would declare a mistrial. He said the Indians who had entered the case failed to show any actual damage from construction of the dam. He added that the tribal fishermen should not make any settlement then because they would be able to obtain only a small fraction of the potential damage to the entire run of salmon. Without a ruling in the condemnation suit, the War Department was not willing to make improvements on the four acres it would turn over to the Indians. The Indians, thus stalled, were reluctant to drop their damage claims. Johnson, the Yakama Agency superintendent, said in a letter to the Commissioner of Indian Affairs, however, that he thought the Indians would be willing to drop the suit if the Army would go ahead with the improvements. "The fact that the War Department has been unable to fulfill any of the agreement that they made with the Indians, in my opinion, is one of the prime reasons why it was not possible, to settle this action out of court," Johnson said. It was months before he got a reply. The impasse was typical of the delays that would occur repeatedly during the next half century. The Corps, officially, was willing to compensate for the damage it had caused the Indians. But the officials, both military officers and civilians, who were assigned to deliver the compensation viewed the problem as legal and procedural. To the Indians, of course, it was a matter of food on the table and money for other necessities. The urgent human need does not seem to have penetrated the bureaucracies, either Corps or Bureau of Indian Affairs.

The commissioner to whom Johnson wrote was John Collier, who is considered the strongest advocate for Indian rights ever to head the Indian bureau. But his record on fishing rights was lackadaisical at best, according to Donald L. Parman, author of the 1985 "Inconstant Advocacy: The Erosion of Indian Fishing Rights." Collier had been drawn to reform the federal government's treatment of Indians through tribes in his native Southwest. He seems to have retained his focus there, never taking the trouble to sort out the complex issues involved in the Northwest treaties. Parman also says that Collier may have viewed the Northwest tribes as "a cultural lost cause" because many appeared to have been assimilated into the larger society in dress and language. If Collier did believe the Northwest tribes had been assimilated, he was wrong. The commissioner may have mistaken the Northwest peoples' adaptability for assimilation. They have long adapted the materials—and sometimes the beliefs—of other cultures to their own traditions and purposes. Centuries as trading people taught them to take whatever could be useful and meld it into their own lives. Lewis and Clark found river people using brass teakettles they had obtained in trade from coastal tribes who had contact with ships. The explorers also found them wearing quantities of the colorful beads carried by European adventurers for trading purposes. Northwest artists early adapted the beads into exquisite decorations on moccasins, dresses, shirts and bags. If Levi's were more practical than buckskin, then fishermen wore Levi's. If canvas could add insulation to a tule mat tepee, they added canvas to the structure. If strong twine was available and hemp was not, they made fish nets of twine. Northwest tribes are dynamic societies, not static museum pieces. Whatever he believed, Collier did little to protect the Northwest people from attacks on their fishing rights.

As time dragged on and the Corps acquired no fishing places for them, a few Indians asked about getting money instead of the sites. Johnson, the Yakama Agency superintendent, reminded them that the tribes had made an agreement based on their own request that they get land, not money. He did not comment that the Corps of Engineers also made the agreement. Indians were not the only ones showing impatience at the lack of progress toward buying sites. Mary Jessup supplanted her husband in hectoring Davis, the Indian agent at The Dalles, about government purchase of the family's land at Drano Lake. In July she wrote Davis that the couple "cannot act as a public servant in caring for the Indians who have been flooded off their accustomed fishing places." She said the government would have to arrange payment "for premises occupied by the unfortunate Indians." Drano, at the mouth of the Little White Salmon River, was one of the sites the Corps planned to purchase when it got the money. Davis, in forwarding Mrs. Jessup's ultimatum, added his interpretation: "I believe this lady means that they are getting tired of waiting for the War Department."

The wait was going to get longer. The $50,000 the Corps sought to buy and develop the Indian sites was in its appropriations bill in 1940. But President Roosevelt vetoed all new construction—except defense work. Construction of the powerhouse at Bonneville Dam was considered national defense work; compensating for the dam-caused damage to Indian fishing was not. The Interior Department asked the Corps again in 1941 to request money for the sites, but with war growing imminent, the Army got no money for fishing sites. The Corps, however, did not drop the in-lieu sites entirely. In a startling example of business as usual, the Portland District Engineer wrote a letter December 8, 1941—the day after the Pearl Harbor attack plunged the nation into World War II—suggesting a solution to the Underwood impasse involved in the government's condemnation suit for Northwest Electric Co. land. Lt. Col. C.R. Moore proposed paying Northwest Electric Co. $10,000 for the right to flood forty-four acres of company land. The plan also included an easement over a little more than four acres for the U.S. Fish and Wildlife Service, and title to another unflooded four acres for the Indians' exclusive use. An additional payment of $521 would compensate Pacific Power and Light Co. for moving a power line. The companies had agreed to the figures, and the suit remained unsettled only because of the Indian claims for damage to their fishing sites. Moore suggested the Indians could be placated by guaranteeing them delivery of discarded salmon carcasses as long as the government operated the hatcheries.

The colonel noted that the proposed site was adjacent to a traditional fishing place now under water. He quoted Indian Agent Johnson as saying the new site "placed the Indians in practically as good a position as they were prior to construction of Bonneville Dam." They would, however, now have to go 3,600 feet upstream by boat to obtain the hatchery carcasses. The number of Indians involved in the suit varied in different reports from forty to one hundred, and the individual amounts claimed for lost fishing from ten thousand to two million dollars apiece. Moore implied the Indians need have no say in the settlement. They are wards of the government, he said, and their claims should be settled by the Fish and Wildlife Service, the

Bureau of Indian Affairs and the War Department "without resort to court action." The undersecretary of War approved three weeks later, finally making a single site available to replace the two dozen lost.

For the Indians who fished upstream at Celilo, 1941 was a good year. Indian Agent Davis at The Dalles described the season as "hectic . . . with the largest catches on record." As salmon began returning in the spring, the *Oregon Journal* had crowed, "Indians Admit Sages Fail And Salmon Passing Dam." The newspaper labeled the traditional first salmon ceremony at Celilo a "thanksgiving ceremony to the Great Spirit for a plentiful supply of salmon." Thanksgiving, the news report said, represented "admission by headmen that they have erred in predictions that Bonneville Dam would end salmon fishing."

Although fish appeared to be plentiful, the year brought other problems. Part of the reason for an increased catch at Celilo was an increase in the number of fishermen there. At a June meeting of the Celilo Fish Committee, Chief Tommy Thompson of the Wy'am complained that Omar Babcock, the Umatilla Agency superintendent, had "brought in a lot of people to fish." Before Babcock's tenure only Celilo residents fished there, Thompson complained. Others came to trade for fish, not catch them. Babcock's tenure, of course, coincided with the flooding of all the fishing sites on the Bonneville pool, and at least some of the dispossessed fishermen moved to Celilo. Henry Charley, for example, told Thompson that he and John Polk used to fish between Big Eddy and Celilo, "but now those places are flooded by the dam." John Culpus, whose family had lived on the river since long before white explorers found the Columbia, tried to fish elsewhere but was told to move. A white man claimed prior rights to the spot because he had been there five years. So Culpus, too, went to Celilo. Non-Indians, meanwhile, were muscling into the good fishing at Celilo, placing nets in the river where they would keep the fish away from the Indian sites. Seufert Brothers, the giant canning company that controlled much of the upriver commercial fishing, used set nets that also interfered with the Indians' fishing. Seufert had an Oregon state license for the nets, which were illegal for anyone else to use. When the Indians objected, the state said Seufert was there first.

And that winter in Washington state, author L.V. McWhorter, who lived on the Yakama Reservation, told Agency Superintendent Johnson about rumors that the next legislature might try to rescind its permission for the Yakama to fish at Priest Rapids. That area was home of the Wanapum Band in the big bend of the Columbia far upstream from Celilo. "Knowing the bitter animosity of the fisheries head we should not sleep on the situation," McWhorter said. Johnson scoffed at the idea. "I do not anticipate that we are going to have any serious difficulty with the present Washington State Fish Commission on matters pertaining to Indian fishing at ancient and accustomed sites off the reservation," Johnson wrote. McWhorter was not convinced. "I was instrumental—in fact brought about—the legislative act permitting them to take fish for their own table and they hate me like h—," he wrote. Washington continued to restrict Indian fishing as much as it could. And in May 1943 Warm Springs Superintendent Jasper W. Elliott wrote Indian bureau attorney Kenneth R.L. Simmons with concern about the "ill feeling which is building up between the Indians and state officers" in Oregon. Nevertheless, Oregon's legislature fell in line with the 1942 Tulee ruling and voted to let Indians fish without a license.

There was even extortion on the river. In the spring of 1942, Indian agent Davis discovered that the owner of Brown's Island, one of the ancient Indian fishing sites at Celilo Falls, was charging Indians 25 percent of their catch for the use of the island. The Indian bureau apparently stopped the practice by calling the island owner's attention to several Supreme Court decisions.

Adding to the Indians' worries in 1941 and 1942 was the presence of Edward G. Swindell Jr., a Bureau of Indian Affairs attorney who had been dispatched by Commissioner Collier to make another study of Indian fishing sites, rights and practices. Celilo Fish Committee members feared that his study was connected to the possible construction of another dam, one that would drown Celilo Falls. During the June 1941 meeting, as Swindell began his survey, Chief Thompson's son, Henry, challenged Swindell directly. "By destroying the fishing sites it is just the same as if you destroyed the chief's fireplaces where he cooks his food," Henry Thompson said. "You have taken the means away from him for feeding himself." Johnson, the Yakama Agency Superintendent, assured the fishermen that Swindell was there "to help with hunting and fishing rights" not to make studies for another dam. He said money was being set aside to buy fishing sites on the Bonneville pool. He didn't mention that the president had vetoed the funds. Swindell was more circumspect. He said he could not assure the Indians there would be no additional dams, but the Indian bureau was not planning one. The Corps of Engineers was, however—as Swindell and Johnson must have known. In fact, Swindell said little more than a year later it was "not beyond the realm of possibility" that a dam would be built near The Dalles and flood out the

Indians' major remaining commercial fishery. Fourteen years later the Indians would lose Celilo Falls. The Corps included a dam near The Dalles in its initial survey of potential Columbia River development in the 1920s. By 1942, inland agriculture and business interests had been agitating two decades for dams and locks to take barge transportation as far as Lewiston, Idaho. The question really was: when would another dam be built, not whether there would be more. The Dalles site was included in the original report, known as the 308 Report, that laid out potential navigation and hydroelectric development for the entire Columbia Basin. A pictorial representation of future Columbia River development published in the Sunday *Oregonian* October 1, 1933, included The Dalles site. By 1943, the Corps was conducting the review of the 308 report that led Congress to authorize the project in 1946. Col. Theron D. Weaver, the Corps' Portland district engineer, formally recommended building The Dalles Dam in May 1946. Because the public closely followed—and sought to influence—the Corps' development activities, Johnson and Swindell were naive at best and deceptive at worst in indicating they knew nothing about a dam at The Dalles.

With the coming of war, most of the younger fishermen and those who would become leaders entered military service. Delbert Frank moved his high school graduation up to April 1942, lied about his age, went into the Navy at seventeen, and served as a gunner on transport and cargo ships in the Pacific. Nelson Wallulatum joined the Navy when he was old enough late in the war. Percy Brigham of Umatilla was an Army sharpshooter, occasionally using his skills to provide wild boar for his unit's dinner on New Guinea. Walter Speedis of Yakama was drafted into the Army and served in the Pacific. Robert Gunnier of Yakama went from Chemawa Indian School at Salem, Oregon, into the Air Corps. He served four years before coming home at war's end to fish. Virginia Beavert, a Yakama tribal member, enlisted in the Women's Auxiliary Army Corps and served with the Cavalry at Fort Riley, Kansas.

Every reservation has a monument to its veterans, and the lists of names are long in relation to the total populations. I once asked an Indian veteran why, given this country's treatment of Indians, so many tribal members willingly went off to fight for it. Two things, he explained: the warrior tradition and defense of the land. Not the nation, the land.

While the young fishermen were away in uniform, Indians remaining at home, such as Henry Charley, Sampson Quaempts and James Jim, persisted in their efforts to obtain the sites. And the government continued to deal with the matter after a fashion. In February 1942, W. Barton Greenwood, the acting commissioner of Indian affairs, wrote to Yakama Superintendent Johnson telling him the War Department lacked authority to buy the sites. However, he said a bill before Congress would allow the Corps to use money appropriated earlier. "It is apparent that the War Department is making a sincere effort to carry out its agreement," he said, adding " . . . it is hoped that the Indians will be patient and not begin further legal action with respect to their fishing rights in the Bonneville Pool. It is our opinion that within a reasonable time new sites will be available to the Indians." He did not define reasonable. Already, four fishing seasons had gone by since the dam flooded the fishing places.

Meanwhile, the Yakama Indian Nation was, as usual, engaged in a court battle with Washington state over treaty rights. Both the U.S. Supreme Court decision in the Yakama case involving Sampson Tulee of the Klickitats and Indian bureau attorney Swindell's report on fishing rights came in 1942. The Tulee case laid the groundwork for some later decisions upholding the Indians' rights, but its immediate effect was to uphold most state authority over the Indian fishing except the requirement to buy a state license. Swindell's report, grandly titled *Report on Source, Nature and Extent of the Fishing, Hunting and Miscellaneous Related Rights of Certain Indian Tribes in Washington and Oregon,* focused on the Tulee decision's approval of state control. The court ruled that the state could regulate the Indians' fishing as long as the rules were designed to conserve the fish and applied to everyone. Swindell said the ruling inhibited the federal government from enlarging Indian fishing rights but the states could do so, at least for subsistence fishing. He had that in mind in including in his report descriptions of the way Indians lived before white settlement and "until conservation measures became necessary." He suggested that his report could be used to justify laws recognizing the rights the treaties were supposed to reserve. Swindell either did not understand or chose to ignore the fact that neither Washington nor Oregon had any interest in expanding Indian fishing rights. The two states' efforts were aimed at limiting Indians' fishing, not enhancing it. Their regulations—applied to both whites and Indians—banned weirs and traps, which were the Indians' traditional fishing tools in some places. But the rules permitted gill nets and fishing rods, which whites used and Indians at that time did not. At this time, even state fishery officials estimated that the Indian fishers took less than 9 percent of the commercial catch in the

Columbia. The Indians' 160,000 fish amounted to just under 65 percent of the commercial catch above Bonneville Dam because most non-Indian commercial fishers abandoned the upper river after the dam was built. As always, by far the largest share of fish was caught in the ocean and in the lower river.

Swindell recommended that the Indian bureau instruct the tribes in their limited rights and urge them to quit fighting the state rules. He acknowledged that convincing older fishermen would be difficult, if not impossible. But, like the agents who packed children off to boarding school, he had higher hopes for younger fishers. He also suggested that the Indian bureau set up on-reservation hunting and fishing rules unless the tribes adopted rules that met the agency's idea of accepted conservation. While the tribes and river people had no formal rules for conserving fish and game, their practices of taking only as much as they needed and not fishing at certain times had served for centuries to preserve both fish and animals.

Swindell concentrated the Columbia River portion of his report on Celilo Falls, where he said the principal problem was that "there are so many more Indians participating in the fishing than in the early days." The increase was caused partly by the Indians' desire to make money in a money-based economy. Fishing only for subsistence was no longer possible at many of their other traditional places, either because the fish runs had been destroyed or the type of gear effective in specific spots was banned by the states. And, he said, nothing could be done about whites grabbing a share of Celilo sites because the treaties said "in common with" other citizens of the territories. Like many others before and after him, Swindell did not fully understand the significance of the treaty language and the rights the Indians had retained. It remained for federal judges Robert C. Belloni and, more specifically, George W. Boldt in 1969 and 1974 rulings to spell out the full extent of "in common with." The two rulings said, in essence, the Indians were entitled to continue obtaining their food and livelihood from the fish and must be allowed a fair share of the resource. Swindell filed his massive report in July of 1942. As he prepared to leave the Bureau of Indian Affairs for the Army that December, he complained to a friend that there had been no reaction from his bosses to the report on which he had spent a full year. He had been gone for weeks before Walter V. Woehler, assistant to the commissioner, wrote with appreciation for his "extensive and creditable" report. If the BIA ever made use of Swindell's report, it is not evident.

Swindell's was not the only study of salmon and Indians done that year. Indian Agent Davis made one of his own, documenting the importance of salmon to the Indians. In a sample of five families, he calculated an average annual salmon consumption of more than 5,000 pounds of fresh, dried and salted fish and "liquid sauce." His report did not include fish traded or sold, but he noted that "during the summer the normal family at Celilo feeds quite a number of additional people who stay with them and fish at the falls." Accompanying his report to Yakama Superintendent Johnson was a list of Indian homes in the Columbia River area from Stevenson to Alderdale on the Washington side and Hood River to Arlington on the Oregon side. It included the year-round residents at Celilo. His list of seventy-four families named a dozen at Rock Creek and ten at Spearfish on the Washington side and eleven at Celilo on the Oregon side. Some members of those families still live along the river. Others were forced to move by later dams. Illustrating the fishing people's distrust of the states, Davis told Johnson that Chief Thompson had asked that the fish consumption figures be used only by federal agents and not shared with the states. Johnson took Davis's figures, did a little calculation and came up with a yearly total of 315,000 pounds of salmon consumed by the river families. A similar survey on the Yakama Reservation indicated average consumption of 1,800 pounds per family per year, or 900,000 pounds a year for the five hundred reservation families. The total for the two groups: 1,220,000 pounds. The commercial catch on the river during that period varied from 1,879,880 in 1939 to 4,830,625 in 1941. State conservation measures, however, were aimed chiefly at the Indian fishery.

While the Corps of Engineers stalled, the Bureau of Indian Affairs dithered, and Swindell and Davis studied, several dozen families clung to the river and tried to fish. At Underwood, government officials considered that a problem. Samuel J. Flickinger of BIA, Howard Polinger of the Corps' Real Estate Branch and Milton C. James and Clifford Presnell of the Fish and Wildlife Service got together in Washington, D.C., and agreed on a solution. When the Fish and Wildlife Service was taking eggs from salmon at the fish traps on the Big White Salmon River, the agency would take the stripped carcasses daily to Indians camped at the mouth of the river at Underwood, eliminating the Indians' need to fetch the dead fish. "... every reasonable effort will be made to see that the carcasses will reach the Indians in good condition," wrote Charles E. Jackson, the acting Fish and Wildlife Service director. The agency would make a similar effort at Spring Creek and the Indians could have the dead salmon from the Little White Salmon River traps if they would fetch them by way of the road. Jackson, in his memo to the commissioner of Indian affairs outlining the plan, said the Corps intended to give the Indians definite assurance they could camp at the mouth of the Big White Salmon River. The Army also would assure the Indians it would seek funds to improve all the planned campgrounds "after the paramount needs of war have been fully met." He added: "It is hoped that the Indians can be persuaded to do their part in conserving this important resource without resorting to costly litigation, at least for the duration of the war. The slight inconvenience that may be caused by the temporary inability of the U.S. Engineers to improve the Indian camp grounds is just another of the things that all citizens must cheerfully face during wartime." The fact that Jackson considered loss of their major food supply "a slight inconvenience" shows how completely government agents failed to understand the Indians. No wonder that the tribal people remained skeptical. At a mid-October Yakama Tribal Council meeting, David Miller, a Yakama tribal member who was chairman of the Celilo Fish Committee, expressed doubts that the Corps would ever build the sites. He pointed out that the agreement was made in 1939 "and nothing further had been accomplished."

Both the Yakama and the Celilo Fish Committee complained about the Big White Salmon site (Underwood). The water had risen higher than anticipated, leaving less room to camp and no room for drying sheds. The ground was steep. The water was stagnant. There was no place to dispose of the fish remains except the river, where strong current formerly carried away the offal. Now, however, rotting fish clung to the shore, creating a health hazard and an odor that made the site nearly uninhabitable. The problem was left for winter to solve. As another fishing season approached, in March 1943, the only visible action regarding the sites was concern by the Indians that the Army would tear down their fishing shacks when it removed other houses from the site. The Army assured them it had no intention of removing Indian property, but it said nothing of its earlier plan to leave the seven houses there for the fishing families.

Efforts to win Congressional approval and funds for the sites continued throughout the war. A bill was drafted in 1943 but nothing happened. The measure reappeared the next year. Once more it was pigeonholed despite a plea from J.W. Elliott, the superintendent at Warm Springs, to attorney T. Leland Brown of The Dalles to do anything possible to get the bill brought up in Congress. Finally, March 2, 1945, with the war nearing an end, President Roosevelt signed a bill authorizing post-war construction of 291 rivers and harbors projects. Included in the $382-million bill was $50,000 for restoration of Indian fishing grounds destroyed by construction of Bonneville Dam. However, the $50,000 would have to come from the Army Corps of Engineers' appropriations for maintenance and improvement of existing rivers and harbors projects; there would be no additional money for the Indians. The measure sparked bitter recriminations among the Indians. Minutes of the April 4 meeting of the Celilo Fish Committee record a people besieged. The state of Washington was trying to deny tribal fishing rights, arresting Indians for fishing at a traditional site on the Klickitat River. A new dam threatened to destroy more fishing sites than Bonneville had. Younger members of the Yakama Tribe lacked interest in preserving their rights. The $50,000, even if spent as proposed, was not enough to compensate for the losses. Andrew Barnhart, a crusty Umatilla fisherman, blamed younger Indians for accepting such a small amount and accused them of taking "side money to sell out other Indians."

Despite their differences, the committee members laid plans to present a united front to the Corps of Engineers. Committee member Jim Billy, a river resident, reminded them all that whatever their differences "preservation of the fishing rights under the Treaty of 1855 is important to the welfare of the people of Indian descent." With the war over and congressional approval of money for the sites, the Indians hoped they would have fishing and camping places before the end of 1946. As William Zimmerman Jr., assistant commissioner of Indian affairs, saw it, any number of the Army's various appropriations were available for the work. The Army saw it otherwise. Secretary of War Robert P. Patterson wrote Secretary of Interior Harold Ickes explaining that the money "is either obligated or programmed for other essential requirements and cannot be made available for the acquisition of the new sites." His reply is a succinct indication of the low priority the Army gave the in-lieu sites. Patterson added, however, that because of "the long outstanding agreement" with the Indians the War Department would try very hard to squeeze money out of its 1947 appropriations, then pending before Congress.

# 4

## DAMS AND DELAY

*You have spoken in a round about way; speak straight.*

—Yellow Serpent, Yakama delegate,
treaty conference 1855

Like a lot of other Northwest Indians, Delbert Frank came home from World War II and went fishing. In the late 1940s, as many as two thousand fishermen thronged to Celilo, the best of the few remaining fishing sites on the Columbia. The ex-servicemen were home to their roots, their traditions and their way of life, catching their families' main food supply and earning enough cash to buy whatever else they needed. Frank's voice reflects the exuberance of those days. "That was an enjoyment to me. I always loved to fish." The fishermen rode hand-pulled cable cars over the rapids to islands, and filled gunny sacks with salmon—"all that we could pack." If he caught more than his family could use, he gave the surplus to other Indians. Some he sold to the nearby Seufert cannery, which, Frank says, gave the tribal fishermen a fair deal. "He wanted to get it all. We caught the fish and took them right to him. He had good relations with the Celilo people basically. He treated them well. He'd loan money in the winter." Now an elder statesman on the Warm Springs Reservation, Frank lets an edge creep into his voice when he talks about the in-lieu sites. "In 1938, they made all kinds of promises that have almost never been kept. They promised to replace everything that was inundated. That meant fishing sites and home sites . . . . I get angry. I fight for this country, then get that kind of treatment."

Like salmon caught in a net, the fishing people struggled to get their promised fishing sites. But, like the salmon, no matter where they turned, they were stymied. The Corps of Engineers took its time allocating money for the sites. The Army and the Bureau of Indian Affairs demanded that the tribes make new, time-consuming decisions on old issues. The two agencies tossed diversions into the site-buying process. The states tried to block both Indian fishing and the fishing sites. And more dams were coming.

Looking back from the last decade of the twentieth century, with its vigorous debates over environmental issues and the merits of growth, it is difficult to capture the fervor for development that gripped the Northwest at mid-century. The debates then were not about whether to develop the region's waterways but about the order of dam construction and whether projects should be built by the federal government, private companies or local utilities. There were then no environmental impact statements for even the most massive of construction projects. There was little thought given to healthy rivers, wildlife, or the natural landscape. Dams were development. Development was progress. Progress was good. Fisheries people—state agencies, commercial fishers, sports fishers and tribes—tried in vain to slow the dam juggernaut. Richard T. Pressey, a biologist who spent thirty years with federal and Washington state fisheries agencies, was one of those who objected to more dams. He remembers the battle sadly. "We predicted many years ago that the dams would kill the salmon. We were voices in the wilderness. We were told by the governors and everyone else to keep our mouths shut—we need the electricity." Gladys Seufert, widow of the last president of Seufert Brothers Co., the fish canners, recalls angry reaction to her husband's testimony opposing The Dalles Dam. She says some people in their hometown of The Dalles never spoke to Francis Seufert again.

In 1945, the same year Congress authorized the Corps of Engineers to spend $50,000 to acquire new fishing sites for the Columbia River people, it also authorized construction of McNary Dam near Umatilla, Oregon. McNary, 145 miles up the Columbia from Bonneville, was the next step in the plan to turn the Columbia and Snake River system into a series of lakes. The next year, while the Corps was left to squeeze the Indians' money out of its existing funds, Congress allocated the engineers $2.6 million to start McNary. Industry, farmers, barge companies, civic boosters in inland towns all clamored for more dams—more electric power for more industry, more irrigation, more river transportation. In Washington state, the federal Bureau of Reclamation was rapidly developing the Columbia Basin Project, made possible by Grand Coulee Dam, which was completed in 1941. Within a few years, new farmers would flock to the dry prairie steppe of the Columbia's big bend. Along with water, they would pour fertilizer and pesticides onto fields that drained into ditches that poured the polluted water back into the Columbia, giving the salmon another hazard in their already danger-fraught lives.

The Corps of Engineers thrived on dams. These were big projects costing big money, and they put the Corps at the center of the Northwest world. As it got the first funding for McNary Dam in 1946, the Corps' division engineer recommended construction of The Dalles Dam just upstream from the eastern end of the Bonneville pool. That was an immediate threat to the Indians' fishing. The dam, eight miles downstream from Celilo, would cover the falls under thirty-five feet of water. The Indians objected, of course, and they were not alone. Within three weeks of the recommendation, Milo Moore, director of Washington state's Department of Fisheries, protested to the federal Board of Engineers for Rivers and Harbors No. 2, the Corps' body that approved such projects. Moore vehemently opposed the dam as a threat to the $10-million-a-year commercial fishing industry on the river. "Proper planning for the use of our water resources would avoid the building of this costly structure and at the same time give us all of the power needed," he said.

But the focus of his letter was even more vehement opposition to a part of the plan that suggested fishing sites for the Indians to replace Celilo. The War Department had no authority to grant Indian fishing sites, Moore said. That authority belonged to the states, and he was sure Oregon and Washington would not permit tribal fishers anywhere near the dam. "The fishing done by these tribes is not a small matter done for subsistence purposes," Moore wrote. Instead, "practically all of the" Indians' catch, as much as three million pounds a year, was sold commercially. (The states' official fisheries report for 1946 lists the Indian commercial catch at Celilo Falls—virtually the only Indian commercial fishing site—at 2.3 million pounds, just over 12 percent of the total commercial landings on the Columbia that year.) Moore needn't have worried about new fishing sites on The Dalles pool. Even at that early date, it was clear the government would not repeat the Bonneville pool promises. C.L. Graves of the BIA's area office in Portland wrote the Indian commissioner, then located in Chicago, in March 1947 describing the possibility of substitute sites as "a play in words." Based on the experience on the Bonneville pool, Graves said there was little likelihood the government could find grounds that would adequately replace Celilo and Spearfish, across the river from Celilo. The Corps was more concerned with placating non-Indian fisheries interests, which vigorously objected to The Dalles' construction, than with compensating the Indians. Before its first negotiations with the tribes, the Corps informed Oregon and Washington fisheries officials of its plans and assured them the Corps would not offer additional fishing sites. Later, Col. T. H. Lipscomb, the Corps' Portland district engineer, told non-Indian fisheries representatives that the dam would, on balance, improve the salmon runs by eliminating the Indian fishery.

Moore, the tribes, and others opposed to the dam got their say before a congressional fisheries committee in August 1946. But the response from more powerful forces was immediate and strong. The Inland Empire Waterways Association, an amalgam of upriver interests led by Walla Walla, Washington, Mayor Herbert G. West, combined with downriver shipping, irrigation, and utility leaders to debunk the fishermen's fears. Federal officials from the Corps and Bonneville Power Administration helped frame the association arguments. Their theme was simple: Development of the Northwest depended on construction of Columbia and Snake River dams. Safeguards were built in to protect the fish, which were at more danger from the commercial harvest than from the dams. In the political climate of the late 1940s that was enough. There were more hearings with the same arguments. Henry Charley, the long-time leader of the Celilo Fish Committee and great grandson of a treaty signer, told one hearing in 1947 that the Corps with its dams "cut the heart out of the Indian." He reminded the Army officers that white men had promised the Indian protection. Where, he asked them, were the buffalo, the elk, the deer, the salmon? He answered his own question: "White man's conservation took it all away." And, if more dams are built, he said, the Indians will soon starve.

Even the heavily conflicted Department of the Interior came down on the side of eventual development. Interior at that time included the power-marketing Bonneville Power Administration, along with the BIA, Fish and Wildlife Service, National Park Service, Bureau of Reclamation, Bureau of Mines, and Bureau of Land Management. Some of those agencies were charged with developing natural resources; others were charged with protecting natural resources against development. In a 1947 memo to the federal Columbia Basin Inter-Agency, Assistant Secretary Warner W. Gardner outlined the issues and the department's recommendation. The Fish and Wildlife Service believed that construction of The Dalles and five planned

Snake River dams would wipe out the salmon runs. The commercial fishery in the river had a wholesale value of $6 million to $10 million a year. Added to the ocean catch, the capital value of the fishery was $125 million. Salmon made up 70 percent of the diet for members of the three treaty tribes, and the commercial value of their catch was $375,000 a year. Gardner placed a capital value of $15 million to $20 million on the Indians' fishing rights. The National Park Service estimated a capital value of $20 million for recreation fishing on the Columbia and its tributaries. But, Gardner said, BPA estimated regional electric power needs of nearly four million kilowatts by 1955. That required added generators at existing dams and building half a dozen new dams in addition to McNary, already under construction. Neither irrigation nor flood control would be greatly affected immediately. Gardner said navigation issues lay outside his authority, but included an annual loss to shipping of $3 million from failure to build The Dalles and Snake River dams. After weighing those figures, Gardner concluded: The Department agrees that the Columbia River fisheries should not be allowed indefinitely to block the full development of the other resources of the river. The fish could be saved by not building eight dams on the Columbia and five on the Snake. But that would mean loss of five million kilowatts of low-cost power, no deep-draft navigation above The Dalles, no barges on the Snake, and ultimate sacrifice of one million acres of irrigation. "It is difficult to precisely equate these potential benefits against the value of the present Columbia River salmon, but all concerned within the Department agreed that they are the foundation of the ultimate development of the Pacific Northwest and that they considerably outweigh the resulting cost to the commercial fisheries, the Indians and the sportsmen . . . . Overall benefits to the Pacific Northwest are such that the present salmon run must if necessary be sacrificed." With that decision, the battle for fish was lost although skirmishes went on.

He suggested some ways to ameliorate the fish loss. First came developing salmon runs in the lower Columbia and coastal streams, where Indians had almost entirely given up fishing. Second came "Indian readjustment," to include payment for their fishing rights, a share in the downstream fishery, and "alternative economic opportunities" for the Indian fishing population. "There is no difference in principle between flooding out a white man's factory and an Indian's fishery," Gardner said. As compassionate as Gardner's statement sounds, it assumes that the salmon were a mere economic matter. To the Indians the fish were far more. Their culture, their religion, and their diet were based on the fish. Losing the salmon meant not finding just another way to make money; it meant finding another way of life. Gardner estimated that both amelioration programs would require ten years to develop, and suggested that The Dalles and Snake River dams be delayed while upriver projects were hastened. But even that modest proposal was rejected in the push to develop. Eight months later, the inter-agency committee turned down Gardner's plan in favor of intensifying the effort to transplant salmon runs to downstream tributaries.

Nature bolstered the dam builders in the spring of 1948. Late spring floods poured across half a million acres in the Northwest, killed fifty people and caused $102 million in property damage. The Corps of Engineers already was updating its comprehensive plan for river development in the region. President Truman ordered the agency to review the plan in light of the disaster, adding weight to flood-control arguments in support of dam building. Engineers concluded that a system of storage dams throughout the region was needed to avert similar disasters. Dam construction moved ahead. Nine years later, Celilo Falls was gone.

The Cold War and Korean War also sped construction of The Dalles Dam, as expanding aluminum and plutonium production gobbled massive amounts of electric power. In November 1950, William E. Warne, assistant secretary of the Interior, suggested that The Dalles be the next constructed dam "if defense requirements demand another additional large block of power." A few months later, in April 1951, Indian Commissioner Dillon S. Myer told E. Morgan Pryse, the Portland Area BIA director, the bureau could not oppose the dam "because of urgent national defense need for power." Pryse, the top BIA official in the Pacific Northwest, had urged his superiors in Washington to object to the dam. Both the Warm Springs and Umatilla tribes later, reluctantly, approved the dam as a defense measure. In January 1952, the Corps' Lipscomb said the Korean War greatly increased the urgency to develop hydropower. "The Dalles Dam is being built earlier than even its most ardent enthusiasts could have hoped." Construction got under way a month later.

As planners in Washington plotted the long-term demise of their fishing, the river people faced more immediate threats closer to home. Nels Helmick, who owned a service station and small store near the Celilo fishing village, had leased from the Seufert Brothers Co. cannery a stretch of shore land west of his store. He planned to build a motel on the property, and asked Indian Agent Davis whether he would face any opposition when it came time to get rid of the adjacent Indian camp. An outraged Davis told his new boss at the Yakama Agency, L.W. Shotwell, that he had given Helmick a lesson in history, treaties, and the Indians' right to fish and erect drying houses on lands bordering their fisheries. Helmick was not one to give up easily. He suggested that if the land fell within the "bordering fisheries" definition, perhaps the Indians could all use one large house instead of "having the place cluttered up with a lot of such shanties." Davis appeared to splutter as he wrote, "He seemed to be of the opinion, as gained from talking with William Seufert, that he could just go ahead and use a bulldozer on the Indian shacks and clear them all out of that space and we couldn't do anything about it. I informed him that the minute that I discovered any such action I would get in telephone communication with you and possibly with the United States attorney." Shotwell agreed with Davis and added that the Indians could make Helmick pay heavily if he attempted to destroy their shacks. Davis discussed Shotwell's response with Helmick. There was no further correspondence regarding Mr. Helmick or his motel, nor is there a motel there today.

That problem was more easily resolved than the conflict with Oregon and Washington, which continued while tribes and state fisheries officials tried to prevent the Corps from building The Dalles Dam. The two states each year closed commercial fishing above Bonneville Dam for a period to allow salmon to escape upstream to spawn. They had not tried to enforce the closure on the Indians, agreeing to what they called the tribes' "alleged necessity" to fish for family food. However, the top fisheries officials of the two states notified Interior Secretary J.A. Krug in the summer of 1946 that they planned to begin enforcing the closure against the Indians on August 25 that year. The state officials, Milo Moore of Washington and Arnie J. Suomele of Oregon, said in recent years the Indians had sold catches during the closed season, resulting in too few fish to spawn. Dams had made the situation worse, they said. The Yakama, Warm Springs and Umatilla tribes promptly adopted resolutions opposing the enforcement. They wrote Krug complaining that the action would violate their treaty rights. In a separate telegram the Yakama Nation told William Zimmerman, assistant commissioner of Indian affairs, that the closure would cause hunger and hardship, and asked the Bureau of Indian Affairs to intervene. The BIA, however, refused to support the tribes. Zimmerman suggested instead that they ask the states to allow fishing for personal use during the closure. Sports fishing continued unrestricted. The Celilo Fish Committee, composed of representatives of all three tribes and the people who lived on the river, finally condemned commercial fishing by Indians during the closed season. But the resolution also urged the states to impose similar restrictions below Bonneville Dam, where 90 percent of the fish were caught. The Wy'ams—mostly the residents of Celilo Village—adopted their own resolution later opposing the closure. They said that dams, not Indians, impeded the salmon runs. As the dispute continued through the fall, Washington Governor Mon C. Wallgren suggested paying the Indians and buying them fish to keep them from fishing. Wy'am Chief Tommy Thompson started a petition campaign opposing the governor's plan. The *Skamania County Pioneer* newspaper reported, "The Dalles Chamber of Commerce, under the direction of W.A. Nelson, well known Gorge booster, is behind the Indians." Residents of The Dalles long considered the Indian fishermen at Celilo a tourist attraction that brought business into their city. Wallgren's plan died quietly. The fishing issue was not wholly resolved until the 1980s and still flares on occasion.

During the late 1940s, the number of disputes at Celilo increased between Indians, who claimed exclusive rights at the falls, and whites, who muscled in for a share of the fish. Frustrated Indians destroyed white fishermen's platforms and wound up in jail. The Wy'am chief, Tommy Thompson, traditionally had settled disputes over sites, but non-Indians ignored him. A bill was introduced in Congress to give the Secretary of the Interior unlimited power to regulate fishing at Celilo, even to deciding who could fish there regardless of treaty rights. The Yakama Nation reacted sharply, saying it would prevent the tribes from defending their own treaty rights. The bill never passed. Pryse, director of the newly-created Portland Area Office of the BIA, suggested instead that coordination of Celilo fishing be moved to the new office from the Yakama agency. In February 1947, the assistant commissioner designated Pryse coordinator of all fishing issues in the Northwest and ordered him to cooperate with state authorities. At the same time on the Washington shore, Klickitat Indians in a resolution "to whom it may concern" demanded to know what right the state had to destroy Indian fishing gear or throw it into the river. "It was lying idle for a month or more. It would be different if I was caught fishing in the river. Nets cost $200 or more each." The resolution was signed by Cecil Wesley, Chairman, and Caples Dave, chief. Milo Moore, the Washington Fisheries director, said it was state policy to observe treaty rights—but Indians had to obey state rules. Whether accurate or not, Wesley's and Dave's complaint was a common one. Former Oregon Fisheries Director Robert W. Schoning, who started his career as a department biologist on the river, recalls there were cases of Washington fisheries officials cutting or tearing up Indian nets. On the Oregon side of the river, the fishermen complained that Seufert, the canning company, had taken the cable supporting the cable car on which the Indians traveled from the river bank to their island fishing sites. Seufert claimed the cable passed over its property and filed suit, charging the Indians with trespassing on its land as they rode the aerial cable car. Neither of those incidents alone caused major disruption of the Indian fishery, but they were typical of the skirmishes the fishing people have fought almost continuously since the 1850s to maintain their fishing rights.

Against this background of development and conflict, the Army did, as promised, allocate money for the Indian fishing sites, and in 1947 resumed discussions with the tribes and river people. It was the tenth season since their usual and accustomed places had disappeared beneath Bonneville's waters. Now it was the Bureau of Indian Affairs tossing the monkey wrench. Without explanation, the bureau suggested diverting a portion of the $50,000 site money to the village at Celilo, which had not been flooded by Bonneville Dam. The Indian bureau created further delay by insisting that the tribes reaffirm their 1939 resolutions approving the six-site agreement and that the new resolutions be in a form specified by the Indian bureau. To make matters worse, as the fishermen gathered at Underwood, the Big White Salmon in-lieu site, for the spring season, they found a log dump at their campsite. A white logger had built a road where Indian homes had been and was dumping logs into the White Salmon River, blocking the shore where the Fish and Wildlife Service delivered hatchery fish to the Indians. The logging operation made it impossible for the Indians to use the only in-lieu site the Corps had acquired.

Mary Underwood Lane, a Cascade Indian who lived along the river, called Davis' attention to the loggers impinging on the Big White Salmon site. She sent a handwritten note June 12 reporting excavation for a log dump on the property planned for the Indian camp. Davis promised to investigate and sent an inquiry through the agency channels. Area Director Pryse asked the Corps to consider the Indians' rights when deciding whether to approve the application of Rogers Brothers Logging Co. to build a row of piles and dolphins in the White Salmon River. Although excavation was under way in June, there was an August 1 deadline for protests. The Corps promised to remove the logging operation if it interfered with the Indians.

The Corps did order the company to move. It refused. The Army passed the matter along to the United States attorney for Western Washington, who filed suit accusing the firm of illegally building on government property and obstructing a navigable stream. Rogers Brothers sent a company attorney, John W. Coughlin, and a Mr. Nelson, to talk to Davis, the Indian agent. The two convinced Davis that the company had some legal right to the site, and that long litigation could keep the Indians from using the camp for some time. They said the company was willing to cooperate with the Indians, however. Davis, instead of seeing this as a threat, suggested it might be a good deal for the fishermen if the logging company would level the ground and build a camp for them. He said the Indians would be drying fish there, not fishing, so the loggers would not interfere with fishing. He did not speculate on the effects of the logging operation on the salmon trying to reach the White Salmon River. The loggers stayed. Later, the company tried to get the site away from the Indians by offering the Yakama Nation land farther up the White Salmon River in exchange for the Underwood property. The Yakama refused.

The struggle over The Dalles Dam, the debate over Celilo, the conflicts with the states over fishing rights, and the gadfly attacks of Helmick, Seufert and Rogers Logging all helped set off a round of squabbling among the Indians. Rivalries between, and within, tribes go back centuries. Whether the Bureau of Indian Affairs and Corps intentionally exploited those rivalries cannot be proved, but the government had a long record of successfully using the divide and conquer technique as whites moved west. In addition, the Indians' process of making group decisions by consensus was a much more difficult and time-consuming process than deciding matters by majority rule.

Residents of Celilo seem to have gotten wind of efforts to enhance Celilo well before the Indian bureau broached the idea to the fishing people publicly. The Celilo people dispatched a delegation to Congress in January 1947 after hearing that the Warm Springs, Yakama and Umatilla tribes were trying to get thirty-four acres at Celilo. They feared the thirty-four acres would take in the seven-acre village Congress granted the river people in 1927. About two hundred people lived in the village and at Rock Creek across the river. John Whiz, their spokesman, said, "We want to make it clear that the Celilo (or Columbia River) tribe is not in any way affiliated with any of the above named tribes." The issue was soon entangled with the Bonneville in-lieu sites. Indian Agent Davis first raised the possibility of diverting in-lieu site money to Celilo in a March 1947 notice announcing a meeting for "Indians who have lost fishing sites by the building of Bonneville Dam." That notice may help explain why some of the few Indians who remember him did not consider Davis a friend, although his correspondence indicates he was the Indians' staunchest ally in the bureaucracy. Percy Brigham, an eighty-eight-year-old Umatilla fisherman with a vivid memory and firm opinions, had one word for Davis: bad. Even the judicious Chief Wallulatum describes the agent as no particular friend of the Indians. Walter Speedis of Yakama, however, recalled him as "a handy man" in helping resolve problems. In his notice of the March 27, 1947, meeting, Davis said the BIA was seeking a decision on use of the money promised by the War Department. He listed potential uses as providing camps at Herman Creek, Wind River, Big and Little White Salmon rivers and Big Eddy—all in-lieu sites long agreed on—and "fixing up the camp at Celilo, Oregon with new houses for the fishermen, including leveling of the grounds, providing water and so forth." He added, "Since the Celilo fishery seems to be the most important it would seem to some that the money from the War Department should be spent there instead of in the other camps."

The meeting in The Dalles City Hall included representatives from the tribes, the river people, the Army Corps of Engineers and the BIA. The morning session was devoted to discussion of the previously selected in-lieu sites and what the Indians wanted done with them. At Big White Salmon, Henry Charley said the fishermen wanted dry sheds and living quarters rebuilt plus level ground, running water, an incinerator and drying racks. Henry Roe Cloud, the new Umatilla superintendent, and Jones Spencer of Yakama emphasized replacement of living quarters. Several other Indians also stressed the importance of housing. Significantly, Davis' five-page summary of the meeting notes that Don E. Meldrum, the Corps land officer, agreed to building living quarters providing there was enough money. Twenty years later the Bureau of Indian Affairs would contend that the sites were never intended to contain homes, leading to a major court case. There was some argument about whether Herman Creek was indeed a traditional site. (Percy Brigham's family fished there then and continues to do so.) There was discussion about whether a site should be at Spearfish Village or Three Mile Rapids at the eastern edge of the pool. Spearfish Village would be under water if The Dalles Dam were built. "It appeared to be the policy of the War Department to refrain from placing improvements where they would be lost by inundation due to dam construction," Davis wrote. The proposed Tenino site faced a similar problem, and the Indians suggested using Lone Pine Island instead. When The Dalles Dam was built in the mid-1950s its north footing covered the Big Eddy site, which at 225 acres was to have provided more than half the promised 400 acres.

Floyd H. Phillips, the BIA district forester in Portland, opened the afternoon session by proposing that $15,000 of the $50,000 allotted to the Bonneville sites be diverted to Celilo. The government had an option to buy thirty-four acres there from Seufert Brothers for $2,100, but did not have money to complete the purchase. There were a number of houses ready to be erected at Celilo but no money for the work, he said. Robert Quaempts, speaking for the residents of Big White Salmon, said he was unwilling to divert the money if there would not be enough to make the Underwood improvements. Superintendent Elliott of the Warm Springs Agency said he thought using the money at Celilo would be a good thing but only if those who suffered losses on the Bonneville pool agreed. Mary Underwood Lane, a Cascade Indian, said most of the displaced Bonneville fishermen were now using Celilo, so that money spent there would benefit them. Alex Saluskin, a long-time Yakama leader who fished at Celilo, reminded the gathering that no amount of money was specified in the original agreement. The War Department was obligated to spend whatever was needed to acquire and improve the sites, Saluskin said. Meldrum confirmed Saluskin's statement. He said the Corps initially thought $50,000 would be enough, but rising prices made the sum inadequate. Two standing votes on diverting the money were muddled. Some delegates voted both for and against the diversion. Davis said, however, it was evident the majority opposed diversion. Phillips then said the tribal councils would have to reconfirm their approval of the original plan. If any money was left over there would be another meeting to decide what to do with it.

The Indian bureau certainly understood the Indians' wishes and was aware that there would be no money left over for Celilo. Edward Swindell, who had made the 1942 fishery study, had become the agency's district counsel in Portland. He wrote about the issue to Kenneth Simmons, who had left the agency and included the Yakama Nation among the clients of his Billings, Montana, law office. Swindell said he assumed Simmons had the same information he did, "namely that the powers that be in the War Department in Washington were of the opinion that the money or a portion could be diverted to Celilo." He added, "However, the Indians at the meeting turned thumbs down on the proposition and it's probably just as well for the reason that the $50,000 is far from adequate to do all that was agreed on several years ago. If the amount of $15,000 as was considered at the meeting was diverted, the War Department could use the diversion as a basis for claiming the Indians had agreed to accept much less than was originally agreed upon." And he noted Meldrum's assurance that the Corps would carry out its obligation. Pryse, the area director, wrote superintendents of the three tribal agencies a few days later urging them to get quick tribal council action on the new resolutions. He said the Corps was demanding the new resolutions before acquiring sites. Davis in his report of the meeting said the order came from Phillips of Pryse's office. Davis was there; Pryse was not. But the Corps later used the lack of new resolutions to delay action.

The issue of using the Bonneville money at Celilo did not go away. Two weeks after the Indians rejected the proposed diversion of funds, U.S. Senator Guy Cordon, an Oregon Republican, lent some support to the diversion proposal. In a telegram to T. Leland Brown, an attorney in The Dalles, Cordon said Congress had not limited the money to Bonneville pool projects, and it could legally be spent anywhere in Oregon or Washington. Brown, who was attorney for the Warm Springs, passed the telegram on to Pryse and said he also would inform the Warm Springs tribes. Brown said he believed it was "generally understood between all of us" that at least $15,000 should be spent at Celilo. It would be at least two years before any other money could be obtained from Congress for Celilo, he said, and even then it would be difficult to get. He was sure when the Indians understood "the true situation" they would agree. "I know our Warm Springs Indians think along this line," he said. But no Warm Springs delegate supported the diversion at the March meeting. Only Mary Underwood Lane of the Mid-Columbia spoke in favor. Brown, at the time, also was attorney for Seufert Brothers, although in those days such a situation was not necessarily considered a conflict of interest.

During this period, the late 1940s, tribes began to have increased influence over their own affairs. High-handed actions, such as Davis's with the loggers, were on their way out. Each tribe by then had hired lawyers that, although requiring BIA approval, represented the tribes, not the government. The attorneys gave the tribes a source of advice independent from the paternalistic BIA. The Yakama Nation already had a tradition of pursuing its treaty rights through the courts, and Alex Saluskin as chairman continued to use the legal system. Saluskin's stepdaughter, Virginia Beavert, a graduate anthropologist, recalls Simmons, the attorney, a handsome man with silver gray hair, visiting the family home and talking law for hours with Saluskin and her mother. The move to tribal government also helped the tribes deal with the world outside their reservations. Warm Springs tribes had established a governing council in 1938 soon after the Indian Reorganization Act encouraged the creation of tribal governments. The Yakama Nation established a formal government in 1944 and the Umatilla tribes in 1948. Before the new councils were formed, most business affecting the tribes was handled by the agency superintendent, often without consulting the Indians. The Yakama's committee of leaders from the various tribes and bands dealt largely with planning ceremonies and powwows and making sure that salmon and the other traditional foods were available for the events. That council had no authority over the member tribes and bands of the Yakama Nation. The Umatilla worked through chiefs and headmen, who took most matters to the superintendent. Some things the leaders handled themselves. For instance, if an Indian rancher had cattle to sell, he probably would take them to his chief or headman, who would market all the animals from that band. With the rise of tribal governments, leaders began efforts toward economic development of their reservations with tribal enterprises, such as the furniture factory started by Chairman Alex Saluskin at Yakama. Not all these efforts at self-help met with approval from BIA officials. Owen Panner, who came to Bend, Oregon, from Oklahoma after World War II, was the long-time attorney for the Warm Springs tribes before becoming a federal judge. Panner recalls a heated discussion with the area director for the BIA, who told the attorney he should not be giving economic advice to his client tribes. "I don't want them to be getting rich," Panner said the director, Don C. Foster, told him. "If they get washing machines, they'll just tear them up." Panner said maybe this generation will but the next one won't. "I learned in Oklahoma that when a rich Indian got drunk, there was someone to pick him out of gutter. When a poor Indian got drunk, there was no one to pick him up. I want them to be better off." But the rise of tribal governments signaled a loss of influence for the river people, the ones most affected by the loss of villages and fishing sites. As the tribes formed governments, the BIA dealt with those entities. As Pryse explained to Henry Charley, most of the river people were enrolled in one or another of the tribes and therefore were represented through those tribal governments. The Klickitats, for example, were among the fourteen tribes and bands with signers of the Yakama treaty. But the river people, as exemplified by John Whiz's statement about the addition to Celilo, always have felt themselves apart, and many still feel they are not fully represented by tribal government. To make their voices heard, the river people in 1947 formed the Mid-Columbia Indian Rights Council, made up of the nine chiefs of the river tribes. The council, under various names, has continued at changing levels of activity.

The Umatilla's transition came just as the vital issue of in-lieu sites required decisions, which the new leaders were not yet ready to make. Attorney Brown's attempt to divert site money to Celilo might also have made their tribal leaders wary. The Seufert Brothers Co. commercial fishing operations often opposed Indian fishing interests. Although some Indian fishermen sold to Seufert and felt he paid them fairly, the company's owners generally preferred buying fish from the white commercial fishermen who at that time were still operating in The Dalles area. And Brown represented Seufert.

As these changes were taking place, the tribes also were dealing with new people. Don Meldrum, the Corps land officer who seemed determined to carry out the in-lieu site mandate, died. His replacement, Harry H. Rockwell, pledged to carry out Meldrum's wishes, but the promise fizzled into indifference. The more sympathetic Earl Woolridge replaced the imperious Henry Roe Cloud, who had succeeded Omar Babcock as Umatilla superintendent in 1939. L.W. Shotwell succeeded Yakama Superintendent M. A. Johnson. Davis remained, but he would soon leave and his office at The Dalles would be closed. Many of the old tribal leaders continued their roles. The generation of World War II veterans had not yet moved into leadership. The Umatilla had Sam Kash Kash, a fisherman who pursued fishery issues for three decades, dealt shrewdly with government and other tribes, and represented the tribes in Washington. There also was Steve Hall, a tribal chairman described by attorney Charles F. Luce as "steady Eddy, a highly respected man," and Louis McFarland, another fisherman who effectively lobbied Congress. For Yakama, Alex Saluskin led efforts to get the fishing sites, urged young tribal members to obtain an education, and established an industrial park to provide jobs on the reservation. Wilson Charley served as secretary of the Celilo Fish Committee and left a legacy of leadership that resulted in the naming of a Reservation Road in his honor. At Warm Springs, Nelson Wallulatum's uncles, Chief Joe McCorkle and Jim Palmer, were members of the tribal fish committee active in the site issue. Wallulatum, recently back from Navy service, drove his uncles to the innumerable meetings and listened to the talk. It seemed to him as if every day was a word battle over fisheries rights. "I recall that many times we sat and met until 2 a.m. over words to sustain our right to that fishery." Wallulatum lived on the Warm Springs Reservation but fished for several years in the early 1950s "when there were fish."

Both the Warm Springs and the Yakama tribes acted quickly after the March 1947 meeting to reconfirm their approval of the agreement although the Yakama made some additions. That tribe suggested a study of developing the Lone Pine Island site and consideration of improvements at Spearfish, the Indian village on the Washington shore two miles east of the Bonneville pool. The Yakama resolution also stated that if there was money left over after the Bonneville work, the tribe would be willing to discuss uses for the money. And the resolution once more emphasized that the sites were compensation only for loss of fishing sites, not for any loss of fish.

The Umatilla Tribes, struggling through the shift from traditional tribal government to management by an elected board, did not take action until the summer of 1949. The Corps adamantly refused to do anything until all three tribes passed resolutions to the Army's satisfaction. It spent months quibbling with the Yakama over their additions to the standard form. Area Director Pryse urged the agency superintendents to push their tribes into clarifying their positions and making them unanimous. However, he did nothing to push the Corps to do something about those sites that had never been subject to disagreement. The Indian agency's district lawyer, Swindell, waited three months after the Yakama council acted, until July 26, 1947, before advising Yakama Superintendent Johnson that the Yakama resolution needed some revision to meet Corps objections. He provided the wording needed, covering substitution of the Lone Pine site for Tenino, improvements at Spearfish, and use of the Bonneville money elsewhere if any was left over. Swindell added the clarifying phrase that improvements be completed before the money could be considered left over. The Warm Springs tribes wavered over the substitution of Lone Pine for Tenino, not wanting to eliminate Tenino and not opposing Lone Pine as an alternative.

Pryse recorded his increasing embarrassment at being unable to get tribal unity while Henry Roe Cloud, then still the Umatilla superintendent, grew more and more impatient with the tribes' delay. He authorized the use of two government cars to take a dozen Umatilla men to a Yakama Tribal Council meeting January 28, 1948, to discuss the site substitution. "My personal opinion about this Lone Pine matter is that this trip is wholly unnecessary as in five minutes the Business Committee here could pass on it," he fumed in a letter to Yakama Superintendent Shotwell. Swindell registered his own growing impatience by refusing to attend a tribal meeting to explain the substitution. When Davis wrote Roe Cloud on July 20 on behalf of the Mid-Columbia people asking about the status of the Umatilla resolution, he drew an exasperated response. Roe Cloud quoted tribal members as fearing the site substitution would result in a loss of treaty rights or that the government would take the tribes' share of the $50,000 out of tribal funds. Some felt the money was meant for the Rock Creek people who fished on the Bonneville pool, and the Umatilla had no right to take action. He said no amount of reasoning seemed to change their minds. "... unfortunately Indian reasoning does not coincide with the necessities required by legal technicalities," he wrote.

Although Indian himself, Roe Cloud seems to have had little empathy with the residents of the Umatilla Reservation. Alphonse Halfmoon, now vice chairman of the Umatilla Board of Trustees, recalls Roe Cloud as interested only in education and hunting, not in fishing rights. A Winnebago from the Plains, Roe Cloud hunted with Halfmoon's father but otherwise seems to have had only formal contacts with the tribal people.

Through the fall of 1948, the Corps, the Indians and Davis haggled over a legal definition of the proposed Lone Pine site, hoping specific boundaries might bring specific agreement. Spring floods washed sand away from the favored site, leaving only bleak rocks. A site on Lone Pine Island looked promising, but it would require a bridge for access. Finally, on October 22, the Celilo Fish Committee approved an area on the south shore of the river near Lone Pine Island. A small amount of dynamite would take care of many large rocks that dotted the site, the committee said. The Warm Springs Council approved the site November 5. The Yakama Council concurred February 8, 1949. There is no record that the Umatilla tribes ever approved. But on September 30, 1949, Lt. Col. D.A. Elliget, Acting District Engineer for the Corps, wrote John Whiz of the Celilo Fish Committee that the Army expected to have the sites in time to discuss proposed improvements early in 1950.

Colonel Elliget's estimate, like so many others involving the in-lieu sites, turned out to be wildly over-optimistic. A year and a half later nothing had been done. World War II had ended nearly six years earlier, but the government was still blaming the war for delaying acquisition of the sites. Swindell, the BIA attorney, assured James Jim, an Indian living on the river shore, in early 1951 that the matter was still "under active consideration" and no doubt would be finished soon. Another over-optimistic estimate.

Two weeks later, B.L. Price, chief of the Corps' real estate division in Portland, reported to E. Morgan Pryse, director of the Portland Area Office of the Bureau of Indian Affairs, on the status of the six planned sites. Little had changed since 1949. The Corps had obtained a little over four acres at Big White Salmon and was trying to condemn a Skamania County road on the tract. It also had acquired four acres at Wind River but didn't expect a federal court trial of its condemnation for the remaining nineteen acres until sometime in 1952. After the Corps filed to condemn the land, the owner logged all the timber worth selling.

After several years of silence, the aging Mr. Jessup, who began pestering Indian Agent Davis to buy his Little White Salmon property for the fishermen in 1939, turned up again in 1946, offering six acres for sale. This time he made the offer to Henry Charley of the Celilo Fish Committee. Jessup even offered to help the Indians fight the politicians "who will deprive the Indians of all and everything they have if they have the opportunity." But buying land was up to the Corps and the Corps wasn't buying then. By 1951, when the Corps was ready to buy, it had to deal with Mary Jessup, and she had decided she didn't want to sell the land for the Indians' use after all. The Corps was negotiating for nine acres of the Lone Pine site. Seufert Brothers Co. owned the land and did not want to sell it for Indian use. The Corps also was meeting opposition from both the private owner and the state in acquiring the Herman Creek site. The state, emphasizing its displeasure at plans for a site near a fish hatchery, quit providing spawned-out carcasses to the Indians. The Indians argued that the hatchery should not have been built near their promised site.

The Corps was assured of one real success with its land acquisition. The 225 acres of Big Eddy—more than half the promised 400 acres—was to be acquired from the state of Washington through condemnation proceedings scheduled to begin May 15, 1951. However, Price acknowledged that within a few years the property would be taken for The Dalles Dam, not used as an Indian fishing site. In a final irony, The Dalles Dam would also drown the irreplaceable Celilo, the largest and most significant of the Indians' traditional fishing places.

In late May 1951, the Yakama tribe tried to nudge the Corps into action. It asked for a meeting with Corps officials in Washington, D.C. The BIA demanded an update from Pryse before the Yakama delegation reached the Capital. His outline differed little from the Corps' report earlier in the month but added that the total appraised value of the sites was $19,248, an estimate he said was probably too low. Adding the Corps' administrative costs and $30,000 for the leased logging and log-booming rights at Wind River and Little White Salmon, Pryse estimated the total cost of acquiring the sites at $55,650. He gave no estimate for the promised improvements. But he noted that the sites' importance and value would increase enormously if The Dalles Dam was built. In reality, the dam already was a foregone conclusion. Construction of the dam began nine months later, and some of the first work was at the Indians' site. The only record of the Yakama meeting with the Corps is a June 8 letter from the commissioner of Indian affairs, Dillon S. Myer. Myer said everyone agreed the Corps had a responsibility to acquire the six sites, make improvements and build access roads. But the Corps doubted that the $50,000 appropriated for the project would cover all the costs, a notion borne out by Pryse's estimates. The Corps said it might have to ask Congress for more money.

At the same time, the Corps suggested the Indians might prefer building improvements on the sites already in hand while it waited to acquire the rest of the sites. Pryse thought this was a fine idea. He arranged for the Indians to inspect the sites again and then meet again to tell the Corps "their current views." But the views were mostly those of the Corps and the meeting, conducted on July 20, marks the point when the Army began to back away from its commitment. A.D. Stanley, a civilian Corps official, brought up new problems: difficulty in obtaining a satisfactory water supply at Lone Pine; a possible substitution for the Little White Salmon site; whether to hold out for eliminating roads at Big White Salmon. And the Umatilla tribes had never given formal approval to substituting Lone Pine for Tenino. Adding to problems—in the Corps' view—was the BIA, which did not want to take over responsibility for any of the sites until all six were acquired and improved. Lt. Col. J. W. Sloat, the Corps district executive officer, said conditions had changed since the 1939 agreement. He suggested both that the Indians share the sites with logging interests and accept improvement of one or more sites with available funds instead of waiting to acquire all the sites.

But Henry Charley, secretary of the Celilo Fish Committee, reminded Sloat that the $50,000 had been only an estimate of the cost and the Corps' responsibility would not end until all the sites were purchased and the improvements made. He listed the improvements as building drying houses and living quarters, leveling the ground and providing running water, incinerators and sanitary facilities. Sloat argued that the $50,000 was appropriated only for site acquisition although the 1945 act authorizing the appropriation states "to acquire land and provide facilities." Thomas K. Yallup, harking back to the Yakama's recent meeting in Washington, D.C., told Sloat the Army had assured him it would ask Congress for more money if the $50,000 was not enough to complete the work required by the Engineers' agreement with the Indians. Strangely, the minute-taker—no doubt one of the government people—wrote "alleged agreement," another indication the Corps might be looking for a way out of the project. Yallup, long a key leader for the river people in the Yakama tribes, was always positive about the government's promise; he would not have called it an "alleged" agreement. Despite his insistence that the appropriation was for acquisition only, Sloat said the Big White Salmon site was ready for improvement. In addition he said Wind River, Little White Salmon and Lone Pine could be purchased within three months after the tribes once more gave specific approval.

Through the years, whenever the Corps was attempting to steer things in a new direction, it demanded that the tribes re-approve the old one. It is difficult to determine from the record whether this was simply the military mind at work or a devious effort to avoid the issue by creating the inevitable delays involved in tribal decision-making. With its dams, once the Corps got congressional authorization and funding, it moved ahead. If changes in design, or even location, were needed—as with Bonneville—the engineers made the required adjustments and moved on. With the Indian sites, if every comma in tribal resolutions didn't match, the Corps asked that new action be taken. Although the tribes had long agreed on four sites, the Corps repeatedly delayed work on them while seeking agreement on the final two sites. Whatever the Army's motive, the ploy served several times to slow progress on the sites.

At the urging of Frank Suppah of Warm Springs, the Fish Committee adopted a set of recommendations to guide the Corps. Suppah sought immediate action by the committee on grounds any delay would keep the fishermen from the promised sites that much longer. In making its suggestions, the committee acknowledged certain physical changes since the original approval of the sites. The committee made a series of recommendations. It suggested that the Corps look for a better site than Herman Creek, that it substitute eight acres near Cook, Washington, for the Little White Salmon site and that purchase of Big Eddy await further investigation. The resolution recommended that the Lone Pine, Wind River and Big White Salmon sites remain as previously agreed on. The committee set development of Big White Salmon as the top priority followed by Little White Salmon, Lone Pine and Wind River. A final piece was added to the resolution: "That the Fish Committee feels that the War Department should replace the living quarters and drying sheds destroyed by the Bonneville pool in addition to other facilities agreed on." (Although the War Department was merged with the Navy Department to become the Department of Defense in 1947, records—including Army correspondence—continued the use of "War Department" for a number of years.) The Yakama Tribal Council approved the resolution four days later, but added that it would like Big Eddy acquired as No. 5 on the priority list. The other tribes also approved.

Although the July 1951 meeting appeared to have resolved any conflict over sites and priorities, two new disputes loomed almost immediately. One was between the Corps and the BIA, the other between the Corps and the Indians. Perry Skarra, the Yakama Reservation superintendent, raised both issues in an August 3, 1951, letter to his boss, Pryse, the BIA area director. Skarra foresaw an attempt by the Corps to shift responsibility for building the site improvements to the Indian bureau, once the Corps had purchased the land. He suggested to Pryse that the Corps could get additional money from Congress for the work more easily than could the Indian Bureau. Since the Corps was at that time a congressional favorite, Skarra's assessment was no doubt correct. Skarra also saw another controversy coming, one that continues despite a legal action that reached both the Supreme Court and Congress in the 1980s. This one was whether the Corps was to replace the living quarters destroyed by the dam. "The Indians believe that the Washington Office of the Engineers has committed itself to providing living quarters and drying sheds, while the District Office of the Engineers believe that the improvements consist only of sanitary facilities, leveling of ground and providing water," Skarra wrote. Most of the Indian living quarters destroyed by the dam were seasonal homes. But they nevertheless were family homes for half a year or more. There is no record that any Indian was ever compensated for the loss of a house at a fishing site. Dozens of people whose families were displaced have said neither they nor their relatives ever received new homes or money for the property destroyed. Lillian Tahkeal, whose family had a house and drying sheds at Underwood, works in the Yakama Nation Higher Education Department. She believes the government told her parents they would get a better home. However, "They never did get it." One handwritten internal Corps memo states, "following housing is needed at various lieu sites." In addition to drying sheds it lists: "Big White Salmon Residence 1 ($10,000.00)." Bessie Quaempts had mentioned at the July 20 meeting that her permanent home at Underwood had been destroyed. Apparently no one else at that meeting discussed a personal loss, although several times over a period of fifteen years lists were compiled of people who lost homes along the river.

Skarra was right about the Corps' intent to foist the site construction work onto the Bureau of Indian Affairs. A handwritten unsigned chronology of the in-lieu sites lists an April 6, 1950, letter in which the district engineer indicates intentions to transfer any of the $50,000 left after land purchases to the Indian agency for improvements. And on December 7, 1951, Stanley, the Corps' civilian, told a Yakama delegation that water, an incinerator and sanitary facilities were all that would be built on the Big White Salmon and Wind River sites "at this time." Those items, he said, were all that was originally contemplated in the 1939 tribal resolutions. Stanley had more bad news. It would cost $40,000 to fill the Big White Salmon site to provide more space. That was too much, he said. He suggested that more land be purchased nearby if Congress provided more money.

Little more than a month later the Corps stopped all work on the sites. Sloat, the Corps' district executive officer, said planning for immediate construction ceased in response to instructions from an unidentified higher authority issued January 10, 1952. Exactly what prompted the order is uncertain, but it came in an internal memo from the North Pacific Division engineer in Portland, one step up the Army chain of command. Lt. Col. L. W. Correll, the division executive officer, said the chief of engineers had ordered that no construction take place until after all the sites had been purchased and then only if there was money left from the $50,000. He repeated the Corps' earlier statement that the money was intended only to buy land. And he said the law authorizing the land purchases did not specify a number of sites. However, the agreement between the Corps and the tribes, embodied in the 1939 tribal resolutions, clearly listed six sites. Correll said if the Indians would be satisfied with four, the Corps would begin development of those. Sloat told the tribes the reason for the delay was differences in the tribal resolutions adopted in the wake of the meeting between the Celilo Fish Committee and the Corps July 20—six months earlier. He apparently was disturbed by the Umatilla resolution calling for all the sites to be purchased before improvements were made on any, and for spending equal amounts improving each of the sites, specifications not included in the other resolutions. He did not say why the difference became a problem in early 1952 although he must have been aware of it in December 1951 when he told the Yakama delegation work would begin soon on several sites. There is no indication there was any disagreement over at least four of the sites. Correll, in his memo, was clearly miffed at criticism of the Corps for the delays in site acquisition. He said the tribes should be told that the Corps would take action as soon as the tribes agreed. But if they delayed agreement, work would be delayed.

The Corps' action likely was based on the politics of the times. The Portland District of the Corps was prepared to break ground on The Dalles Dam in 1952. This was a key project for the Corps. It was big. It had political support from just about everyone except the fisheries people, who were considered a minor nuisance. It would carry barge traffic into the wheat country of Eastern Oregon and Washington. It would generate large amounts of electricity to fuel the region's growing industry. It was, in short, a real winner for the public relations-conscious Corps. At the same time, according to Donald L. Parman in "Inconstant Advocacy: The Erosion of Indian Fishing Rights in the Pacific Northwest 1933-1956," there was a mounting congressional hostility toward the Bureau of Indian Affairs. Indifference to Indian welfare was growing. In addition, the states, especially Washington, were hostile to Indian fishing. "The Indian fisheries seem never to have been looked upon by the state as genuinely legitimate fisheries," the American Friends Service Committee reported in 1970. "The view of both the state and the Bureau of Indian Affairs seems to have been that Indian fishing, although legal, is a nuisance and an anachronism, something which should be expected to disappear in the course of events." So stopping work on a "minor" Indian project was a politically expedient action for the Corps.

There was, however, one thing in the Indians' favor, and Sloat appeared to recognize this. The Dalles Dam would destroy the Indians' premier fishery at Celilo Falls and the Corps was preparing to negotiate with the Indians over compensation for its loss. And by this time, the Indians had some shrewd attorneys working for them. In his February 7 memo, Sloat said he would wait for approval from higher authority. But he suggested that water and sanitary facilities be constructed at one site on each side of the river—Big White Salmon in Washington and Lone Pine in Oregon. "Construction of such facilities prior to the 1952 fall fishing season should indicate to the Indians more than any other action which can be taken, that progress is being made in the acquisition and improvement of the Bonneville Fishing Sites," he wrote. "Such actions should also materially benefit pending negotiations with the Indians in respect to their fishing rights in connection with The Dalles Dam." He estimated the cost of a shallow well, pit chemical toilets and an incinerator at Big White Salmon at $1,800, and a 250-foot well and pit chemical toilets at Lone Pine at just under $6,000. In a letter the next day to Pryse of the Bureau of Indian Affairs he reversed the Corps' long-stated policy. The Corps would not ask Congress for more money when the $50,000 was gone. The Indians could use the Big Eddy site until they got in the way of dam construction, he said, but then they must choose another site. He also asked for another decision on Herman Creek: in the face of state opposition, choose another site or give it up. He also passed along Correll's edict that the Corps would do no work on the four sites agreed on and purchased until the Indians made new decisions on Big Eddy and Herman Creek.

The tribes knew, however, that they sometimes could gain more by going directly to Washington rather than dealing with bureaucrats in the field. Wilson Charley, chairman of the Yakama Fish and Wildlife Committee, led the committee to Washington to ask the Corps there about the stop-work order. That applied only to Big Eddy, the Corps replied. Charley fired off a letter to Sloat March 12 informing him that the Corps' Washington people said work on the other sites was supposed to continue. For good measure, Charley reminded Sloat that the Celilo Fish Committee had taken a unanimous stand on the site issues the previous July at the Corps' request. In Charley's view, that cleared up any questions about what should be done and he urged the Corps to get on with it. Sloat by now was thoroughly confused. He asked the Division Engineer to resolve what he considered conflicting instructions before a meeting with the Celilo Fish Committee and the councils of the three tribes scheduled for April 3, 1952. The Chief of Engineers then told the Portland District to go ahead with improvements so long as it held back enough money to buy the remaining sites. Despite that instruction, issued March 24, the Corps was still delaying its first work at Big White Salmon nearly five months later. The agency was waiting to start work on that Washington site until it had purchased the Lone Pine site on the Oregon shore, Sloat wrote on September 11. The Lone Pine site was tied up in the Corps' land acquisition from Seufert Brothers for The Dalles Dam. However, he said the Corps would start drilling the well at Big White Salmon within the month. Other work would have to wait. The fall fishing run was under way and the Indians' presence would interfere with construction. The Corps would wait until the fishing was over and the Indians gone. The Indians also could move onto the three acres purchased at Cook's Landing (the substitute for 160-acre Little White Salmon). Wind River should be available in a few days. And Lone Pine probably would be in government ownership by October 15—after the fish quit running.

Ironically, part of the land the government condemned for the Wind River site was part of a homestead patented in 1899 by Isador St. Martin whose Indian descendants still owned the land. St. Martin's great-granddaughter, Lonna St. Martin, a Cascade and Chinook Indian, is bitter to this day. The in-lieu site is on the east bank of the Wind River about two miles upstream from its mouth on the Washington shore of the Columbia. A lumber mill occupies the area where the two rivers meet. A well-kept state-operated boat launch and basin for recreation boaters is just upstream on Wind River, easily accessible from Washington Highway 14. Sitting in the spacious living room of her two-story house in the woods a bumpy two-mile ride above the Wind River site, Lonna St. Martin tells her family's story. "The sawmill by the Columbia River is the sacred site that should have been returned to the Indians. When the site was designated, they took that land from my father. Business bought off the government. Government took twelve acres of our homestead. It was taken from the Indians to give to the Indians. Our homestead went to the river. We have some left."

The Warm Springs and Yakama tribes complicated the situation in the fall of 1952 by filing claims for Bonneville Dam's damage to the fish runs and their resulting loss of income. The Warm Springs included a claim for the loss of their fishing sites submerged in the Bonneville pool. If the Warm Springs won their claim for the sites, Sloat told his boss, they might be entitled to damages from 1938, when the pool was raised, until the in-lieu sites were turned over to the tribes. Both Sloat and the Justice Department, however, said the sites should not be turned over to the Bureau of Indian Affairs until the Warm Springs withdrew the site portion of their claim. Sloat also suggested that the Corps continue to take no action on the Herman Creek and Lone Pine sites until the Warm Springs withdrew their claim. The Warm Springs leaders, meanwhile, said they might be willing to withdraw it if they got a satisfactory settlement for the coming loss of Celilo. Congress established the Indian Claims Court in 1946 to provide a forum for tribes that believed they had been badly underpaid for land and other resources, largely minerals. To the Yakama and Warm Springs the fish they could no longer catch were at least as valuable as the Black Hills were to the Sioux. By 1952, both tribes had their own attorneys and they had grown increasingly impatient with the lack of action on their promised sites. In addition, they had negotiations coming up with the Corps over the loss of Celilo. The claims gave the tribes an added bargaining chip.

The Corps was moving ahead with the land purchases despite the tribal claims, and there was hope of getting one site, Big White Salmon, improved that year. Then another blow fell. The Corps decided to raise the level of the Bonneville pool by six feet October 9, 1952. It had done the same thing in 1951, flooding out the Indians' drying racks and tents. This time, Jasper W. Elliott, then an Indian Affairs administrative officer, stopped off at Underwood (Big White Salmon) to warn the Indians while he was en route to the Yakama Reservation. He found Robert Strong and his family loading fish and preparing to move to their winter home in Klickitat. Five women also were there, two of them camped below the 78-foot level where the river would rise. When he returned from Yakama, Elliott found Bessie Quaempts, Mrs. Henry Charley and Eliza Slim Jim loading their possessions on a truck to move to nearby White Salmon. Josephine Washins remained in her tepee in the danger zone awaiting relatives to move her to higher ground. The Indians asked Elliott what would happen to their drying sheds and living quarters when workmen began the site improvements that fall. He told them "I felt sure that they would be advised of any plan to remove or destroy any of these facilities." But Johnny Jackson, the chief of the Cascade band who lives on the Underwood site, says that didn't happen. He motions to a steep, bare hillside next to the site. "They even took down two houses up there," he said. "The water didn't get anywhere near there." But the water rose and the fishing site shrank. And the Indians got no more compensation.

But the Corps did make some progress on the sites. By early 1953, it had built an incinerator and dug a well at Big White Salmon. It had its "order of possession" for Lone Pine, the only assured site on the Oregon shore. It had both sections of the Wind River site. The Big Eddy site already was being used to build The Dalles Dam, but the Corps charged its acquisition cost—$3,700—to the Indian sites anyway.

# 5

# ANOTHER LOSS

*The loss of this historic falls [Celilo] was the darkest day in the common psychological history of the tribe in the current century. The policy of termination was incarnated in the destruction.*

—Richard LaCourse, Yakama historian

State and federal fisheries managers agreed there was one good thing about The Dalles Dam: It would end Indian fishing at Celilo Falls. Although the fisheries people fought the dam down to the start of construction, they took comfort from the expectation—or at least hope—that drowning Celilo Falls would end Indian fishing on the Columbia and disperse the Indians. Eliminating the Indian fishery would remove a major threat to survival of the salmon, they said. At the time, the late 1940s, the states' own figures showed that the Indians were taking about 10 percent of the salmon caught commercially in the Columbia River. The total figures didn't include the large ocean fishery or the number of fish taken by recreational fishers, both exclusively non-Indian activities. But it was the Indians at Celilo the states considered the major threat to the salmon runs. In 1951, as the last ditch fight against the dam was being waged, Samuel J. Hutchinson, acting regional director of the federal Bureau of Commercial Fisheries, made a mèmo for his files of a conversation with Herbert Lundy of *The Oregonian,* Portland daily newspaper. "He asked as to the effects of The Dalles Dam," Hutchinson wrote. "I stated that the beneficial effects would compensate for the detrimental conditions that exist there at present. In brief, it would be easier for the fish to go over a ladder in the dam than to fight their way over Celilo Falls. The Indian commercial fishery would be eliminated and more fish would reach the spawning grounds in better condition." Another government assessment from Corps of Engineers files states, "Except for the loss to the Indians, this conservation benefit will be shared not only by the commercial fishery on the lower Columbia, but by sports fishermen and the general population of the adjoining States." And Col. T.H. Lipscomb, the Corps' Portland District engineer, told the Columbia Basin Inter-Agency Committee in 1952, the elimination of the Celilo Falls fishery would be "an important boon to conservation." The prevailing belief seems to have been: get rid of the Indian fishing and there will be plenty of fish for the rest of us, despite the small percentage of the catch taken by Indians.

The Indians fought the dam too, but they seemed to know from the start that it was losing battle. After all, the white men had been planning this dam a long time. Their deeply ingrained suspicions are reflected in the fairly common belief that the railroad bridge across the river just west of Celilo was built high off the water in anticipation of a dam. The 1912 bridge connecting the SP&S tracks on the Washington shore to the Oregon Trunk Line on the south shore did not have to be rebuilt to raise it above the new dam's pool but its construction was a matter of railroad track levels, not foreknowledge of dams. Before water rose behind The Dalles Dam, the bridge was 150 feet above the low water line and touched both shores well above the current high water mark. Fishing people who lived along the river used it to reach fishing sites or visit friends and relatives on the opposite side of the river. Chief Howard Jim of the Wy'am recalls it from childhood; it was where he caught his first fish when he was twelve years old. Jim lived at Roosevelt, Washington, forty miles upriver from the bridge. He remembers the fish well. "My grandpa brought me across the bridge. I had to go down a cable ladder—150 feet. He asked if I could do that. I said, 'I climb trees.' I made it. First time, I caught a steelhead." The next day, his grandfather took him to the tracks on the Washington shore, where the boy, lugging his fish, caught the eastbound passenger train. Once he got off the train, "I had to pack it four miles up the creek to home."

Families like Jim's were not to be easily removed or stopped from fishing. Jim, seventy-nine, lives at the transplanted Celilo Village now, kept from his fishing boat by illness. But he hasn't been kept from fishing. He got a pole and throws a line in the river occasionally "like the sportsmen," he says with a smile. Sports fishermen have been among the loudest voices opposed to Indian fishing. Former Yakama Council Member Lavina Washines, also

from a river family, explains the fishing people's determination to stay on
the Columbia: "No one could force them from the river. That is where
their heart is. The river is a part of their life."

And they battled to stay there.

After ten years of struggling for the Bonneville replacement sites, the
Indians were determined they would do better with The Dalles Dam. Early
in 1947, E. Morgan Pryse, the district director for the Bureau of Indian
Affairs, told the agency's reservation superintendents the Indians wanted
an early agreement on compensation for The Dalles Dam damages. They
feared delay would mean they would not be properly compensated, Pryse
wrote. "In that connection the Indians point out that promises made to
them for the settlement of loss of ancient fishing sites flooded by the
Bonneville Dam have not to this day been resolved." But Pryse said there
were no other sites to give the Indians and suggested they settle for annual
payments from the dam's power revenues. Members of the Celilo Fish
Committee discussed their concern about plans for both McNary and The
Dalles dams in April 1948. Several suggested that they begin preparing
lawsuits immediately to assure more prompt compensation. Work on
McNary already was under way, but Congress had not yet authorized The
Dalles.

The Umatilla and Yakama tribes sought a court order to halt work on
McNary almost as soon as it started. But U. S. District Court Judge Sam
M. Driver said there was no proof the preliminary work then being done—
the coffer dam—would stop the fish run. Driver agreed with the Indians
on one important point. They did have a property interest in the fish and
rights that are unique and irreplaceable. Money could not compensate for
loss of those rights, he said. For the moment, that was no help. Driver's
ruling has particular interest in light of federal admissions in the 1990s that
salmon runs have declined so badly that several need Endangered Species
Act protection. On April 15, 1948, Driver described "the apparently
irreconcilable conflict of interest between two great public policies." He
said, "One is the conservation of the Columbia River fisheries, and the
other is the development of the hydroelectric power potential of the
Columbia River and its tributaries." Development interests argued that the
fish were making it over Bonneville Dam and hatcheries could make up for
any losses. But testimony in the court hearing from experts on fisheries and
especially on the Columbia River salmon was unanimous that more
hydroelectric development would make the river's salmon industry a thing

of the past. The Chinook and the Blueback would go the way of the buffalo. But that wasn't the issue before Driver's court.

Despite the testimony from those fish experts in state and federal agencies that more dams would mean the end of the salmon, Congress authorized construction of The Dalles Dam in May 1950. While the Indian and non-Indian fishing people and the fishery agencies deplored the expected loss, the irrigation, power, barge, and recreation people had long ago decided their uses of the river were more important than the salmon. However, Congress made a bow toward fulfilling its obligations to the fishing people. It devoted a chapter of the appendix to the 1950 Rivers and Harbors Act, which included The Dalles authorization, to "The Indian Fishery Problem." Discussing the Columbia River situation, the report stated piously, "Alternate fishing sites to replace those inundated must be established—by artificial means if necessary, or the Indians paid just compensation for the sites taken." It suggested that paying the Indians to abandon their fishing rights altogether should be "resorted to only in extremes." The report noted that some Indians will insist on continuing to live in their traditional manner, including fishing, "to the millennium"—the year 2000 then seemed very far away. Ominously, the report added, "It would appear that the long-range solution to the problem lies in the integration and assimilation of these people into society at large." The Bureau of Indian Affairs was working on the problem, the report said. It was trying to help the tribes develop a sound economic base and encouraging young Indians to become educated so they could manage their own affairs. The agency's goal: "relieving the Government of necessity for supervision at the earliest practical time." Within a few years Congress had written that goal into a federal policy known as termination. That policy called for the government to end its formal relationship with the tribes and dissolve their reservations . For "terminated" tribes it withdrew the education, health, housing, and economic assistance the federal government had provided tribes since they were forced onto the reservations. For most of the "terminated" tribes the result was loss of whatever economic stability they had achieved. Tribal members, forced out of familiar social structures, suffered the predictable problems— poverty, alcoholism, despair.

Congress had been studying the possibility of ending its responsibilities for Indian tribes since 1928. It formally approved the policy in 1953 and President Eisenhower's secretary of the interior, former Oregon Governor Douglas McKay, enthusiastically put it into force. Only the Warm Springs, Umatilla, and tiny Burns-Paiute among Oregon's tribes escaped the federal ax. Although none of the tribes involved in the in-lieu site issue was terminated, the threat served as a distraction for tribal governments. It was just one more thing to deal with. To the tribes, programs such as termination and relocating tribal members to cities away from their reservations were attempts to destroy tribal cultures and renege on treaty-provided responsibilities. Although the termination policy has long since been reversed, many Indians remain suspicious that new efforts to provide tribes with as much independence as they want are simply a new means to the same old end. Lavina Washines, a former Yakama Council member, expresses a common view that the government still in the late 1990s is trying to end its role in Indian affairs: "They want us to assimilate into the public but they will not succeed. They are doing everything . . . . One way is with education to destroy future generations' minds."

Even after Congress authorized building The Dalles Dam, both the tribes and other fishing interests tried to prevent or delay its construction. Fisheries agencies urged that dams be built on upstream tributaries instead while they studied effects of Bonneville and McNary, then under construction. One proposal would have saved Celilo Falls by moving the dam a few miles upstream. But that would have resulted in less power production because the dam would have been lower. And it would not have provided for river traffic around the falls, a key element in the eyes of inland farmers and civic boosters who saw their little river towns becoming bustling port cities. The year 1951 was crucial. Money to begin construction was in President Truman's budget that he sent to Congress in February that year. Pryse wrote Indian Commissioner Dillon S. Myer that there was no way to compensate the Indians for destruction of their fishery that would result from building the dam. "This office has vigorously protested construction of The Dalles Dam," he said. Myer rejected his plea. Fishing interests had a brief moment of triumph in June when a congressional committee carved one-fifth of the money out of the dam-funding Rivers and Harbors Act, largely on grounds that dams would destroy the salmon. But the victory lasted only a few weeks. Development interests won out again. The money, including funds for The Dalles, was restored in the final version of the Rivers and Harbors Bill that Congress approved for the fiscal year beginning July 1, 1951. Work on the dam was scheduled to begin in the spring of 1952.

In spite of the Indians' hope for an early settlement of their claims for the loss of Celilo, it was only in late 1951 that Congress approved negotiations with the tribes. The approval declared that Congress recognized the tribes' treaty rights, then required them to give up both those rights and any fishing sites if they accepted a settlement with the government. The *Oregon Journal* reported that Warm Springs attorney T. Leland Brown of The Dalles drafted the bill and sent it to Senator Guy Cordon, an Oregon Republican, for introduction. If true, that seems a major betrayal of his client. The last thing any of the tribes would agree to was giving up the right to fish. Even the frequently insensitive Corps of Engineers recognized this. Many of the values attached to the soon-to-be lost fishing area were intangible and sacred to the Indians, the Corps said in an interim report on the negotiations. It was impossible to place a price on those values. So the Corps recommended that the residual value of any future fishing should not be deducted from the settlement but instead should be considered a partial offset for those priceless values being lost. The Corps might resent becoming entangled in the complicated, time-consuming and, in the mind of the engineers, tiny project of in-lieu sites. But its officers and civilian managers often exhibited a sense of fairness. And the Corps had no axe to grind over fishing. Its only concern was that fishery interests did not delay its important work—building dams.

Just as the tribes and the Corps prepared to begin negotiations over compensation for Celilo, the states renewed their attacks on Indian fishing. Corps representatives met with fisheries officials of the two states November 17, 1952, the day before opening discussion with the tribes. In a later memorandum, Milton C. James of the Washington Department of Fisheries outlined the discussion concerning the proposed agreement between the Corps and the Indians. The state officials, he said, provided "detailed explanation of the reasons why the states considered that the document should extinguish the fishing rights once and for all with no language which would lend any encouragement to the belief on the part of the Indians that they could expect any further consideration."

In June 1953, fisheries officials of both states wrote a series of biting letters challenging the Corps' authority to provide the Bonneville in-lieu sites or substitutes for Celilo and the Indians' rights to fish from them. The Washington Department of Fisheries also fomented some outside opposition to the Indian sites. In May 1954, an official of the Washington Department of Fisheries, Donald R. Johnson, wrote to a Richland man, R.F. Foster, outlining state objections. He said Foster could use the information contained in the letter but asked that the letter be considered "personal" rather than official; in other words, Foster should not publicize the involvement of a state official in undermining the Indians but could use the material from the letter in his own opposition to the fishing sites. Johnson then suggested that sportsmen might protest acquisition of the sites to the Corps of Engineers. The locations, he said, "are all too liable to be excellent fishing sites for the Indians." Foster apparently took the hint. Soon afterward, the Washington State Sportsmen's Council, at the urging of the Richland Rod and Gun Club, passed a resolution asking the Corps not to provide any fishing sites for the Indians.

The Celilo settlements reached in 1953 and 1954 made the Indians' fishing rights around the dam subject to the Corps' dam construction and operations but left their rights unaffected elsewhere. The settlements totaled nearly $27 million after the Nez Perce Tribe, whose headquarters is Lapwai, Idaho, won a share. The recognition of the Nez Perce as a Columbia River fishing tribe, based on the Celilo settlement, brought that tribe into the continuing fishery battle. It also created resentment among some members of the other tribes and the river people, who claim the Nez Perce were not among the traditional Celilo fishers. However, at some time each of the tribes has claimed that it alone had rights to Celilo and other Columbia River fishing spots. The settlement also created long-lived resentments between the river people and the tribal governments. Some of the river people were not enrolled in any federally-recognized tribe, scorning tribal affiliation and insisting that fishing was their aboriginal right that had never been surrendered. Wy'am Chief Tommy Thompson, the aging patriarch of the river, was one of those who retained his independence. But, departing from its looser policy on Bonneville Dam, the federal government negotiated the Celilo settlement only with the tribes that had signed treaties—the Yakama, Warm Springs, Umatilla and Nez Perce. Olney Patt Sr., then both a fisherman and a Warm Springs Council member, took part in those talks. He was one of the few Celilo fishermen involved. However, Chief Thompson did some of the talking. Patt remembers, "He was good. I liked to hear him. The government would send their best out to talk to the Indian people. They used highly trained attorneys. Regardless of what we said they would turn it around in some way and use it against us instead of for the good of the tribe . . . A lot of guys we thought were friends turned out different from what we thought. That really hurt. We trusted people and maybe shouldn't have. The old chief at Celilo (Thompson) never trusted anyone."

The money went to the tribes, not directly to individuals. All the tribes except Warm Springs distributed most of their settlement money to members on a per capita basis. Warm Springs alone retained the bulk of the money in the tribal treasury as seed for development and made only small per capita payments to its members. The Warm Springs' investments made them the region's most prosperous tribes before Indian gaming began in the 1980s. River people were forced to enroll in a tribe or lose any benefit, and the tribes pushed fishing people to enroll to boost the size of the settlement, which was based on tribal populations. Many of the river people resented the fact that reservation children who never came to the river got as much money as fishermen who had made their livelihood there for decades. That aspect of the settlement still annoys Percy Brigham, a Umatilla fisherman who made his living on the river. "Little kids got as much as I did. It was a dirty trick. Everybody got the Celilo settlement. Not 25 percent of them fished." Celilo was a good living for Brigham. He recalls being able to put $10,000 in the bank in twenty days there.

The per capita distribution was the biggest disappointment for Charles Luce in his time as the Umatilla attorney. The tribes' Board of Trustees wanted to use the $4.6 million—equal to $40 million now—for enterprises and employment on the reservation. But Indians were coming from all over claiming to be Umatilla, and, Luce recalls, some of them were. They would go to board meetings and demand that the money be distributed to individuals; they didn't live on the reservation and thought they would not benefit from tribal enterprises. The board faced a tough problem: The people who wanted individual payments could vote the trustees out of office. So the board put together a plan to buy out those individuals at 50 cents on the dollar, giving them the money immediately. The tribe would invest the rest. But Morgan Pryse, the district BIA director, vetoed the plan on grounds it was unfair. Luce believes the reason was to make termination easier. "Most of the time I was their attorney the policy was to get rid of the reservations. If they had approved something to make tribal enterprise possible, it would have been harder to get rid of the reservation." Termination did not reach the Umatilla, but the tribes struggled to fund job-creating businesses until they built one of the region's most successful casinos in 1995.

To be fair, the Warm Springs tribal government did get to keep most of its share of the Celilo money, but its membership was more willing to leave the money in tribal coffers. Also, the Warm Springs reservation remains isolated from population centers and even in the 1950s appeared to have few resources that whites coveted. Umatilla, on the other hand, lies just outside Pendleton, a major town in Eastern Oregon, and includes some of the richest wheat land in the Northwest.

Indians lost more than fishing places behind The Dalles Dam. Backwater also flooded two villages in an area where people had lived for thousands of years. The village on the Oregon shore was larger and got more attention. In fact, it had been getting attention, either critical or benign, for at least forty years. The Oregon village first got in the way of the Corps of Engineers in the early 1900s, when the Corps built the Celilo Canal. The builders tore the Indians' houses down and promised to build new ones after the canal was finished. It didn't, as Jerry Bruneau related in his 1937 affidavit with the tale of Old Smykes's smokehouse. Indians rebuilt on their own and finally, in 1927, Congress recognized their occupancy of the land by transferring 7.4 acres, wedged between the river bank and the Columbia River Highway, to the Department of the Interior for the fishing people. Responsibility for the little reservation was shuttled among the three big reservations and no one paid much attention to it. Perhaps a dozen families lived there permanently before Bonneville Dam's displacement sent others crowding in. During fishing seasons, hundreds, like Art Parr of Umatilla, came for a few days, a few weeks or a few months. Parr, who quit elk hunting in 1997 at age ninety-four because the Forest Service clear-cut his favorite hunting area, fished in the 1940s and 1950s just for his own family. If he wanted to buy a new pickup truck, he'd stay at Celilo a few extra days. If he got more fish than he needed, he gave the surplus to the Salvation Army. Most of the year he raised wheat, beef cattle, and chickens on his reservation land.

At Celilo Village, sanitation was minimal. Living quarters were often haphazardly built. And, as more Indians gathered there to fish after World War II, it became the scene of conflicts. In 1950, the Warm Springs and Umatilla tribes asked Congress to give them law enforcement authority over the little reservation. They presumed a dam eventually would destroy Celilo Falls, but in their request to Congress they estimated it would be "maybe ten or fifteen years." Congress denied their request. Through the years, non-Indians at The Dalles occasionally suggested either improvement or removal. Congressman Robert R. Butler, an Oregon Republican, tried unsuccessfully to get $75,000 for the village in 1931. Later, store owner Nels Helmick had suggested bulldozing the whole settlement. The Bureau of Indian Affairs tried to siphon some of the Bonneville in-lieu site money to add land to the Celilo village and make some improvements in 1947. It failed in that effort but did buy thirty acres for added camping and fish-drying space adjacent to the original village. Change finally came in 1949.

The government purchased thirty-four acres south of the highway, and built a new village with a water system, a sewer system and ten new houses. The Corps persuaded the Indians to accept the site, on the narrow bench between the Oregon Trunk Railroad tracks and a basalt bluff, by saying it provided the only opportunity for a good water supply. There the tank could be high above the homes to provide pressure in the system. Author Martha Ferguson McKeown Dana, a longtime friend of the Celilo people, wrote later that the new houses were built from badly warped salvaged World War II surplus materials. The wood had been shipped to the Pacific and back, then left lying in weeds at a railroad siding. The houses had no closets and no cupboards. But Chief Thompson, by then in his nineties, moved to the best of the new houses. His son, Henry, also moved. But others refused. Tom Frank said he did not want to leave the place where he was born and raised and where his ancestors lived before it was a reservation. He stayed and died there before rising water covered the old village. When the Corps was ready to move everybody out in the face of the rising river in 1956, about two dozen families were living at the old village.

In the memory of Indians who grew up there from the 1930s through 1950s, life at old Celilo was idyllic though sometimes harsh. Their sense of loss remains acute. Nathan Jim Sr., born in 1937, lived there with Chief Thompson and his fourth wife, Flora, Jim's grandmother. Thompson was the village authority and arbiter of disputes. Boys like Nathan, wearing only moccasins and overalls, were free to roam the village and nearby area. "I'd have a dried salmon in one pocket, dried meat in the other, stay out all day . . . . We'd throw rocks at the trains and put rocks on the tracks. We'd put pennies on the tracks and the train would flatten them." But there was work even for a five-year-old. Jim's daily chore was to make the quarter-mile trek to Helmick's store and return with two buckets of water. The store was the village's only source of drinking water. Johnson "Chief" Speedis, a contemporary of Jim and a great grandson of Thompson, recalls climbing the cliffs at a slightly older age. The fishermen were a major tourist attraction, and Mamie Smith remembers selling fish at the roadside. Smith chuckles at one memory: "One big one got curled up from drying in the sun. A white guy from New York asked about it. I told him he was curled up from being caught while going around a corner. He wanted that fish, even said he'd pay double for it. So many comical things happened."

Russell Jim, a Yakama who sold soft drinks near the grocery store as a boy, remembers seeing Jay Minthorn, a Umatilla, with a salmon bigger than the boy. Jay was twelve or thirteen and had the salmon over his shoulder. "The tail was dragging on the ground. He'd go a ways and the fish would fall down. He'd sit down. Two white guys were trying to buy it. He said he had to take to his grandma. He wouldn't sell it." Minthorn laughs at the story. "We had to make sure to get the salmon back for the family." Lillian Tahkeal, whose family spent part of the year at Celilo, remembers it as a place with a lot of children to play together. Older children gathered at Helmicks' in the evening to play games. Some of the Indian girls worked at the Helmick restaurant as waitresses.

Smith lived there later with her husband. While he fished, she worked in The Dalles, first in the state tuberculosis hospital and later managing a laundry. "There was spring fishing, fall fishing. We saved the money from each season, living on that. It was a cycle. Meantime, between his fishing and my working at The Dalles we were doing all right till they flooded us out."

By the time Jim, Smith, Speedis and Tahkeal were growing up there, the village was crowded, unlike the original sprawling settlement. First, the railroad came through in 1884, forcing the village closer to the river bank. Then the canal, completed in 1915, took part of the land. Finally, the Columbia River Highway pushed through in 1916, forcing everyone closer together. Reginald Winishut, who lived there after Bonneville Dam flooded his family's home, explains that government construction compressed the village so that four or five families were forced to live under one roof. "The white man forced that, then complained about dirty, smelly Indians."

The Dalles Dam was about to "solve" that problem too. The Corps of Engineers went about obtaining land on The Dalles pool in a different way from its Bonneville acquisitions. For Bonneville, the Corps obtained "flowage easements," which gave it only a right to flood the land where the pool rose. If Indian allotments or homesteads were held in trust by the government—as most were—records indicate the Corps made its deal with the Bureau of Indian Affairs, not the Indian owners. For The Dalles, the Corps bought the land outright, including the Indian allotments. Of course, for both Indians and non-Indians, there was no choice; if the land owner didn't like the price or didn't want to sell, the Corps condemned the land and paid a court-determined price. But this time, the Army was meticulous about dealing with Indian owners of land and of buildings on private land. A preliminary report lists twenty-one Indian-owned parcels totaling 1,428 acres. Some of the flooded allotments were at the Indian village of Spearfish on the Washington shore near Big Eddy, which the Indians had chosen as a Bonneville in-lieu site. Like Celilo, Spearfish was drowned by the dam's backwater.

The Corps' property acquisition policy was standard procedure. But its unintentional effect was to leave more than two dozen Indian families homeless. Most would get far less for the flooded houses than they needed to get a new place to live. A Corps appraisal sheet for houses at the old Celilo Village lists only two houses considered worth more than $1,000. Some buildings (possibly drying sheds) were valued as low as $5. Most were appraised at $200-$800, hardly enough to pay for even a shack elsewhere. The Bureau of Indians Affairs estimated that modest replacement homes would cost about $7,700 each. The Bureau, tribal governments and local government officials at The Dalles, eleven miles downstream from Celilo, saw the problem. The local officials feared the displaced Indians would move to higher ground nearby, build new shacks and create "an unsightly and unsanitary condition." County Judge (the equivalent of a county commission chairman) Ward Weber led the effort by the Wasco County Welfare Board to arrange for moving the dispossessed people. Although a majority of the families said they preferred remaining in the Celilo area, one component of the county plan was persuading the Indians to move somewhere else. Weber's plan called for a $500 bonus for any family agreeing to move more than ten miles from Celilo. He said the sanitary situation was very poor and "will become increasingly so if additional houses are built on government land south of the railroad track"— the new Celilo Village. Eventually, the Celilo residents scattered over five counties in two states. The county proposal included only the permanent residents of the old village, not the dozens who may have lived there one year or who lived there six months of the year, then moved elsewhere. One provision of the plan was that all the houses, drying sheds and other buildings between the highway and the river be demolished "and under no circumstances be rebuilt or reoccupied." The Corps needed five and a half of the Indians' seven and a half acres for dam-related construction. Weber recommended that any of the Indian village land not flooded by the dam be turned into a park. Today, a public park with brick and concrete restroom buildings, a boat launch, picnic tables, camping sites, green grass, and trees stretches eastward from the site of old Celilo village. Across Interstate 84, the Oregon Trunk line, and the Union Pacific Railroad lies the "new" village, its sewage system working only part time, its dirt road rutted, and many of its buildings crumbling amid brown weeds.

Congress appropriated $210,000 in May 1950 to relocate displaced families who were permanent residents of land taken for The Dalles project. The appropriation measure required that the entire seven-acre old village site be transferred back to the Corps of Engineers. And it omitted one provision of Weber's proposal—that the new Indian homes be built on established reservations, other communities, or the Bonneville in-lieu sites. It appears the plan to relocate river people displaced by The Dalles might have triggered some thought of equal consideration for those displaced by Bonneville, although there seems to be no written record of any such proposal. However, lists of Indian people who owned houses near various flooded fishing sites before Bonneville was built appear in government files with the records of Celilo property owners. The Celilo counts were made in 1955; the Bonneville site lists were dated 1953. Unfortunately for the displaced Indians, the Corps was moving faster on construction than the BIA and county officials were on relocating people. The Corps needed the land to relocate railroads on both sides of the river by July 1955. Congress approved money for the relocation July 15, 1955. The Corps had been unable to find the promised fishing sites in sixteen years; it moved the fishermen out of the way of its dam in a matter of weeks. As the Corps hastened the fishing people out of Celilo, its officials suggested some of them be housed temporarily on vacant portions of the thirty-four-acre new village site. Lillian Tahkeal, whose family was not considered permanent residents of Celilo, moved to the new village. Tahkeal remembers living there. "They promised us better cabins. They were never built. The only ones built were for permanent residents. What the rest of us got were cement slabs and Army tents. They were terrible. In the wind they were really bad. They'd fall over." Winds in the Columbia Gorge are famous for their velocity and intensity. The Army tents soon began to shred. The tents were taken down after Celilo flooded and there was no annual influx of fishermen. By February 1956 the BIA was just beginning to determine who was eligible for a new permanent house. Some claim they got nothing. Mamie Smith and her husband were simply told to leave their home next to the railroad, she said. With sarcasm she explains, "If you had a $50 house, they'd give, say, one candy bar. They gave other people twenty candy bars for what they got us. That was our year around home. They never considered that. We went."

The money measure was meant to include ousted residents of Spearfish as well as those at Celilo. But the Corps said in April 1955, three months before the money measure passed, that all fourteen families at Spearfish had already moved without help. The Corps suggested the government could cut $40,000 from the proposed relocation cost if it eliminated the Spearfish families. In the tradition of Washington state's antagonism toward Indians, officials of Klickitat County, site of Spearfish, did not get involved in relocation. At least some seasonal residents got nothing. "It was not only our livelihood but we didn't get anything for our homes. That's what hurt most," recalled Walter Speedis, who had been a seasonal resident since his family moved to the Yakama Reservation when he was a child. He is a great grandson of a treaty signer and the grandson of Martin Speedis, who took an early active part in the in-lieu site effort. Martin Speedis pursued the issue until he died. Walter Speedis, who worked in the Yakama Cultural Department, did the same. "I'll walk in my grandfather's moccasins," he explained. Sisters Elizabeth Henry and Virginia Harrison shared a family allotment several miles upriver from Spearfish. They got little for it; the government said it was virtually worthless. A few families with nearby allotments got substitute houses, some fifteen miles from the river, others high on a cliff back from the river above their old village. The land there is so rocky they cannot build a satisfactory water system. Halfway down the hill toward the river is a tiny cemetery with family names that loom large on Celilo and Spearfish documents. Below, on the river, is Horsethief Lake State Park, a green expanse of lawn and trees with picnic sites, access to the river and running water. The water didn't cover this former Indian land after all. A metal plaque on the park restroom building announces: Wishram Village. National Historic Site. There is no other evidence of the people who called it home for hundreds of years.

There was one last fishing season in the fall of 1956. Then the gates of the dam closed in March 1957. Weeping Indians stood on the shore and watched as the white man's dam drowned their homes, their livelihood and the center of their culture. To Yakama historian Richard LaCourse, "The policy of termination was incarnated in the destruction."

# 6

# HALF A LOAF, OR LESS

*The intent of the federal government, of course, was to
separate the Nch'i-Wana [Columbia] Plateau People from
their ancestral lands and resources, and to obtain lands for
the railroad and for the benefit of the immigrating farmers.
To the Yakama peoples this meant leaving religious,
spiritual, cultural and traditional areas ... being torn from
their ties to the past, a traumatic deprivation that would
leave them alone in the present.*

—Yakama Nation comments,
Corps of Engineers System Operation Review, 1994

Ted Strong was ten years old when The Dalles Dam flooded his family from
its home at Celilo. He recalls vividly the trauma of being dispossessed, a
trauma that was intensified for his father because the veteran fisherman could
no longer catch the salmon to feed his family. Instead, to survive, the family
was forced to accept a recurring gift of dead hatchery fish. Strong, long-time
executive director of the Columbia River Inter-Tribal Fish Commission,
describes the scene at the Underwood in-lieu site, where his family moved:
"We were made to line up in a circle. The dump truck would come and
dump the many fish. These fish would be thrown at our feet. It was a
methodical distribution. The hatchery men with pikes would go around the
circle and give each person a fish, around and around until the fish ran out.
And watching men who . . . were proud fishermen, now having lost their
dignity, lost the immediacy and the worship services that went with the
taking of the fish from the water . . . .These men were now relegated to

standing in a circle and having fish thrown at their feet. It changed the culture and it changed the traditional values the people held."

The Strong family joined a settled community at Underwood. Strong's grandmother, Celia Johnson, had a house near the top of the hill. His grandfather, Jim Umtuch, also lived at Underwood, as did all of Johnny Jackson's family. Strong recalls it as an exciting time for the children. There were new acquaintances and exploring new surroundings. "At the same time we were rewarded with some of children's economic opportunities. We could still sell a salmon or two to tourists, still sell some (salmon) eggs to non-Indian fishermen. Collecting pop and beer bottles and turning them in for refunds by the sackful could be lucrative for the young."

Fall, however, drove home to the children the change that had been made in their lives. Sent to public school in White Salmon three miles east of Underwood, Strong remembers, "We found a hostility that was beyond just new kids on the block." They had come from a school that was mostly Indian. Now they were taunted by the majority whites as "dirty Indians" and challenged about their right to be there at all. "Not having developed any debating skills," the Indian boys soon turned the challenges into schoolyard fights. "We learned very quickly to band together as tribal kids and dared not be found alone by white kids on the playground. The playground became our battle ground."

Hiding their grief and guilt at losing the ancestral fishing grounds, Strong's parents, James and Margaret Strong, told their children the world was changing and they would have to change too. "They encouraged us not to fight with white kids and to be good students . . . . It was a lesson in perseverance." The move to Underwood did not allow James Strong to continue fishing. Dip net fishing was limited by the lack of good sites. Although it was illegal, some of the younger men went upriver to use their dip nets from boats. James Strong returned to farming on the Yakama Reservation near Granger, Washington, sixty miles north of the river. But he continued to spend midsummer to late fall at Underwood, where he built drying sheds for others, and his family dried the surplus fish brought from the state and federal hatcheries and distributed to the families. The fish were good for drying and smoking and would keep the families through the winter. Their food value was high but their commercial value was very low— and the states agreed to give the Indians the fish only on condition that they not sell them. Nevertheless, "sometimes we would take two or three salmon and try to make sales," Ted Strong recalled. They would get only four or five cents a pound.

Strong remembers the uncertainty the loss of Celilo brought to the fishing people. "I believe that every family was faced with the same questions: Where do we go from here? Every man felt a certain loss of dignity and every woman felt a loss of family security with the disappearance of the fisheries and all of the many fish that would be yielded from these great fisheries. In place of the abundance so fully and graciously provided by the Creator we had more promises by the federal government of superior access to a livelihood. Among those promises were in-lieu sites—sites that were intended to provide a similar lifestyle—that are still today empty promises. The tribal people of my parents' generation have died never seeing those promises fulfilled." Celilo Indians experienced two other major changes as a result of moving to Underwood. The site is closer to Portland than Celilo, only sixty miles. So the move brought some of the older teenagers in contact with the city and its temptations for the first time. And the immersion in non-Indian society spelled the near end of the native languages. Public schools sharply discouraged both the Wasco tongue and traditional dress. The Indian children adapted.

The Strongs coped. Others did not. There was virtually no Indian fishing on the Columbia during the next three years. Percy Brigham, who survived to fish again, says many big time fishermen drank themselves to death after Celilo was gone. Brigham turned to sturgeon, then to gillnetting salmon from boats. He traded for property at Cascade Locks, and his sons still fish from nearby Herman Creek. For Mamie Smith, the end of Celilo fishing meant hard times. Her husband had no place to fish and they had no place to live. She worked two years to make the down payment on a house in Wapato, Washington, on the edge of the Yakama Reservation. "I did waitress work, picking fruit—apples, plums, grapes, peaches, everything I could pick—bartender. I spent twenty-two years as a maid in Wapato. I had to pay for the house. I had no choice." Her then-husband, demoralized by losing the only occupation he had known, did "not much of anything" after Celilo drowned.

By 1958, the BIA said all the permanent residents of old Celilo Village had been "provided with comfortable homes at various places up and down the river and elsewhere." Under the BIA's tight rules, only a small portion of the people who considered Celilo home qualified as permanent residents. Part of the thirty acres that BIA bought in 1947 for campsites and drying sheds would go to the state for a park. There was no suggestion that it could become an in-lieu site or a permanent Indian village. Although the BIA itself had suggested that dispossessed Celilo residents move into the drying sheds until they had new housing, the agency now complained that "transient Indians" had done just that, creating health and social problems. The agency said it helped them find new places to live elsewhere. It would be difficult to overstate the damage that losing the Celilo fishery did to the Indian people of the inland Northwest. Loss of the Bonneville fishing sites had enhanced the importance of Celilo, for centuries a gathering and trading place as well as a premier fishing location. Non-Indian towns moved to make way for the various dams contained residents whose roots there were no more than three generations deep. Indians, who look back to the seventh generation for guidance and consider their own actions in light of effects on the seventh future generation, had roots that extended beyond counting. The dispersal of people whose life centers on family and tribe tore the heart from their society.

Despite their preoccupation with getting the Celilo settlement and the pain of losing their premier fishing site, the Indians never retreated from the effort to get the Bonneville in-lieu sites. Nor did they back away from their right to fish. But they suffered some major defeats.

In early 1953, the Army Corps of Engineers thought it had found the ideal alternative to the Herman Creek site so adamantly opposed by the state of Oregon. The government already owned the land at Cascade Locks, about five miles east of Bonneville Dam. Government buildings on the property included sanitary facilities. The city and port of Cascade Locks, Oregon, had turned down a chance to get the property cheap when the government offered it. And the area was part of what had been a major tribal fishing area until construction of the Cascade Locks in the late 1800s. However, it had since become a popular spot for recreation anglers. The states' acerbic letters objecting to Herman Creek as an in-lieu site paled against the storm raised when the Corps suggested Cascade Locks. An Associated Press story datelined Cascades Locks April 10, 1953, began, "Columbia basin Indians are going to get part of a popular fishing site here . . . ."

Three days later a delegation representing the city, the port, businessmen and other local residents called on Col. T H. Lipscomb, the Corps' Portland District engineer. They wanted information and time to prepare a protest. Lipscomb promised them both. The group, organized as Cascade Locks Citizens Committee, opened the controversy with a letter asking in effect "why us?" Denying any racial discrimination, the group said Indians, unlike industry, would bring neither new taxable wealth nor jobs. That, the writers said, would leave the "entire burden" of additional schools, churches and recreational resources to the present 650 residents. The letter was signed by Russel H. Nichols, chairman of the committee, Mayor V.F. Wigren and John E. Springer, secretary of the port. They asked Lipscomb for clarification of several points, which essentially were the group's arguments against an Indian fishing site. Their issues included number of Indians—fifty or five thousand? "The answer will affect the entire economic and social status of the Cascade Locks community," they wrote. The writers said they were concerned about exclusive fishing rights for Indians and "inevitable conflicts" between Indians and sports fishermen. And they were very worried about sanitation facilities and fish drying. ". . . will this be the typical dog-ridden village such as existed for so many years at Celilo and other Indian fishing sites?" they asked. Had the Corps considered the effect fish drying "in the heart of town" would have on property values? The letter concluded, "If there are those of the opinion that our objections to the establishment of an Indian fishing camp in the heart of our community are not valid or of sufficient import, we invite them to imagine what their sentiments would be if a similar project were proposed within a stone's throw of their own homes."

Lipscomb told the division engineer he also had a call from a businessman, whom he did not name, who favored the Indian fishing site and indicated Nichols and his group did not represent the majority in the town. The colonel also met with the citizens committee, suggested they work out some recommended rules for the site and submit them to the Bureau of Indian Affairs. Nichols was not about to compromise with the Corps. He wrote to his congressman, a freshman Republican named Samuel H. Coon, a staunch advocate for private power in the public vs. private power controversies of the time. Otherwise, he seems to have slipped from Oregon's collective political memory; even the Indians, whom he attempted to thwart, don't remember him. Nichols couched his plea in hyperbole and misinformation. Indians would be welcome in Cascade Locks, he said, if they would live like everyone else and "not want a lot of extra rights." He also told Coon, " . . . the Indians want exclusive fishing privileges to an area, the Cascade Canal, that never was an Indian fishing spot. It is man made and the Indians have never fished in it." Nichols either did not know or didn't want to know that the first full-scale report ever made of Indian fishing in the Northwest listed the Cascade Locks area as an Indian fishing site. In his 1889 report on the Indians' "usual and accustomed places," special Indian agent George W. Gordon wrote of a dip net fishery on the Oregon side of the Columbia. "This fishery is on land condemned and appropriated by the government for the purpose of constructing the Cascade Locks—now under construction."

Coon sprang to the aid of his white Cascade Locks constituents. He showed no evidence of considering his other constituents, the Indians of the Warm Springs and Umatilla reservations, both within his district. Coon asked the chief of engineers to investigate but left no doubt where his sentiments stood: "I can well understand the citizens of this town being unwilling to agree to this situation," he wrote. "It is a small community and would be unable to cope with the situation as outlined in the letter . . . . I wish to protest the proposed transfer of this property to the Department of the Interior for use by the Indians." There was more correspondence between Nichols of the Citizens Committee and Lipscomb, culminating with Lipscomb's request that the committee name someone else to deal with the Corps because of "the insulting tone of Mr. Nichols' letter."

In the same letter to the committee's W.W. Cameron, Lipscomb provided an icy destruction of the committee's objections item by item. Statements by members of the committee indicate the city has more problems with transient fishermen then using the land than it would with the Indians, he said. Congress determines uses of government property, including the Locks site. As for the frequent references to the site being "in the heart of town" the Corps knew of no residences within 150 feet of the site. In another letter, he noted, "The only access across the tracks is an underpass under the railroad which also gives access to the Government land now used as a city park." The seven acres on an island was 580 feet from the nearest part of the business district. Lipscomb appeared particularly galled by the committee's questions about sanitary facilities. "It should be noted also that the area leased to the city for park and recreational purposes contained a 'Chic Sale' latrine which was burned on May 22, 1953." He had explained earlier that the government buildings on the site contained the same type of indoor plumbing no doubt in use in most of Cascade Locks. He wrote much the same in response to Coon's inquiry.

Despite Lipscomb's defense of Cascade Locks as a site, Coon's intervention had an effect. The Corps sold the land to the Port of Cascade Locks. Congress had ordered the eight acres turned over to the Port of Cascade Locks in 1940, Lipscomb said in a letter explaining his proposal that it fulfill part of the Corps' in-lieu site obligation. However, Congress said to get the land, the port would have to pay not less than 50 percent of its appraised value. The land and improvements were appraised in 1941 at $19,194. "The money

*The Dalles Dam, showing Lone Pine in-lieu site and north footing where the largest site was supposed to have gone. Photo by Bob Heim, July 14, 1988. Courtesy U.S. Army Corps of Engineers.*

was never paid," Lipscomb said. "District's files indicated that the Port of Cascade Locks objected to provisions of the Act which limited the use of the land and improvements to municipal parks and docking purposes." He cited correspondence from May 1949 indicating the city and port of Cascade Locks "were no longer interested in purchasing the property from the government." Lipscomb obviously believed that, with the city and port turning down the government offer, he could make other arrangements to dispose of the property. But the idea that Indians wanted the land revived the local bodies' interest. And Coon apparently persuaded the Corps brass that the local community should have a second chance. Lipscomb explained to one Indian fisher that the Corps was forced to sell to the port under a 1940 law with which his office was not familiar during negotiations with the Indians. It was the same law Lipscomb had cited in reminding the port and city they had passed up their chance at the land. He obviously had not foreseen how much difference a congressman's interest could make in interpreting a law.

The controversy discouraged some of the river people. Nora Woodward Evans wrote the colonel in June 1953 saying that, in view of the dispute, she and her family would rather have a cash settlement for their rights. "With the public feelings as they are, we have all agreed on this," she wrote. "Perhaps this will be the time for us that promises won't be broken." Lipscomb had to tell her there was no provision for cash settlements, only the in-lieu sites. In a second, plaintive letter to the colonel the following February, Evans said her family had been under the impression the river people could dipnet at Cascade Locks that spring. "Now we understand that you have sold that site," she wrote. "It seems to me we Indians are losing our beloved Columbia River. Have you another site in place of this one. My earliest ancestors up through my father and brothers dipped at the Locks. My sons and I fished with pole after we could not dip there."

The answer to Evans's question about another site was, No. The Cascade Locks Citizens Committee had suggested two. One, on Bradford Island, which serves as foundation for Bonneville Dam, was under military security restrictions and not open for fishing. The other, a former camp for conscientious objectors at Wyeth five miles upstream from Cascade Locks, wasn't considered even worthy of suggesting to the Indians. However, the Corps was still looking for sites to replace both Herman Creek and Big Eddy. A.D. Stanley, who was in charge of property acquisitions for the Corps, suggested in September that he could find several to replace Big Eddy if the Indians would accept camping and fish drying sites rather than fishing sites. He thought the Corps might be able to pressure them to do so after they got a financial settlement for The Dalles Dam fishery losses. In view of the pressure put on the Indians to accept Cascade Locks, he also urged that the Corps be sure it could acquire a site before suggesting it to the tribes.

Nora Evans was not the only one getting discouraged by the on again, off again nature of site selection. Andrew Barnhart, a Umatilla fish committee member, suggested to the Celilo Fish Committee in May 1954 that they just drop the whole thing. "We are spending too much money for the delegates to go here and there," he said. "They're always traveling. We have been talking camp sites for twenty years and nothing has been done. The white man is making a fool of us. We go see one camp site and select it and the next meeting we don't have a campsite." The committee took no action.

Just as Lipscomb was being forced to back down on the Cascade Locks site, the states of Oregon and Washington attacked him concerning all the sites. Robert J. Schoettler, director of the Washington Department of

Fisheries, warned that the state was considering closing all commercial fishing "at some or all of the sites acquired for the benefit of the Indians." The Indians have no special fishing rights at those sites or anywhere else in Washington, he said. The state has a right to control fishing and would enforce its regulations against Indian violators. Before Schoettler wrote to the Army, his agency had devoted more than a month to marshaling its arguments, trying to enlist the U.S. Fish and Wildlife Service as an ally and picking at the original premise of lost sites. In one internal memo, the department's Milo Bell suggested that the government was equally obligated to furnish substitute sites to white recreation fishermen whose favorite angling spots were drowned. Schoettler's attack was followed by a similar outburst from John C. Veatch, the chairman of the Oregon Fish Commission. Veatch conceded that treaties protected Indian rights at their usual and accustomed places but added that "conditions are no longer such that such rights can be lawfully or practically projected to other locations." He devoted several paragraphs to denouncing the large amount of fish taken by Indians. "We formally protest the granting of these sites to the tribes," he said, "for it is our belief that the major use to which they can be put is that of fishing and the fishing is a threat to the continuance of the salmon runs." Almost as an afterthought, he added that the two states intended to finally close the Columbia to commercial fishing above Bonneville Dam after The Dalles Dam was built. They did so in 1957.

In 1953, when commercial fishing was still open to non-Indians above Bonneville Dam, the commercial catch above the dam by Indians and non-Indians combined was about one-fifth of the total Columbia River commercial catch. By that time, few non-Indian commercial fishermen were operating on the upper river, leaving most of the upriver catch to the Indians. That year the Indian fishermen got 17 percent of the total river commercial catch, one of their highest percentages ever. In 1957, with the states' closure of commercial fishing above Bonneville, the upriver catch, all by Indians, fell to about 1 percent of the total river catch. Although Veatch railed about the damage Indians were doing to the fish runs, the states did not begin to reduce the number of fishing days for lower river, non-Indian fishers until 1957. Robert W. Schoning, whose twenty-four years with the Oregon Fish Commission included eleven as director, remembers the policies of his time. Traditionally the states "didn't give consideration to the Indians." For years they set fishing seasons "basically for downriver protection of fall Chinook." He notes also, "In Washington State there was a much more stringent anti-Indian philosophy on fishing."

The Corps tried to mollify the states. Colonel Emerson C. Itschner, the Army's division engineer at Portland, told Schoettler the principal use of the sites would be for camping during the fishing season to receive fish carcasses from nearby hatcheries. He said the sites wouldn't increase the Indians' catch because there were few fishing locations on the sites. "Although the virtual elimination of the Indian fish catch by dip-net operations on the lower Columbia has not been at any time an objective in our activities, it nevertheless will be the inalterable result," the colonel wrote.

Despite the states' complaints and Itschner's assurance there would be little, if any, Indian fishing, the Corps went on working on the sites. Its land acquisition staff intensified the search for two more sites and came up with half a dozen possibilities. In January 1954, Lipscomb asked for authority to purchase two of the sites. There was still money available. After the Cascade Locks fiasco, he said he wanted to make sure he had authority to buy the sites before he asked the Indians to approve them. He was also still complaining about the "most difficult and time consuming" process of obtaining tribal approval. Nothing came of the proposed sites; there is no evidence the tribes were asked to approve any of them. But the Corps did finish work on the Big White Salmon and Lone Pine sites in 1954, fifteen years after its initial promise of six sites and four hundred acres. Each site had an incinerator, toilets and a well. In addition, the Underwood site had been leveled with 2,800 yards of fill. But the Corps did not build living quarters or drying sheds at Big White Salmon as requested by the Indians, because it said its remaining money was needed to buy the additional sites and build the minimal facilities there.

Now the Army wanted to transfer both completed sites to the Interior Department, parent of the Bureau of Indian Affairs. Lipscomb clearly wanted to get the whole project behind him. "The matter has been pending now a considerable length of time, in large measure due to the very difficult problem of securing the approval of the Indian Tribes and others involved of sites selected or alternate sites to be selected." But the Justice Department blocked the transfer for several months because the Yakama and Warm Springs claims for damages to the fish runs had not been settled—although even the government agreed the claims were not related to the in-lieu sites. The acting area director for the BIA also stalled the transfer. In a letter to the commissioner of Indian affairs in March 1954, L.P. Towle, the acting area director, offered several reasons to avoid accepting the transfer. "The status of 'in-lieu' sites is presently subject to such uncertainty as to prevent the submission of definite recommendations at this time," he said. Towle provided most of the uncertainty. He said it would be undesirable for BIA to take responsibility for the sites because of "lack of funds and personnel, and our general policy of terminating responsibility for Indian affairs." He suggested several possibilities, all of them avoiding BIA responsibility. He favored turning the lands over to the tribes without any further government involvement and let the tribes use or sell them as they wished. It really didn't make much difference, he said, because under their treaties the fishermen could use any of the sites that were usual and accustomed fishing places regardless of who owned them. Besides, except for Big White Salmon, where the Indians obtained hatchery fish, the sites had little value "other than as sites for occasional, itinerant camping, or as sites for the establishment of more permanent residences." The sites weren't really compensation for their lost fishing sites because the type of fishing the tribal people practiced no longer existed in the Bonneville pool, Towle said. He also called continuation of the sites "undesirable" because they would "sooner or later resemble the Celilo shack village."

The Indians used the two sites anyway without objection from the Corps. Wasco County, Oregon, officials and the Oregon Fisheries director, M.T. Hoy, objected, however. Donald E. Heisler, the Wasco district attorney, said conflict was arising between the county and Indians who were adding their own buildings to the facilities provided by the Corps. The Indians were simply doing as they had always done, building drying sheds and homes to serve during the fishing season, from April to August or early September. The Corps was anxious to avoid any complications that might further delay getting rid of the sites. It asked John Whiz, chairman of the Celilo Fish Committee, to pass the word there should be no changes to the sites until Interior took over. But the Interior agency directly involved, the Portland Area Office of the Bureau of Indian Affairs, continued trying to avoid responsibility. E.W. Barrett, a BIA range conservationist, suggested to the new area director, Don C. Foster, that the official opposition to the sites strengthened the case against BIA acceptance. Foster agreed and strongly recommended to Indian Commissioner Glenn L. Emmons that the department refuse to accept the sites. Towle, by then Foster's assistant, outlined Foster's reasons in a letter: Because their value as fishing sites is practically nonexistent they did not fulfill the requirement of the law to provide fishing grounds. BIA didn't have enough money or personnel to administer them. And their acquisition would complicate termination of federal responsibility for the tribes. Foster too recommended that the sites be turned over to the tribes as private land, not tax-free trust land, the normal status of Indian lands. Foster seems to have been eager to implement the termination policy although none of the fishing tribes had been targeted. Federal efforts to shed governmental responsibilities to the Indians were never stated as a reason for delaying the in-lieu sites. But there is evidence, such as Foster's attempts to avoid accepting them, that the policy played a larger role than is evident. The National Archives and Records Administration alludes to the issue in a summary of Northwest BIA files in its Seattle Regional Repository. The primary function of the regional BIA office "from its inception" in 1946 to 1965 was carrying out termination and paying claims, the notation states. Congress did not establish termination as national policy until 1953, but both Congress and the Administration had been studying ways out of involvement with tribes for at least a decade previously. The concentration on termination may explain why the BIA did little to push the Corps to fulfill its promise to the Indians. Foster became area director only a few months after Congress passed the Termination Act. Secretary of the Interior Douglas McKay, former Oregon governor, was happy to use his own state as a showcase for the new policy. The government shed all but three Oregon tribes. Foster had every reason to expect they too would fall to the termination ax. At the same time Foster was trying to avoid taking on the in-lieu sites, he was warning the tribes that they might have to assume full financial responsibility for Celilo Village because of the coming termination. Reginald Winishut recalls that when Foster showed up at meetings the Indians' reaction was, "God, that man's here again. We'll have a battle."

A few months after Towle's second letter, Foster's new assistant, Perry E. Skarra, questioned acceptance of the sites "at a time when we should be planning in terms of withdrawal or at least diminishing custodial responsibilities." The in-lieu site issue was closely related to that of Celilo Village, he said, because many of the displaced Celilo residents had said they planned to move permanently to the new in-lieu sites. In the end, Foster couldn't duck the sites. The Indian commissioner told him that the law didn't give Interior the option of accepting or rejecting—it just required the Corps to turn the sites over to Interior for the Indians. The early 1950s mark the low point in BIA's support for the Indians, which never was very effective.

However, the tribes weren't ready to accept the sites either. At a special meeting of Umatilla tribal members the day after Towle's initial letter, several people stated their suspicions that the sites would be of little use, and that tribal ownership was another white man's trick. Said Charley Johnson, "What good can we benefit from using these sites when there are no fishing sites? We in time will have to pay taxes on them. Take Celilo, for instance. Everything is going to be destroyed and as long as the white man is going to have a little jurisdiction over them, in time they will do the same with them as they have done with Celilo." In 1956, the Umatilla Tribes' Board of Trustees formally refused to accept the sites. William E. Ensor Jr., the superintendent of the Umatilla Reservation, told Area Director Foster in January 1957 the board probably was influenced by a notice that the Oregon Fish Commission planned a hearing on commercial fishing on the Columbia. The state had said for several years it planned to close commercial fishing above Bonneville after The Dalles Dam was completed and so the Indians had no assurance they could fish from either of the two sites. In addition, Ensor said, the board felt that the Corps "had shown marked reluctance in carrying out the board's understanding of the in-lieu site law."

The Celilo Fish Committee protested the proposed fishing closure on grounds such action would be contrary to the treaties between the United States and the tribes. Charles F. Luce, the Umatilla's attorney, asked the commission to exempt Indians from the ban on commercial fishing. Veatch, the commission chairman, said the commission couldn't make an exception unless their treaty rights included commercial fishing. Luce pointed out that the Indians traditionally sold a portion of their catch. In fact, salmon had been the major trade item on the river before white settlement. Veatch said the state had never conceded that "preferential rights applied to any Indians" except when they were fishing at usual and accustomed places when the treaties were made. As for commercial fishing, the only concession had been that they could get a commercial license "without the requirement of citizenship" if they lived in either Oregon or Washington. Since Indians all had been citizens since 1924, that wasn't much of a concession. And Veatch complained that the Corps went ahead fulfilling its 1939 promise in spite of the states' announced plans to close commercial fishing above Bonneville and their written objections to the sites. The treaties don't apply to the in-lieu sites, Veatch said, and the closure is necessary for conservation. Bonneville had depleted the salmon and The Dalles would cause more loss. Luce responded—correctly—that Congress specifically stated the in-lieu sites would have the same status as treaty sites. And the states were allowing commercial fishing to continue below Bonneville Dam, where 85 to 90 percent of the fish were caught. If conservation was the issue, the states should place more restrictions on the lower river fishing. The states finally conceded that the Indians could dipnet commercially while the commercial season was open downstream, but at all other times they could not sell any fish and the states would take strong measures to stop any Indian gill net fishing. Because The Dalles Dam had destroyed the last dip net sites that yielded commercial quantities of salmon, that restriction left the Indians with barely subsistence fishing—perhaps enough to feed their families, but not enough to support them.

Later that year, the Umatilla Tribes, attempting to hold onto their fishing, refused to approve plans for drying sheds at Lone Pine until the Corps agreed to do everything possible to provide the promised fishing grounds. That included arrangements with the Oregon Fish Commission. In a bitter letter to the Corps' district engineer, David S. Hall, the Umatilla executive secretary, said there was no point in discussing drying shed construction without considering whether there would be any salmon to dry. He wrote, "It was because we were assured of other places to fish that our tribe did not present a damage claim for the destruction of the fish sites by Bonneville Dam." He said the tribal fishermen needed to know where they could fish, and he believed the Corps had an obligation to help resolve that issue. If there was no agreement, he added, the fishermen probably "will go ahead and fish in the Bonneville Pool and the whole problem may wind up in the courts." But the ploy didn't work and there still was no place to fish. Except for Lone Pine, the available in-lieu sites bordered no eddies, no swift flowing water, no spot for a dip netter's scaffold. The river had become two lakes between Bonneville Dam and Rufus, Oregon, seventy miles upstream. The lakes covered the most productive half of their traditional fishing grounds. In the 1960s John Day Dam would take the remaining half.

Meanwhile, over the objections of the states, Congress gave the Corps an additional $185,000 in 1955 to finish buying sites and building the sanitary and other facilities. "Illegal and unwise," huffed the Oregon Fish Commission. While the bill was working its way through Congress, realtor Charlotte Chandra of Stevenson, Washington, offered the Corps six hundred acres at an unspecified location on the river at $200 an acre, "a bargain." But the Corps responded that it wasn't buying, although it still owed the Indians two sites and more than three hundred acres. A few months earlier, the Corps had turned down an offer of land near White Salmon, also saying it had no need for more. The added money from Congress allowed the Corps to go ahead with construction at Wind River and Little White Salmon and add drying sheds at Underwood and Lone Pine. The BIA continued its efforts to avoid taking responsibility for the sites. In 1956, Foster's assistant director, Perry E. Skarra, teletyped Foster, who was in Washington on business, that he was unable to find the original tribal resolutions accepting the Corps' proposal for in-lieu sites. Skarra recommended delaying BIA acceptance until all the sites were finished or the issue was resolved. Later that year, Foster once more told the Indian Commissioner that the area office objected to the transfer on the basis that the land was more campsite than fishing site. A few months later BIA suggested that the counties get title to the sites and take responsibility for them. There was no provision in the in-lieu site law for any kind of county involvement and the counties generally avoided taking on any Indian related projects; the idea was quickly dropped. A reluctant BIA finally agreed to take title to the two sites. In 1959 the Warm Springs Tribes formally accepted them, agreeing to assume responsibility for policing and maintaining Lone Pine. However, the tribal resolution also implored the Secretary of the Interior to insist that the Corps clean up a hazardous fish wheel shaft on the site. Yakama was to take responsibility for sites in Washington, but Alex Saluskin, the Yakama tribal chairman, told Foster the tribe objected to accepting the sites before the Corps finished all the work it had promised to do. "In the future we will take jurisdiction and see that there are proper sanitary conditions," Saluskin wrote.

By this time the Corps was ready to tell Congress it couldn't do any more and ask for a release from further efforts. It had been twenty years since the Corps agreed to find and develop six sites totaling four hundred acres. With the completion of Wind River and Little White Salmon, it had developed four, totaling just under forty acres. Then Cascade Locks came up again. In early 1960, the tribes renewed efforts to persuade the Corps of Engineers to acquire the eight acres it had originally proposed as the Cascade Locks site. Commissioners of the Port of Cascade Locks voted that April to allow the Indians to fish on the north side of the old locks, a 1.6-acre piece of the property, but only if the non-Indian community approved. The Corps agreed to take another look at the site despite the fact that it could be reached only by boat, there would be no sanitation facilities and no space to camp. Nothing happened. Merle E. Lietzke, chief of the Corps' real estate division, told the Umatilla Board of Trustees in December 1960 that the Corps was still exploring the possibility of fishing rights at Cascade Locks. But he added, "there is a serious question if it is a worthwhile site." And, he said, the possibility of acquiring two sites in addition to the four already finished "appears very remote." He said the Corps would have to notify Congress and return the unspent money to the treasury unless the three tribes agreed on some satisfactory solution.

As for the tribes' complaint that the Corps had destroyed Indians' buildings on the finished sites, Lietzke said the Corps didn't know who owned the shacks, and they were in the way when the Corps began building drying sheds. So the Corps posted notices to remove them, then tore them down. He concluded that the Corps "has fully met its obligation." The tribes disagreed. Luce told Lietzke all three tribes opposed letting the money return to the treasury and believed the Corps should renew its efforts to find them fishing places on the Bonneville pool. The Corps set a deadline of May 1, 1961, for the tribes to agree on the two additional sites. At the same time, The Dalles *Chronicle*, reporting on a meeting about the sites, said some of the Indians viewed the chance of getting more sites as hopeless. Choice areas had all been taken for other uses. Two months later, Warm Springs attorney Owen Panner prodded Lietzke to find sites and account for the Corps' spending on the project. In October, Panner wrote Lietzke again asking if there was any response to the tribes' request for the Herman Creek site. Umatilla attorney Mark McClanahan asked the same question two weeks later. Nothing happened.

The Umatilla Tribes' Fish Committee report of December 1961 reflects the frustration and discouragement all the tribes felt as government agents agreed to take actions, then found reasons to avoid carrying out their promises. The report also reflects the continued importance of the in-lieu sites to the tribes. First, the Yakama said they had given up trying to find a site to replace the initial Big Eddy site that had become a part of The Dalles Dam. In the same meeting with the Corps the Yakama agreed to let the Oregon tribes acquire sites in addition to Lone Pine on their side of the river before the Yakama asked for construction of improvements on Washington shore sites. Merle Lietzke of the Corps asked the Oregon tribes what additional sites they would like. The Umatilla report recorded the discouraged answer: "Reply was it would be hard to say because any Lieu sites the Oregon Indians asked for the request was always turned down, was not available or could not be bought because of price or was owned by some Oregon State organization." The Indians said they wanted fishing sites, not just camp sites, which would be an expense to maintain and of no use if there were no fish to catch or dry. Tribal and Corps representatives looked at an old ferry landing near Rowena between The Dalles and Hood River. There was an old building and room for camping there. For some reason the proposal was never pursued. The site has since become a premier sailboarding area. The Indians and engineers looked at a site downstream from Hood River, but the Corps said it was quite expensive and would require both crossing permission from the Union Pacific Railroad and construction of an access road. The Warm Springs people once more looked at a site at Herman Creek but the Umatilla delegation didn't bother, because the Corps had already said it was not available. Percy Brigham, a member of the committee, suggested man-made sites, but Lietzke rejected that idea.

In January 1962, the Umatilla Tribes authorized Percy Brigham to request the Port of Cascade Locks to allow tribal fishermen to use the Cascade Locks site. Also, the two Oregon tribes agreed that the Corps should acquire an acre and a half at Cascade Locks and defer improvements on the other sites. The Yakama Council concurred June 12. The Corps began condemnation proceedings to acquire the little site below Cascade Locks, which became known as Lower Cascade Locks. By December of 1963 work on the site was finished. Eugene Greene Sr., now the Warm Springs tribal fisheries director, fished at the Cascade Locks site in the 1960s. He remembers the fishing as good and relations with the sportsmen fishing nearby as generally amicable. Greene's brother had a scaffold at Cascade Locks and stayed in one of the three camping sites there. Eugene Greene fished at night, then drove a hundred miles home to Warm Springs to go to work. "It made for some awful long days," he remembers. He mostly took just a few fish at a time—"just what my wife could handle in a single day—three or four fish." If the fish were Chinook salmon that might be as much as eighty pounds. He also recalls the sports fishermen lining up to watch the Indians pull fish out of the water with nets. "It didn't make us popular," but "most were real nice. A few were not. The majority were OK. We tried not to pick fights." Sometimes, disputes were difficult to avoid. Alphonse Halfmoon, now vice chairman of the Umatilla Board of Trustees, recalls one incident in which rod and reel fishermen tore down an Indian scaffold, claiming it had been built in space used by the sportsmen. The scaffold owner was unable to collect damages. At the time, most of the tribal fishermen at Cascade Locks were, like Greene, fishing only for their own family use. The main problem was that there was room for only three families to camp, and ten families used the site to fish. When it finished Cascade Locks, the Corps had $40,000 left, but it had no prospects for the promised sixth site and 360 more acres.

# 7

# UNDER ATTACK

---

*You will usually find when a treaty is made with the Indians, the white men expect the Indians to observe it to the letter, while the white men observe it if it is in their interest to do so; otherwise they will violate it.*

—Isabel Lear Underwoood,
granddaughter of Chief Chenoweth
and daughter of one of Phil Sheridan's soldiers,
quoted in Chuck Williams' book
*Bridge of the Gods, Mountains of Fire*

Randy Settler grew up on in-lieu sites. It was a life of hard work, frequent hunger, love of school and watching almost constant conflict between his parents and government officials. When state officials weren't arresting his parents and other Indians for violating fishing regulations, federal officials were trying to move them off the in-lieu sites.

Randy was three when the Settlers moved to the Lone Pine site in 1958. That was soon after the site was completed and before the BIA formally acquired jurisdiction. Eventually, the intended drying shed held parents Alvin and Mary, Randy, his three brothers, and two sisters. Randy Settler recalls, "We didn't have electricity. We did not have running water . . . . We froze in winter, roasted in summer." They also sometimes went without food. Randy rarely missed classes at the little country school at Petersburg half a dozen miles from Lone Pine because he got one free meal a day. "It was the best meal of the day," he recalls. "So I got a good education." He missed school only for fishing. When they were not fishing, the Settlers were reading by the light of a kerosene lantern. Alvin Settler, now chief judge of the Yakama

Tribal Court, read law books and the Bible. Mary Settler also read law books. Randy read every book in the Petersburg School Library.

The Settlers were not alone. By 1960, six families were comfortably at home on the Lone Pine site. Marion Lewis raised nine children in a drying shed to which he built additions as his family grew. The school bus stopped right at their door. Lewis moved to The Dalles but at seventy-two continued to fish each year at Lone Pine. Ted Strong recalls the sheds where his family lived at Underwood. Others set up housekeeping in sheds at Cook's Landing.

In using the drying sheds as their homes, the fishing families were being practical. The Corps had promised to replace the buildings destroyed by the floodwaters behind Bonneville Dam. That included the sheds where the tribal families dried their winter's supply of salmon. Indian women had over centuries developed a design for wooden drying sheds that served their purpose perfectly—preserving the fish without destroying its flavor or texture. Indian men had learned to follow their wives' instructions to the last nail.

But the Corps, with its college-educated engineers, brushed aside this practical knowledge. Although Corps documents say the agency built the sheds to Indian specifications, the buildings bore no resemblance to anything fishing families describe. Instead, the Corps built concrete-based metal structures designed to withstand the winds and rains of the Columbia Gorge for decades. They were sturdy and durable, but no good for either air drying or smoking fish. The concrete floors held dampness, which gathered on the metal ceilings, causing them to sweat. "You could feel the water drip down, like dew," recalls Jay Minthorn, a Umatilla Board of Trustees member who tried to use the sheds. "It spoiled the salmon." Metal walls and roofs absorbed the heat of the sun and burned the fish. A single foot-wide window did not permit the river breezes to blow through and do their work. The Corps built places for wood stoves to discourage fire-building inside the sheds, but Minthorn wryly notes that it is impossible to smoke fish without an open fire. Since the Corps had not replaced their living quarters and the drying sheds were unusable for drying, a number of families, like the Settlers, moved into the sheds. With a little work, they made fine homes. Then the fishing people built traditional and satisfactory drying sheds.

By 1960, the Bureau of Indian Affairs had accepted four of the promised six sites from the Corps of Engineers. Within months after assuming jurisdiction, Bureau staff members visited all four completed sites. They found things in fair condition except for the six families living in the drying sheds at Lone Pine. In late October, the federal agents took another look at the sites and started a war of recrimination that continued intermittently for nearly forty years. The BIA sent a report, with pictures, to the tribal governments and asked the tribes to enforce regulations for using the sites. That led to a meeting of delegates from the BIA, Celilo Fish Committee, Corps and U.S. Public Health Service in which the Fish Committee members bitterly accused the Corps of not fulfilling its obligations. They complained of impure water supplies, lack of sanitation and other health hazards, the unusable drying sheds, failure to remove old buildings, failure to clean up trash, and failure to improve access roads.

The Wind River site was reached only by a tortuous road built to service a high power line between Bonneville Dam and the Yakima Valley. The single lane road was—and remains thirty-nine years later—a rutted challenge for anything but a pickup truck or four-wheel drive vehicle. Towing a twenty-five-foot fishing boat over the steep two-mile-long road requires skill, luck and a certain defiance of reality. Virginia Beavert says her family took a motor home to the site during fishing seasons, but had to launch its boat elsewhere. The boat launch filled with silt soon after construction. Sophie George, a noted Wasco beadwork artist whose family also fished there, says authorities promised another road into the site; several official letters refer to building a Wind River road. The site is two miles up the Wind River from the Columbia but the road route is eight miles, including the final two-mile service road. At the mouth of Wind River a lumber mill sits on land the Indians say is the site of their ancient village, and was the intended location of the in-lieu site. They do not know how the lumber mill got the land. Just upstream from the lumber mill, next to Washington Route 14 on the north, is a state built and operated boat launch for recreation boaters and fishers. Its quarter-mile paved access road is a striking contrast to the bumpy, rutted route to the in-lieu site.

Underwood was boxed in below State Route 14 to the south and a steep hill to the north. A county road marks the west boundary and the White Salmon River on the east provides boat access to the Columbia under the highway. Cook's Landing, the substitute for Little White Salmon, is an uneven rocky point of land reached on an axle-threatening quarter mile of ungraded road.

Despite the tribes' complaints that the sites failed to fulfill the promises made more than twenty years earlier, Secretary of the Interior Frederick A. Seaton urged the tribes to make and enforce rules for using the property. In

*Aerial view of Bonneville Dam, with a good view of the river as it is today. The new Bonneville Office in-lieu site is visible, as is Bradford Island, once an Indian burial ground. Graves were dug up and skeletons removed to a north shore cemetery to make way for the dam. Courtesy U.S. Army Corps of Engineers.*

a November 22, 1960, meeting, Northwest BIA officials told the tribes that Seaton threatened to get rid of the sites if they were not "properly utilized." The Yakama Tribal Council refused to accept the sites until they were improved, and said the tribe would take jurisdiction only if the tribes also gained title to the property. Nothing happened on the completed sites until more than a year after the Corps acquired and improved the Cascade Locks site. Then, in December 1963, the Corps and tribes agreed to spend the $40,873 remaining from the 1955 appropriation to improve the other four sites—Lone Pine, Underwood, Cook's and Wind River. Action never came swiftly for the in-lieu sites, however. Before anything could be done, the BIA had to make a survey. That took a year and some prodding from the health departments of Wasco County, Oregon, where Lone Pine is located, and the Clark-Skamania Health District in Washington, which contains Underwood, Cook's and Wind River. The Oregon health officers described conditions at Lone Pine as very bad, and recommended that it not be used for either permanent or temporary residence. By early 1965, the Corps estimated that it would cost $40,000 to improve the sanitary facilities at all four places. The amount coincided almost to the penny with the amount remaining from the 1955 appropriation.

Meanwhile, the BIA spent months asking the Department of the Interior for authority to write rules governing use of the in-lieu sites, and telling county officials it would need enforcement help from the counties whenever rules finally did get written. The Corps in Portland asked its superiors in Washington for authority to spend the remaining money. There was no indication it needed such authority since the appropriation had placed no restriction so long as the money was used for in-lieu sites. But seeking permission let the Corps delay work. Corps officials in Portland got the requested authority, then announced it would make the sanitation improvements only on two conditions: That it would have no responsibility to obtain additional sites and that, if the work cost more than its estimate, the BIA would supply the rest of the money. The deal would meet the Corps' primary goal—ending its involvement in the sites. At best, the Corps always considered the in-lieu sites a nuisance when it had important things to do, such as building dams. However, duty-bound officers continued trying to fulfill the Corps' obligation, although as early as 1951 it was evident Corps personnel were seeking a way out. U.S. District Court Judge Owen M. Panner, then the Warm Springs attorney, analyzed the 1965 proposal: "They wanted to get it out of their hair." It wasn't that the Corps was anti-Indian, he said. "They were just caught in the middle and didn't know what to do." He conceded that the agency faced an impossible task. The destroyed fishing sites were irreplaceable. In addition, "satisfying all the Indians was very difficult." But Panner said the Corps was not above exploiting differences between the tribes or between the tribes and river people to avoid taking action. The deal the Corps offered—build improvements on the five sites and give up on additional land—was a way out for the engineers. And the tribes saw no choice. Reluctantly, they agreed.

But nothing was done that year or the next except for another inspection, which found that all the sites except Underwood had deteriorated since 1964. The Corps finally made most of the requested improvements in 1967. However, it did not build a water supply for Lone Pine because of the expense of hooking it up to the private system that served the adjacent area— $20,000. Nor did the Corps install promised showers at Cook's Landing. The BIA arranged for regular garbage pickup at Lone Pine and at Big and Little White Salmon sites. It arranged a contract for garbage service with Cascade Locks port personnel for that site. There was no one willing to pick up garbage at Wind River, but the site was little used and there was no particular problem there.

While engaged in the continuing skirmishes over the sites, the tribes also were involved in a larger, more intense and potentially more devastating battle over the fishing rights preserved in their treaties. Two decades later that battle and the in-lieu site issue would join to catch the attention of Congress and bring a final effort to fulfill the 1939 promise. Some of the Indians, and many non-Indians, believed that the money paid to the Yakama, Warm Springs, Umatilla and Nez Perce tribes for Celilo Falls bought the tribes' right to fish as well as the fishing site. It did not and was not intended to. But there were few places to fish. Except for Lone Pine, the available in-lieu sites bordered no eddies, no swift flowing water, no spot for a dipnetter's scaffold.

Salmon runs had plummeted after The Dalles Dam was finished. The states were determined to conserve the remaining fish, supplemented by hatchery stocks, primarily for the commercial fishery on the lower Columbia with a nod to sportsmen the length of the stream. On the lower river, the states cut the number of fishing days for the commercial gillnetters, who hauled in tons of fish at a time, to a hundred days a year from the pre-dam hundred and fifty. After considerable argument they allowed that the Indians could sell fish caught during the same hundred days, but they could use only their traditional dip nets in which they caught a fish or two at a time. In a joint announcement in May 1957, the two state fisheries agencies said they had reached an understanding with three tribes to regulate Indian fishing. For the first time, the announcement stated, commercial gillnetting was prohibited above Bonneville Dam. Similar agreements continued over the next few years, but the Indians were virtually stymied in catching fish. Dipnetting was impossible at Celilo Falls. At that time, Indians were still tied almost entirely to their dip nets. These required swift, clear water where the fisherman could see the fish and a rock or platform at the water's edge, where he could reach the fish. Before The Dalles Dam, at Celilo Falls a fisherman taking one fish at a time could catch dozens of fish in a day. But the dams had destroyed nearly all the places of swift, clear water where dip nets could be effective. Some days a diligent fisherman could catch nothing. Gill nets, by contrast, are set in the river, attached either to the shore or buoys, and can be up to four hundred feet long. They catch dozens, sometimes hundreds, of fish at a time. In requesting extension of the 1957 agreement, Yakama attorney James B. Hovis told state officials that a single commercial gill net vessel in the lower river would land as much fish as the total Indian catch upstream. The Indian catch was so negligible, he said, that the states could allow fishing 365 days a year and it would not affect the number of salmon escaping to spawn.

During that period, the Indian share of the river's commercial catch bounced along near zero. In 1960, for instance, the spring chinook commercial catch of 867,000 pounds included only 1,200 pounds of Indian-caught fish, a fraction of 1 percent of the total. Non-Indian commercial fishers took more than half the fish swimming upriver that year. Indian fishermen got barely enough for subsistence. That didn't keep the states from worrying about Indian fishing. Oregon was alarmed over tribal catches from a run headed into Lindsey Creek and complained to the tribes. The Washington Department of Fisheries offered to pay the Yakama tribes if they would not fish in 1959; the tribes refused. The number of salmon returning to the Columbia dropped to its lowest level in a decade that year, but the downriver commercial fishery stayed open just under the normal one hundred days. Informed that Indians had sold some of the hatchery carcasses given them, Milo Moore of Washington's fisheries department asked the U.S. Fish and Wildlife Service to find a better way to dispose of the thousands of spawned-out fish. They belong to the state of Washington, Moore declared, and the Fish and Wildlife Service had no right to give them to Indians.

Salmon are too much a part of the river Indians' lives and culture for the fishing people to be kept from the fish for long. They began finding ways. Although dip nets had long been the favored fishing method, the use of set nets and gill nets had precedents into antiquity. Indians long ago fished from thirty-foot canoes using gill nets made of Indian hemp. They used set nets made of root bark before white men first came to the Columbia. Because the dip net sites at the falls and rapids were so productive, the other methods had been little used for many years. In 1960, however, a few fishermen put out set nets—anchoring them to shore with rocks. The nets stretched out three to five hundred feet, and they captured fish. The states didn't notice. The next year, there were a few more. The following year, 1962, the Yakama Tribal Council set seasons for its fishermen. More Indians returned to the river. The states noticed. The Oregon Fish Commission rejoiced when a Portland judge convicted Portland Fish Co. of illegal possession of Indian-caught fish. The judge reduced the fine to $200 on grounds the company thought the purchase was legal. But the commission was convinced that if it could cut off the market, the state could then "control the Indian fishing problem."

Fisheries officials who served during the 1960s contend their sole concern was the fish. Richard T. Pressey, National Marine Fisheries biologist in the 1960s and 1970s, says the federal agents didn't care who was allowed to catch the fish "as long as there were fish." Oregon's concern was a large commercial Indian fishery, recalls Robert Schoning, director of the Oregon Department of Fisheries during the 1960s. "Where it was just one family (of Indians), it didn't matter." The Oregon officials believed that the flooding of Celilo had left the Indians without a significant fishery and little threat to the commercial industry downstream. Therefore the state took few special measures to restrict them, except for banning them from areas close to fish hatcheries. Washington state, however, maintained a constant battle against Indian fishing on the Columbia and elsewhere. Washington has long had a large and powerful commercial fishing industry and an active and equally powerful sports fishing lobby. They have agreed only on their opposition to Indian fishing.

The Yakama commercial fishing season and regulations, allowing the use of gill nets, set up a direct confrontation between states and tribes over the meaning of the treaties. The Portland Area Office of the BIA frantically sought advice from Washington. Its major question: Under what circumstances should federal attorneys defend Indians arrested by the states for fishing? George W. Dysart, the Interior Department's assistant regional solicitor in Portland, recommended that the federal government refuse to defend Indians caught fishing in violation of tribal ordinances. He said progress was being made in reaching tribal-state agreements but both sides were losing confidence in the Interior Department and, if it did not make decisions soon, the entire effort would be wasted. In a postscript, Dysart said he needed answers now. Washington state had just arrested three Yakama tribal members—Clarence and William Tahkeal and Robert Nelson—for gillnetting in the Columbia River near a closed area. The tribe did not defend the men, who were accused of violating a tribal ordinance as well as state rules.

The next time, a month later, Oregon State Police nabbed Clarence Tahkeal near the Washington shore and Hovis, the Yakama tribal attorney, rose to his defense. That time, Tahkeal was fishing in compliance with a tribal ordinance and within a usual and accustomed area, Hovis argued. And the state had no basis for claiming a conservation necessity for enforcing a ban against Indian fishing. The tribes were allowing only seventy-nine days of commercial fishing in contrast to the hundred days the states allowed downstream, and the downstream fishermen were getting 99 percent of the fish. It was not the last arrest for Clarence Tahkeal. And there were others with similar records.

"It wouldn't have been so bad," mused Clarence's widow, Lillian, "if they didn't use force like we were criminals. They'd handcuff people, hit them, that kind of treatment." Almost worse was the loss of nets; officers confiscated and destroyed them. Myra Sohappy complains that state agents never charged her husband, David, with any offense. That left him with no charge to fight so that he could demand return of his nets if he were acquitted. She estimates he lost thousands of dollars worth of nets in his thirty-year battle against state, federal and tribal governments. David Sohappy's battle against those authorities eventually led him to prison, but it also won court recognition of Indian rights and drew Congress into the fray. Clarence Tahkeal began putting gill nets in the river from Cook's Landing in 1961. Each year, he fished from March until October. In June, when school, was out, Lillian would join him, helping with the nets and the fish until their three sons grew large enough to help—and to get arrested. From June until September, the family lived on the Cook's in-lieu site. The sons still fish from Cook's. Lillian Tahkeal works for the Yakama Indian Nation Higher Education Department at Toppenish. She recalls that the renewed Indian fishing infuriated the states. "They thought they were getting the Indians off the river . . . . They thought with Celilo gone, the Indians were gone." With a slight smile, she added, "It didn't work out that way."

The arrests dampened some of the states' optimism that they were finally bringing the Indians to heel. "Encouraging," said Robert W. Schoning, Oregon fisheries director, after the Yakama passed a regulatory ordinance in May and refused to defend two tribal members arrested for violating it. He was less sanguine in a letter later that year to Senator Wayne Morse, an Oregon Democrat. The Yakama Council had established its commercial season without consulting other fisheries agencies, he complained, then amended it to add fishing days without notifying the other agencies. Dysart, the Interior attorney, also was miffed at the Yakama Council for changing its rules without notifying other agencies. "Such method of operation certainly does not have our support or approval," he assured Schoning.

Increased tribal fishing and the states' resistance had brought delegates from the Interior Department and several of its agencies from Washington, D.C., to the Northwest in an effort to find agreement on fishing rules. The Yakama ordinance change may have been a reminder that the Yakama Nation was a sovereign entity to be heeded, not a subordinate interest group to be pressured into giving up its rights. The Umatilla Board of Trustees also provided a reminder, and that one resulted in a key court ruling in favor of the tribes. The Confederated Tribes of the Umatilla Indian Reservation filed suit against H.G. Maison, the superintendent of the Oregon State Police, and the State of Oregon. The tribes asked for a judgment that the state restrictions on salmon and steelhead fishing were not applicable to the Indians. And they asked for an injunction to keep the state from enforcing its restrictions on tribal fishermen. The U.S. Ninth Circuit Court of Appeals didn't give the Umatilla the injunction, but its 1963 declaration was clear: The state could not impose its rules on the Indians unless those rules were indispensable to fish conservation. And the court said Oregon had not come close to showing such a need. In fact, the court disapprovingly quoted the state's expert witness, researcher H. John Rayner, as explaining that by "conservation" the state meant "the regulations are necessary to conserve fish for commercial and sports fishermen, disregarding the needs of the Indians altogether." That ruling was a major victory for the tribes and impeded the states' efforts to place a disproportionate share of the conservation burden on the Indians.

By then, Dysart and tribal representatives, including tribal attorneys, had begun attending meetings of the Oregon Fish Commission to plead for fair treatment. Washington seasons were set by a department director. So there was no similar public forum in that state. The states were reluctant to recognize tribal authority in the fisheries. Game officers continued to arrest Indian fishermen, and trials brought mixed results. One local court ruled that the state could regulate Indian fishing if it showed it was cooperating with the tribes. The tribes then had no biologists on their staffs, placing them at a disadvantage in setting their seasons and justifying them to the states. States and tribes tried to find common ground but any agreement was tenuous at best. At one meeting, Sam Kash Kash of the Umatilla Fish Committee complained about recent publicity blaming Indians for destroying the fish. There were plenty for everyone before the white people came, he said. And Indians are as interested in conserving the runs as anyone. In a 1964 meeting, Dysart explained some of the Indians' frustration. Non-Indian commercial fishing had been limited to two days (in June) and the Indians had accepted a shortened season also, but sportsmen, who fished both above and below Bonneville Dam, continued without restrictions. It is hard for the Indian to see why he should stop fishing when sportsmen are not restricted, Dysart told the commission.

So some of the fishermen just went on fishing. By then, many Indian fishers were using boats to set their nets in the river and haul in their catch. Duane Clark recalls, "One of the toughest things, there was no place to land. We fished all at night. We were always hassled by the feds and state, mostly the states on both sides. Sometimes they took our nets." The fishermen had to find buyers too. They no longer could sell directly to a cannery since the state deemed their fishing illegal.

To some of the river people, the tribal governments' efforts to work things out looked too much like giving up treaty rights. Those fishermen reasoned that their ancestors had given up a great deal in exchange for continuing to fish. They considered any interference with that fishing, from whatever source, a violation of the treaty and their rights. They refused to abide by either state or tribal rules. Some extended their fishing above The Dalles Dam. On the other hand, the states—especially Washington—wanted full control of the river. Senator Warren G. Magnuson, a Washington Democrat, introduced two resolutions in the United States Senate designed to get rid of the Indian fishing "problem." One would have required that Indians be treated like all others, without regard to their treaty rights, in off-reservation fisheries. The other called for purchasing the treaty rights at twenty-five times the average annual value of the Indian fishery for the previous three years. Congress did not adopt either Magnuson resolution or any of the several other schemes aimed at giving the states total control of the Indian fishery. Theodore T. Bugas, executive secretary of the Columbia River Salmon and Tuna Packers Association, urged the commission to support the Magnuson resolutions. Extinguishing Indian treaty rights would be the best solution, he said, so the management agencies could more thoroughly control the fish harvest. However, the Oregon Fish Commission conceded that any national legislation solving the "Indian problem" would be difficult to pass because President Kennedy had declared that his administration intended to honor treaties with the Indians. Dysart, the government attorney, pointed out to the Commission that the government had paid the Indians $27 million to merely subordinate their fishing rights to The Dalles Dam. Extinguishing the rights altogether would cost much more, he implied—if the Indians were willing even to discuss the possibility. They weren't.

The stage was being set for the major legal battles to come. David Sohappy and his brother, Aleck, had joined the Tahkeal brothers at Cook's Landing. David Sohappy, his wife, Myra, and their growing family would soon move permanently to Cook's. The Umatilla and Warm Springs tribes joined the Yakama Nation in setting tribal fishing seasons. The number of fish coming back to the Columbia rebounded beginning in 1964. More Indians went fishing. A state survey in the spring of 1964 found eighty-seven Indian nets in the river above Bonneville, compared to seventy in the same season the previous year. In 1966 various governments filed two hundred fishing violation cases against members of the Yakama tribes. And the Indians began to catch a measurable number of fish— as much as 2 percent of the river's total commercial tonnage.

Fishing engaged entire families, and it was hard work. Randy Settler, now a Yakama Tribal Council member, describes his childhood as a member of a fishing family during the 1960s: "We had a sixteen- or fourteen-foot wooden boat. Me and my brother and Mom's nephew would fish. We'd sleep on the bank, check the nets, miles from anybody. We'd take the fish, meet the buyer at the boat landing. I was seven or eight years old. He'd get us gas. We'd watch him weigh the fish, write a receipt. Then he'd take us to the store to get food, then go back again and again. My brother was about ten. So was the cousin. That was how we grew up. Work all night. Go to school. I'd sleep in school." Other memories are more chilling. One of the federal agencies put a cyclone fence topped by barbed wire around the Lone Pine site where the Settlers and other Indian families lived. Caucasian families would bring their children to stare through the fence at the Indians. "We were something to see." Randy Settler recalls with some irony. More recently he fished for the Columbia River Inter-Tribal Fish Commission doing salmon research.

The family fished three hundred days a year in the 1960s. Their activities pitted them against their own Yakama Tribe as well as against state and federal fisheries officers. Indian fishing people charge that the state never checked to determine whether Indians were using treaty-protected locations. State game officers simply arrested any Indian tending a net. Randy Settler saw state authorities arrest his mother and tribal, as well as state, officers arrest his father and uncle. His uncle, Homer Settler, studied Indian law in jail. Randy's mother, Mary Settler, escaped a jail term then but later went to Oregon state prison for selling fish. Even as she defied them, Mary Settler won a certain respect from the state and federal agents charged with controlling Indian fishing and fish sales. Richard Pressey, the retired fisheries biologist, recalls state and federal agents silently wishing for Mary Settler to reach the Washington shore safely as she eluded officers on rough water in a Columbia Gorge storm. Pressey's and Randy Settler's versions of the chase differ, but they agree that this tiny woman—barely five feet tall—had the courage to take a small boat across the Columbia's whitecaps, outmaneuvering the larger fisheries enforcement boat. "When she reached the shore safely, we cheered," Pressey said.

The fishing people, however, found little to cheer about in those years. In addition to battling for both their fishing rights and the promised sites on the Bonneville pool, they were losing more fishing grounds and homes. Construction of John Day Dam in the 1960s created another lake, this one seventy-five miles long, stretching eastward from The Dalles pool to McNary Dam near Umatilla, Oregon. That lake completed the destruction of the Columbia River Indians' fishing grounds along the Oregon-Washington border. It also forced dozens of Indian families to find homes on higher ground. They received what they considered a pittance to build new homes. There was no talk of replacing the fishing sites lost there until twenty years later. Even so, Charles F. Luce, Umatilla tribal attorney when work began on John Day and now the retired CEO of Consolidated Edison in New York, got the tribe to identify all its fishing sites for the record. The move paid off when Congress passed new legislation on in-lieu sites in 1988.

Lavina Washines recalls that the Corps forced her grandmother, Sue Walsey, from her allotment at Rock Creek, Washington. "She died from the pain of having to leave the land," Washines said. "The Corps took Grandmother's allotment and gave her so many thousand dollars. My Grandma cried and said she was not leaving. The Corps man said, 'Stay and you'll go under the water.' That's what the man told her—'the water will cover you.'" More than a hundred members of Washines' extended family were affected by the ouster. Like many Indian families, Washines' lived close together with homes on a single allotment sheltering several generations. Walsey and other family members moved to an area near Goldendale, Washington, fifteen miles from the river.

Louise Billy, a Yakama elder, went to the Corps with an interpreter to make her claim. "I made a claim of my residence, my niece's home, and my mother's home whose name the allotment was under," she told the Corps. "We were removed from our land and our homes were demolished because the Federal Government and the Corps of Engineers had lied to us. They said our land would be under water when the John Day pool would back up, but our land is still above water where the Rock Creek Park is now located." Jay Minthorn, the Umatilla tribal official spearheading new efforts to complete in-lieu sites, asks, "Why is it so hard for us?" He invites a look at the town of Arlington, Oregon, relocated by the Corps of Engineers to the shore of the new lake behind John Day Dam. "They moved homes at Arlington. It was an improvement over the old town. We are fighting just for facilities."

In fact, the government spent $3 million to move Arlington, 1960 population 643. That didn't include $500,000 for a new grade school. It cost the government $1.5 million to move businesses and homes at Boardman, Oregon, and an equal amount to build a new high school. Moving parts of Umatilla, Oregon, cost $500,000 and parts of Roosevelt, Washington, $360,000. In all the Corps of Engineers spent $160 million to move homes, businesses, roads and railroads. The Corps also was touting the seventy-five miles of recreation opportunity it was creating on the lake behind the dam. It offered to build nine parks on the Oregon side and eight on the Washington side if state or local governments would maintain them. The corps had taken title to 27,300 acres of shore land on the new lake it created, and was offering the property for industry, fish and wildlife reserves, and general river access. There was no mention of Indians.

Howard Jim, chief of the Wy'am at Celilo, grew up on Pine Creek in Washington state and fished at Blalock on the Oregon side twenty miles east of John Day Dam. He recalls that when he was young, before the dams, the Indians fished anywhere they wanted all summer. Jim was on the Mid-Columbia Council of Chiefs when John Day was built. But he says with some bitterness that reservation Indians took over, and he does not know why there was no effort to obtain replacement sites for places such as Blalock flooded by John Day Dam. The government tried to get all the Indians to leave the river, Jim remembers. "They offered to give us land and to build houses . . . . The water ran us out . . . the Rock Creek people, Pine Creek, Roosevelt." Jim's family got $1,200 for a lost home. The Indians moved higher into the barren hills of the eastern Columbia Gorge, east of the National Scenic Area. Even if the Indians were willing to turn from fishing to farming, "you can't plow the land the Indians got," Jim said. "You can't plant wheat on rocks."

Looking at the value of money in the 1960s and at the Indian homes, many people say the Indians got fair treatment. In economic terms that argument can be made. But to the people of the river, the economics is a lesser concern. The Corps spent $100,000 to move cemeteries at Irrigon and Boardman, Oregon, and miscellaneous graves on the John Day pool. Indian residents complain that they were not even given an opportunity to move the graves of their ancestors.

At Alderdale, a rocky shrub-covered point jutting into the river—now lake—the whole area where Indians lived is under water. So is the island where there were graves. A plaque on the river's north shore has been set on a stone that was taken from the village site now under water. The inscription is headed "Nawai", and it reads:

> Under these waters of the John Day Dam rest the earliest inhabitants of this area. The ancestors of the people we know today are located throughout the Columbia River Basin. At Alderdale these people of the river built their winter lodges of willow poles and tule mats and lived there year around. Following the cycles of their lives some of them would move out in the springtime, taking only such equipment as was needed to gather and dry roots, berries and the meat of wild game and salmon. Always they returned to this great river that was their permanent home base. The names of those few learned from the elders of the elders are also identified and will be honored and respected.

There follows a list of names. Frederick Ike Sr., a Yakama member of the current In-Lieu Site Task Force, points to the second name in the first column—"my mother's name." She was named for the ancestor who lies beneath the water. The whole Alderdale community moved up the river bank. Indians got no compensation for John Day, Ike notes. The Corps built them nothing. Many there were never compensated for lost homes.

Looking out over the water from the rocky point, Ike reminisces: "I used to fish here." It was never easy. After the river became a pool, the Spokane, Portland and Seattle Railway began locking the gates at crossings on roads the Indians used as access to the river. Complaints had no effect. "My mother and stepbrother used to break the locks and the railroad would lock them in." Finally in the late 1960s, Ike and another fisherman visited railroad officials in Portland. The two Indians presented the SP&S with a copy of the 1855 treaty between the United States and the Yakama tribes and of the 1905 U.S. Supreme Court ruling spelling out the Indians' right of access to the river. "Open the gates or we go to court," the Indians said. The gates were unlocked.

On the Oregon side, Union Pacific Railroad still, in the late 1990s, locks the gates on roads across its tracks occasionally and has pulled rocks away from the track to make the crossings impassable, according to Jay Minthorn. The issue remains unresolved despite years of negotiations.

# 8

# BESIEGED

*We will live here as long as there is time—close to the earth
and close to our home, the Chiawana [Columbia River].*

—Puck Hyah Toot, Wanapum prophet quoted by
Click Relander in *Drummers and Dreamers.*

David Sohappy wanted only to live in the traditional Indian way, care for
his family and worship the Creator who sent the salmon that supported life
and family. Instead, he became a central figure in a series of real-life dramas
that defined Indian rights and ultimately led to a renewed effort to fulfill
the government's 1939 in-lieu site promise. The same events swept him
from his beloved river.

Sohappy's stubborn insistence that the Creator—not state, federal or
tribal government—controlled his fishing brought the wrath of state and
federal fisheries authorities down on the Cook's Landing in-lieu site. Sohappy
and his extended family lived on the rocky, windswept point that juts into
the Columbia River from the north shore. Several other families lived there
too from time to time, but only the Sohappys stayed year after year. In the
early 1980s, their permanence and their openness about their fishing made
David Sohappy the focus of both a several-hundred-thousand-dollar
government sting operation—known as Salmonscam—and federal efforts
to remove all permanent residents from the in-lieu sites. Salmonscam sent
David Sohappy to federal prison and hastened his death. But it drew national
attention to his people's struggle to maintain their treaty-guaranteed rights.
The efforts to evict the Sohappys brought renewal of the 1939 promise and
a plan to fulfill it at last.

*David Sohappy in a photograph taken during his trial in Yakama Tribal Court in 1987. Courtesy Jeanie Senior.*

Sohappy was from the family of the nineteenth-century Indian prophet Smohalla and in time Sohappy became a leader of the Feather religion, the offshoot of Washat that Smohalla created. Sohappy believed that the Creator and the Yakama treaty gave him the right to take salmon to provide for his wife and eight children. And he believed he could live where he fished. Those beliefs brought David Sohappy three decades of conflict with government—federal, state, local and tribal. The Wanapum Band, to which the Sohappy family belonged, remained at White Bluff on the arid Columbia River bank after the 1855 Yakama treaty. In 1942, the federal government removed the few remaining families to build the Hanford Nuclear Project. The Wanapum moved upstream and stayed by the river until the mid-1950s, when their last village was destroyed by a public utility district dam. Ironically, the dam was named Priest Rapids after Smohalla. David, born in 1925, grew up on his grandmother's Yakama Reservation allotment, following the seasonal food cycles—game, fish, roots, huckleberries. From April to October the family was at White Bluff where his grandmother had a fish-drying shed. He also visited his grandmother's sister, who had a fish drying shed at Drano Lake, the mouth of the Little White Salmon River, where the Corps of Engineers originally planned to build one of the Bonneville in-lieu sites.

As David grew up, his grandmother wanted him to farm, but his heart wasn't in it. When fishing season began, David went to the river, although he never stayed more than a few days or weeks. He got a job as a mechanic in a government garage, and he married Myra, a childhood playmate. By the time he was drafted in 1946, they had one child. David reached the rank of sergeant in his eleven months in the Army Air Corps, before the service decided to discharge all fathers. David went back to Yakama. He ran his family's farm and worked for another farmer. He held jobs as a carpenter, electrician, plumber and heavy equipment operator. Each year he went fishing for a few weeks in the Yakima River or at Priest Rapids or Celilo Falls on the Columbia. After The Dalles Dam ended Celilo fishing, David's brother, Aleck, began going to Cook's Landing with friends Clarence and William Tahkeal. David joined them, fishing on his days off from March to November. Then he lost his job at a White Salmon sawmill. He and Myra and the eight children moved to Cook's Landing and David went fishing full time.

They ate salmon two and three times a day, traded fish for some staples and bought a few others. Their sons hunted for meat. The family never asked for welfare or surplus commodities. David provided salmon for tribal ceremonies and conducted religious ceremonies in the family's own longhouse at Cook's. "We never took more than we needed," he said. They did not live luxuriously. The cavernous wooden building in which they lived and stored their fishing nets was not insulated. It sits on the point of the inlet, exposed to the raw fury of Columbia Gorge winds. Furnishings were sparse. Myra always had racks of salmon drying. Neither David nor Myra drank alcohol. Myra Sohappy says about Cook's: "We thought that was our country. I see a lot of houses. I don't know what kind of agreement there was. We weren't there very long when the government started harassing us . . . . We lost a lot of nets, stolen by the states and Indian tribes. We were able to get enough fish to live. There was a nice buyer in the Portland area." The Alexander family also lived at Cook's. And the Tahkeals continued to spend half the year there fishing. The inlet became the focus of state efforts to control Indian fishing. And it became the centerpiece of the BIA's efforts to remove permanent residents from all the in-lieu sites.

During the late 1960s and early 1970s, the tribes were so busy fighting for their right to fish they had little time to keep up the battle for the in-lieu sites. They also had to defend their few existing sites from a Corps of Engineers plan that threatened to make all of them smaller. In the background was yet another shift in federal Indian policies and a militant nationwide movement asserting Indian rights. The federal government's enthusiasm for termination had begun waning almost as soon as it cut the first tribes loose from federal supervision and assistance in the late 1950s. Gradually, the policy was forgotten. The Nixon Administration formally abandoned it in 1969. Finally, in 1973, Congress legislated its demise in favor of programs to give tribes more autonomy without cutting the federal strings completely. Most Northwest tribes, with their long history of battling for fishing and hunting rights, were well prepared to manage their own affairs.

The number of salmon returning to the Columbia River hit a low point in 1960, then began a substantial climb. As the number of fish increased, so did the number of tribal fishermen and the states' concern about Indian fishing. The states continued to ban all but Indian dip nets above Bonneville. By 1966 the Yakama, Umatilla, and Nez Perce tribes all were setting their own commercial gill net seasons with restrictions on members, but the states ignored the tribal authority and cited Indian fishermen for violating the state rules. In 1966, Oregon stepped up enforcement, seizing nets and arresting fishermen. Yakama attorney James B. Hovis remembers handling six hundred criminal citations against Yakama tribal members in Oregon and Washington that year. The next year, faced with a Washington Supreme Court ruling that Indians had "peculiar fishing rights in some areas," Washington Fisheries Director Thor Tollefson considered recommending an Indian fishing season. Two county superior courts already had announced they would not accept Indian fishing cases until they had a U.S. Supreme Court ruling. Their stand in effect nullified enforcement efforts. Tollefson still wasn't convinced, but he bowed to reality and allowed Washington buyers to purchase Indian-caught fish.

In 1968, salmon numbers dropped again and all state interests promptly looked at restricting the Indians. Russell Bristow of Columbia River Fishermen's Protective Union (commercial fishers) urged the Oregon Fish Commission to halt all sport and Indian fishing until "we get the number of fish over (the dam) we want." Both state departments expressed concern about the Indian fishery. Oregon Director Robert Schoning said the Indians were fishing on a large concentration of fish below John Day Dam, "where passage problems are critical." But in May the U.S. Supreme Court ruled, in a Washington state case from Puget Sound, that the states could not discriminate against the Indians in setting seasons and regulations. The states for the first time established a commercial season for Indian fishers above Bonneville Dam. That didn't keep David Sohappy from getting arrested for fishing outside the state-prescribed limits. He sat in the county jail at Stevenson, Washington, for three nights and four days. When he got out, he went to court. This time, he was a plaintiff. Attorneys for the National Office for the Rights of the Indigent, based in New York City, entered the issue. David's cousin, Richard Sohappy, a decorated soldier on leave to recuperate from Viet Nam War wounds, led the plaintiffs' list. Richard Sohappy, then twenty, had been arrested with his uncle. Both were given suspended thirty-day jail sentences, and fined $250 with $200 suspended. David's brother, Aleck, and Myra also were plaintiffs in the civil suit along with the Sohappys' Cook's Landing neighbors, four members of the Alexander family, and their former fishing companion, Clarence Tahkeal. In all, fourteen members of the Yakama tribes were listed. The defendants were Chairman McKee A. Smith and the other members of the Oregon Fish Commission and Oregon and Washington state fish and game officials. The fishermen asked the court to define their treaty rights and the extent to which the state could regulate them. Federal attorneys soon filed a similar suit on behalf of the four treaty tribes fishing on the Columbia.

U.S. District Court Judge Robert C. Belloni combined the two suits, and on July 8, 1969, he handed the Indians a stunning victory. He built on the previous year's Supreme Court ruling regarding the Puyallup Tribe, which stated little more than that state regulations could not discriminate against the tribal fishers and must be necessary for conservation. In addition, Belloni said, the states must give separate consideration to the Indian fishery and they must regulate their fisheries so that tribal fishers can take a fair share of the runs. There would be no more regulating the fishery to insure the catch for downriver commercial interests while placing tight rules on Indians' upriver fishery. Not discriminating meant giving the tribal people a fair chance to catch the fish. Predictably, the Indians were generally pleased with Belloni's ruling, and the states and non-Indian commercial and sports fishermen were not. But the reaction was mild compared to the vitriol and violence that greeted a similar ruling by Judge George W. Boldt in Seattle five years later. Neither editorials nor letters to the editor showed up in Portland's two daily newspapers within a week of the ruling. However, Umatilla tribal fishers Robert and N. Kathryn Brigham found cables cut, tanks stolen, and holes in their fishing boat within days after Belloni's ruling. Laura Berg, in an essay on the ruling in the Hastings College of Law *Journal of Environmental Law and Policy*, reported that Belloni was surprised at the adverse reaction. "Fishermen of all kinds, the sports and commercial fishermen, reacted a lot stronger than I ever thought they would," Berg quoted Belloni.

Judge Belloni's landmark ruling in 1969 was the first step toward giving Indians equality on the river. But it did not immediately change the way the states managed the river. Oregon developed a theory it called "equal meaningful time on common stocks." Under that plan outlined by Robert Schoning, the Oregon Fish Commission director, the commercial fishermen below Bonneville Dam and the tribal fishermen above the dam would be allowed the same number of fishing days on the salmon runs that crossed Bonneville Dam. Oregon considered only those salmon stocks that spawned above Bonneville Dam to be "common stocks." The state did not consider runs that spawned in the Willamette and Cowlitz rivers, tributaries that enter the Columbia below Bonneville Dam, to be common stocks because they did not reach the fishing grounds the Indians were then using. That theory allowed the state to continue giving non-Indian commercial fishers below the dam considerably more fishing time and fish than it allowed the Indians. And since there were more non-Indian commercial fishermen with larger nets than the Indians', the non-Indians still would have had a substantial advantage. To the Indians that looked a lot like continued concentration on restrictions and enforcement against tribal fishermen. Both states continued to impose brief Indian fishing seasons, inflexible gear requirements, and rules that generally favored downstream non-Indian commercial fishermen and sports fishermen over the Indians. At the same time, the tribes were setting their own seasons and limits on tribal fishermen, showing that they were as capable as the states at managing the fishery. Some Indian fishers, such as David Sohappy, believed, however, that their right to fish was no more subject to tribal rules than to state rules. It was not that they fished until there were no more. They simply followed their own logic of fishing seasons. "Only the fish know," explains Myra Sohappy. She is angry at the Yakama Nation. "They robbed us of our fish." She— and others—contend that the tribal seasons, like the state's, restricted Indian catches while "the white man takes all our fish."

Not the least of the Indians' problems—and the salmon's—is the confused overlapping of jurisdictions involved in improving, protecting and managing fish runs. The National Marine Fisheries Service is charged with protecting anadromous fish—those that spend part of their lives in the ocean—from poaching. The federal agency also administers protection for anadromous fish listed as threatened or endangered under the Endangered Species Act. The states, through an interstate agreement, set seasons and catch limits on the Columbia, and each state sets its own rules for fishing on the Columbia tributaries. The tribes have authority over their members' fishing. But Indians fishing at Celilo had long obeyed only the edicts of the chief there. It was the chief's responsibility to state when enough fish were in the river for catching to begin and to close fishing when enough were caught. With Celilo fishing gone, and with it the chief's authority, some of the river Indians, including David Sohappy, believed only the river people understood the fish well enough decide when to fish. At the same time, the tribes had begun working with state and federal officials to assure a fair share of fishing for their members. The legal battles of the 1970s and 1980s defined more clearly the authority of each entity, but as Congress created new bodies to deal with the decline in salmon numbers and related issues, the situation grew more complex.

Faced with intensive state efforts to restrict their fishing and disagreement with their own tribal government, river Indians turned elsewhere. Treaty Indians of the Columbia River, Inc., an organization of about one hundred river people, grabbed public attention in 1971 by petitioning the United Nations for help. The Indians asked UN Secretary U Thant to send a peacekeeping mission to the Columbia River and appoint a permanent American Indian delegate to the UN. They also asked UN financing to take their treaty dispute with the United States to the World Court. Several of the signatures on the UN petition were familiar names from the courts, in both civil suits and criminal fishing violations. The Indians said they had exhausted their financial resources while the states cut off their ability to make a living by confiscating boats and nets. Nothing came of it but publicity. However, there are tribal members today who think U.S. tribes should have their own representation in the UN.

There was ample reason to seek a peacekeeping mission to the Columbia River in the early 1970s. Burnie Bohn, longtime Oregon fisheries official, recalls the period vividly. Through 1971, 1972, 1973 and 1974 the state and Indians were in court several times every year over one thing or another. Judge Belloni had kept the 1969 case, U.S v. Oregon, open to assure that the states complied. It remains open as the paradigm for managing salmon fishing on the Columbia. Bohn was deeply involved in the fishery. He recalls, "There was almost no year where there was any peace on the river." Whatever the state did was "never quite interpreted to be consistent" with Belloni's 1969 order. The state rarely won, and there were only a few draws, while the effort cost the agency vast management time. Belloni had not defined "fair share" and, in Bohn's view, that vagueness fueled some of the animosity between tribal fishermen and the state.

Nor was there peace between the river people and the tribes. In 1970, Leo Alexander called a meeting of plaintiffs in the original lawsuit, Sohappy v. Smith, because tribes and the federal government had entered the suit. Alexander said he feared that future involvement in fishing rights decisions would be confined to tribal organizations. The fishing people remained very much a part of the continuing contentious process, however. In 1972 a dozen residents of the in-lieu sites went back to Judge Belloni asking him to prevent the state of Oregon from interfering with their spring fishing season. The Indians said they had reason to believe that Oregon planned to set a spring season above Bonneville Dam beginning May 1, after the spring run had substantially passed the Indian fishing grounds. They asked the judge to prohibit state interference with a tribal season beginning April 17. Their season, with its small share of the fish, would not affect conservation efforts allowing escapement of salmon upstream to spawn. They had a point. During the early 1970s, non-Indian and sports fishermen caught more than 85 percent of salmon that originated in the Columbia River, leaving little more than 3 percent for the Indians and less than 10 percent to escape for spawning. The Indians' request said that despite Belloni's mandate allocating them a fair share of the salmon, "Oregon has continued to place restrictions upon the treaty Indian fishery far beyond those necessary for the conservation of the resource." In fact, they said, "Discrimination against treaty Indian fishing has actually increased since the (1969) judgment." Washington was even worse in concentrating fisheries enforcement on Indian people.

The enforcement only intensified in 1974 after another federal judge, George W. Boldt of Seattle, cleared up the ambiguity that had bothered Bohn about what constituted a fair share for the Indians. Fifty percent, Boldt said in a case involving Puget Sound fisheries. Half for the Indians, half for other fishermen. In the wake of that ruling, "the state of Washington declared war on the Indians," recalls Alphonse Halfmoon, vice chairman of the Umatilla Board of Trustees. A few months later, Belloni applied the 50 percent rule to Oregon and the Columbia River.

While the tribal fishers were winning judicial approval of their right to fish, the BIA was juggling three in-lieu site issues. Simultaneously it was trying to remove permanent residents from the sites, attempting to stop the Corps of Engineers from flooding the sites, and making plans to improve the sites. The dozen years of the late 1960s and the 1970s were marked by bickering and by efforts to improve the sites but no government effort to finish obtaining the four hundred acres promised the Indians.

The Bureau of Indian Affairs first issued rules for use of the in-lieu sites July 1, 1966. An affidavit in a later court case—in which David Sohappy was a principal figure—states that those first rules allowed permanent buildings if they were maintained and if the owner got a permit from the BIA. A year later, Interior Secretary Stuart L. Udall wrote Alvin Settler that Indians then living on the sites probably would be able to get permits if their buildings met health standards. The BIA soon changed its mind and issued new rules to keep the sites tidy. The new rules, effective in mid-February 1969, touched off a controversy that worked its way into federal appeals courts and Congress. Indirectly, the controversy resulted in legislation twenty years later that was designed to provide more fishing sites, if not the four hundred acres promised so long ago. The 1969 rules for the first time placed a ban on permanent dwellings on the sites. Only tents, tepees, campers, and mobile trailers were allowed, and those were to be removed whenever the owners were not catching, drying, or processing fish. Under the rules, BIA would remove or demolish any structure left on a site. Indians who lived along the river, both on and off the in-lieu sites, protested the new rule. Some argued that they had a right to keep a net in the river or fish for sturgeon year-round and therefore could legally remain in the sites all year. Some reminded the BIA that they had lived permanently on the sites flooded by Bonneville Dam, and the Corps originally had promised to restore all the lost buildings, including homes. A few asked Northwest members of Congress to help them. Through the spring and summer, the river residents, the tribes and BIA tried to resolve the dispute. The BIA tried to get the tribes to remove their members from Cook's. No tribe wanted that chore although a number of tribal government officials agreed that the sites should not contain permanent residences. They contended the sites were meant for all tribal members, and the presence of permanent homes discouraged others from using them. Eugene Greene says the Cascade Locks fishermen understood they could not live permanently on that small site. BIA finally asked the Interior Department solicitor for an opinion of the legality of its action. Dysart, the assistant solicitor, responded in October that the housing ban was legal. The treaties, he said, limited the Indians' off-reservation rights to taking fish and erecting temporary buildings for curing them. He said the secretary of Interior could allow permanent homes on the sites but was not obligated to do so.

The BIA stuck to its rule. And some of the Indians stuck to their homes. The Sohappys and a few others were no more willing to give up the homes than they were to give up the fishing. Johnny Jackson moved away from Underwood at first, but the BIA burned the drying sheds the Indians left, and they had to rebuild. Jackson moved back to protect the sheds. He is still there, the only resident. The drying sheds and the nets remain secure under his watchful eye. He fishes some, and in the fall cuts and hauls firewood to elders on the Yakama Reservation. The government also removed drying sheds from Wind River after each fishing season, usually paying the owners less than $100. Sophie George believes it was the Corps of Engineers that burned the drying sheds each fall, although it was the BIA that decreed all buildings must be torn down. George recalls, "Every time we built dry sheds they burned them down. Grandmother used to cry. One cabinet destroyed at Wind River was hand-cut lumber. The material was custom-made for the five-layer dry shed. When they were building it, they were really particular about how it was done."

The BIA has never fully explained why it decided to ban permanent dwellings. There are several plausible possibilities. First, the agency came under severe criticism for the sanitation problems on the sites. Banning permanent residences would reduce the potential problems and lessen the work for BIA staff. Second, some Indians had complained that the permanent residents were usurping the sites. Third, the rule was announced only a few months after the Sohappys and others filed the U.S. District Court suit challenging state efforts to control Indian fishing. Although Dysart, on behalf of the government, represented the Indians in the fishing rights case, titled U.S. v. Oregon, officials at all levels of government viewed the Sohappys as troublesome if not trouble-makers. It would not be surprising if BIA aimed its no-residence rule at them. Still, the BIA took a go-slow approach to enforcing its no-permanent-residence rule, saying it wanted compliance with a minimum of hardship for the people who lived on the sites. In May 1969, Area BIA Director Dale M. Baldwin assured Congressman Wendell Wyatt of Oregon that "it is not our intention to summarily evict them." Assistant Commissioner Charles P. Corkle provided the same assurance to Senator Bob Packwood of Oregon. In meetings a month later between BIA officials and the residents at Lone Pine and Cook's, the fishing people pointed out that before Bonneville Dam some of them had lived in houses along the river all year. They also said their shacks were healthier than tepees, which the rules would allow, and many could not afford the campers and trailers, also allowed. They also were suspicious of the BIA's motives. Some questioned the agency's interest in improving sanitation. Others suggested it might be retaliating against the residents who defied tribal fishing rules. At a similar meeting in White Salmon a few months later, it became evident that the Corps had promised at least some of the people their homes would be replaced. A BIA history of the issue conceded that a number of the Indian people probably had believed since 1933 they could establish homes on any in-lieu site.

Indians argued that several of the in-lieu sites, including Underwood and Cook's, had been Indian villages before Bonneville was built. Graham Rice of the BIA agreed. He reported to his superiors that people had lived at Lone Pine since about 1960, and the site had been used for year-round camping before it became an in-lieu site. Underwood was a permanent Indian village before and after it became an in-lieu site. Cook's had been permanently occupied since 1960, but used for camping and drying before the Corps acquired it. Leo Alexander, a resident of Cook's, explained, "When it became clear to our people that the Army Corps of Engineers had reneged on its promise to rebuild their homes, many of our people commenced rebuilding their own houses." The Corps, of course, denies that it ever promised to replace homes. The written record is ambiguous but there is evidence to support the river residents' claims. Several documents in Corps and BIA files include lists of people who had houses on fishing sites before Bonneville Dam. Several meeting records during the 1940s and 1950s contain statements from Indians about replacing homes lost to the dam, with no contradiction from BIA or Corps representatives who were present. Court files contain pictures of homes on fishing sites taken during the 1930s. Part of the issue is what was a permanent home for these people, who traditionally moved with the seasons to obtain food. Lavina Washines explains that before fish runs were so depleted, her family spent February to November each year on the river, returning to the Yakama Reservation only in winter. The Goudys of Lone Pine argue that they fish for various species throughout the year and therefore have a right to remain near their nets and scaffolds continuously.

Perhaps no other issue has so severely split the river people and tribal governments. Until the BIA began efforts to enforce its no-permanent-residence rule in the late 1960s, the tribes ignored the fact that some members remained on the sites year round. But, forced to take a stand, both Yakama and Warm Springs councils opposed permanent residences. Johnny Jackson, who won the right to remain at Underwood through a long legal battle, is bitter. "The tribes never helped us out on that until the very end. They never done nothing for us. We done what we could. We had salmon bakes to pay our lawyer." Leo Alexander, at a 1972 meeting, expressed the river peoples' resentment of tribal government: "Tribal councils want to protect their authority. The tribal councils are diverting attention from the real problem. They intend to create a climate against the Cook's people. This is an old game of outside interests, including the Bureau, to divide and conquer. Columbia River people are not against the others—just trying to preserve their culture."

One reason the tribal governments opposed permanent residences on the sites was that there was too little camping room for everyone who wanted to fish. That, of course, was a direct result of the Corps' failure to provide the four hundred acres it had promised in 1939. And four hundred acres would have been enough land to accommodate homes for those displaced by Bonneville Dam. The largest site the Corps had agreed to provide, Big Eddy at more than two hundred acres, became a footing for The Dalles Dam before the Corps even made a move to turn it over to the Indians. The site was never replaced. Then the Little White Salmon site, once planned for 160 acres, became instead 3.14 acres at Cook's Landing. Cascade Locks, originally eight acres, became 1.6 acres. Eugene Greene Sr., director of the Warm Springs fisheries program, fished at Cascade Locks during the 1960s. He has no idea why the area shrank. His explanation: "Everything starts to get smaller and smaller" when it is being turned over to Indians. "On the other hand, when word gets out we want to buy property, prices accelerate fast." The only sizeable in-lieu site, Wind River at 23.6 acres, was almost unusable because of silting at the boat launch and a nearly impassable access road. In all, an increasing number of Indian fishermen were being crowded onto 41.3 acres instead of the four hundred they were promised. Adding to the crowding was the loss of Celilo Falls and dozens of smaller traditional fishing sites on The Dalles and John Day pools. At the same time, the non-Indian population of the Northwest was growing, and the Columbia Gorge saw both increased development and increased recreation use. The newcomers crowded the Indian fishermen and made it harder to find more room.

BIA didn't want the Indians living on the sites. Neighboring communities complained about conditions on the sites. The Corps refused to consider building homes as part of its compensation for flooding home and fishing sites. And it seems no one wanted the Indians anywhere else either. Del Webb of BIA discussed the issue with Dick Adlard, resources development officer for the community extension service, in nearby Stevenson. A "reasonable minded person who would like to help the Indian people" had suggested setting up a village for them somewhere east of the current sites because there is not room for sixty-eight people at Cook's. The response was immediately and vehemently negative. The issue clearly worried William T. Schlick, the superintendent of the Yakama Indian Agency. In May 1970, he wrote to the area director saying he could find no evidence of any promise the Indians could live on the sites but that the fishermen feared loss of their gear if they did not remain. The solution to the impasse is more difficult, he said, because of friction between tribal members who used the in-lieu sites and the Tribal Council. The conflict had other aspects, including the legal battles over fishing rights, per capita payments to tribal members, and the authority of tribal police on the sites. A solution is urgent, Schlick wrote.

Tim Weaver, an attorney for the Yakama Indian Nation since 1971, said the residency issue was affected by a lot of tribal politics between the site residents and the council. Some of the site residents refused to recognize and follow the tribes' law and order and fishing regulations. There were fights between fishermen, each claiming the right to a specific site. There was confusion over whether tribal police had jurisdiction over such crimes as assault and liquor consumption. Rumors were rampant. Although BIA had promised ample notification before actually evicting anyone, reports kept cropping up that removal was imminent. In October 1970, Leo Alexander asked Yakama Superintendent Schlick to call a meeting of everyone concerned with the in-lieu sites because of the U.S. position in the U.S. v. Oregon lawsuit concerning Indians residing on the sites. Alexander also cited recent rumors and the request of "another federal agency" to remove the Indians. A day earlier Seattle attorney Lowell K. Halvorson had written to Joseph D. Dwyer, assistant to the area BIA director in Portland, on Alexander's behalf. Alexander was convinced that the government planned to evict the residents, and Halvorson reminded Dwyer that he and government attorney George W. Dysart had given assurances they would inform both the Indians and Halvorson before taking legal eviction action. Just where Alexander got his notion about eviction is not recorded. Dysart had written as part of the government's filings in U.S. v. Oregon that the in-lieu sites were subject to the same conditions as the usual and accustomed places cited in the treaties. He added, "The question of the right of Indians to permanent residence on the sites is a matter of current controversy between some of the residents of the sites and the Department of the Interior" but is not involved in these suits. The rumors didn't die. That summer, attorney Halvorson wrote Dwyer again, this time asking if the eviction plan was tied to the railroad's intention to encroach on the in-lieu sites. There is a long history of conflict between both the Spokane, Portland and Seattle Railway (now Burlington Northern Santa Fe) on the Washington shore and the Union Pacific Railroad on the Oregon side. Both railroads follow the river shore closely, and few fishing sites can be reached without crossing their tracks. But there is no evidence the railroads were involved in the eviction effort, although at least one structure at Cook's turned out to be on railroad property.

Reid Peyton Chambers, a UCLA law professor and Native American Rights Fund attorney, weighed in with a letter to Louis R. Bruce, the commissioner of Indian Affairs, stating that the government had no right to evict the residents. Chambers was in the area representing some residents of Cook's. Even Graham Rice of the BIA and Yakama Superintendent Schlick agreed there was no reason an Indian fisherman couldn't camp on the sites any time when he was legally fishing. Such camping would apply to a tent, camper, tepee, or trailer, and be subject to health and sanitation rules. But the list of acceptable dwellings did not include the permanent wooden houses occupied by some of the Cook's and Underwood residents.

In the midst of the BIA's slow-motion effort to oust the site residents, the Army Corps of Engineers in 1970 proposed flooding part of the sites. The Corps planned to raise the maximum level of the Bonneville pool by three feet to help the Bonneville Power Administration meet demand for electricity. BPA is the federal agency created to market the power produced by federal dams on the Columbia River and its tributaries; the Corps of Engineers operates most of those dams, providing the amount of power ordered by BPA. With the region's growing population using more electricity, BPA developed what it called the Hydro-Thermal Power Program. Under that plan, part of the power needs would be met by building nuclear or coal-fired power plants. These would supplement the hydropower dams that then supplied nearly all the region's electricity. But the use of electricity fluctuates throughout each day. It is cheaper to turn hydropower turbines on and off than to start and stop coal and nuclear plants. So BPA proposed using the Columbia River dams to supply the so-called peaking power during high use periods, such as early evening when most families are cooking dinner. That plan required changing the amount of water flowing through the dams, causing the river level to rise and fall rapidly within a few hours. Bonneville is the furthest downstream of the Columbia dams, and the Corps planned to use its pool to smooth out those fluctuations to avoid disturbing cities, industrial plants and recreation on the densely populated lower river. To handle the changing water volume it needed to raise the maximum pool level, flooding substantial portions of the Cook's and Underwood sites daily and permanently flooding portions of Wind River, Lone Pine and Cascade Locks.

When the Corps completed its plan in February 1972, the Indians were fearful and angry. At a meeting to discuss the matter, Indian fisher Mary Settler, who lived on the river bank, said she would need an appropriation for a boathouse since everything else would be flooded. A typed partial transcript in BIA Portland files describes an acrimonious session in which voices rose and tempers flared. Chambers, the Native American Rights Fund attorney, berated the Corps for secretly retaining a flowage easement over the sites that would allow the agency to flood much of the land it had provided the Indians. A Corps representative identified only as Dougherty defended the action as legally correct. "We are within our rights," he said. But Chambers said even if raising the pool were legal, it was morally outrageous and shameful. "The Corps is becoming the cavalry of the twentieth century," he said, "driving the Indians literally into the river." The BIA's Joseph Dwyer said the Department of the Interior—both BPA's and BIA's parent agency—would not sit idly by. BIA would insist the Indians get some kind of compensation. An unidentified voice asked, "In-lieu in-lieu sites?" There was laughter.

The Umatilla Tribes did not wait. They filed suit asking a federal judge to bar the Corps from raising the pool. Judge Robert C. Belloni, the judge who earlier ordered that Indians get a fair share of the Columbia's fish, issued a temporary injunction March 30, 1972. He told the Corps and tribes to negotiate. The Corps agreed to protect three sites by modifying their shoreline at a cost of $43,000 to retain about the same land area as before. But a 1975 report in BIA files showed only thirty acres in the five sites was above high water mark or protected by dike—only three quarters of the total sites area. And just under twenty acres was usable for camping or parking. The Corps also agreed to ask Congress for authority to look for more in-lieu sites. Chambers toured the river banks with James Alexander and Corps staff members looking at potential sites. Chambers drew up a list of twelve sites that could be developed, but nothing ever came of it. Belloni's order barred the Corps from removing or damaging any structures on the sites unless absolutely necessary—and then it would have to compensate the owners so they could replace the property.

Meanwhile, the two federal agencies involved in the sites appeared to be working at cross purposes. While the Corps of Engineers was planning a project that threatened the sites, the Bureau of Indian Affairs was trying to improve them. It's not clear what prompted BIA's action, but it began about the time that Chambers was checking conditions on the sites. Native American Rights Fund is a national organization that gives legal help to Indians, often in highly publicized causes. And BIA's action probably also had something to do with the fact that Chambers had the ear of Julia Butler Hansen, the formidable member of Congress from Washington's Third District. Her district included the three Washington in-lieu sites. Hansen at the time was chairman of the Interior and Related Agencies Subcommittee of the House Appropriations Committee, which approved BIA funds, and she was a force in Democratic politics. At any rate, Dwyer wrote a memo in July 1970 suggesting some long term solutions "to the number of vexing problems BIA has had in administering the sites." Cascade Locks had only minor problems, he said, largely because it wasn't usable as a campground, and the Port of Cascade Locks was providing maintenance. The four other sites, however, presented a variety of problems that Dwyer considered serious.

He referred to the largely-ignored regulations issued in 1969 that banned permanent residences on the sites. "After the initial flurry of opposition, BIA retreated and the problem remains," he said. A survey in May, three months after the ban was announced, had found twenty Indian-owned buildings on the sites. Dwyer said the sites remained unsightly and had sanitary deficiencies that could result in health problems for both the residents and campers. If BIA did not take some action, he said, the agency "could be held as an accessory to the perpetuation of submarginal conditions." His first recommendation, as a good bureaucrat, was to form a committee. He suggested two representatives from each of the four tribes to work with BIA on a long-range plan. Discussions would need to include representatives from Cook's and Lone Pine "so that they will know what is transpiring." The wording indicated that the river people should be kept informed but should not participate in planning. He then followed with specific suggestions for each of the five sites: Do nothing at Cascade Locks. Dismantle the Wind River drying sheds because the area is not suitable for drying fish. Or the sheds could be improved for temporary camping quarters. Put in picnic tables. Big White Salmon will always be a problem because of inadequate space, Dwyer conceded. He suggested three alternatives. One called for removing the drying sheds, building a caretaker's house, and using the site only for camping. A second called for removing the drying sheds and not having a caretaker. Under the third, the metal sheds would be converted to camping quarters. Lone Pine and Cook's called for larger measures. Dwyer suggested building a caretaker's cottage for each, and contracting with a tribal member to serve as overseer in exchange for housing. The metal drying sheds should be removed, and the space used for camping. Water service should be provided at Lone Pine despite the $20,000 price tag—which Dwyer felt could be reduced. As for the people living on the sites, if they weren't there to fish they should be removed.

Dwyer also proposed that the sites be turned over to the tribes, relieving BIA of administrative problems. That plan had acknowledged difficulties: the tribes probably wouldn't accept them without improvements; the tribes probably wouldn't agree on a plan; and, if the tribes took over improved sites, the areas probably would deteriorate and "they would still have the problem of adverse public reaction to their appearance and conditions." Finally, Dwyer said, BIA could go on managing the sites under its current rules. That would require cleaning up the areas, removing "junk buildings" and dispossessing a number of families. He accurately forecast that dispossession would meet with "considerable opposition and misunderstanding." Apparently nothing happened in response to Dwyer's proposal, and in November 1970 he wrote another memo suggesting that attempts be made to improve conditions on the sites through the Community Action Agency in Stevenson. Stevenson is the county seat of Skamania County, location of the Wind River, Cook's Landing and Underwood sites. Dwyer noted that BIA had no money and no priority for maintaining the sites. A few days later he wrote another memo, this one documenting a visit from Chambers about people living on the sites. Chambers represented the Leo Alexander family, who lived at Cook's.

The attorney assured Dwyer that Hansen would consider an appropriation for improving the sites. Dwyer responded by asking for first-rate facilities—self-contained sewage systems and double restrooms to serve twenty-five to thirty people camping at each site. Chambers also told Dwyer the Native American Rights Fund was prepared to defend any residents of the sites if BIA tried to evict them. A few months later, in February 1971, the chairman of the Skamania County Parks and Recreation Board, Ray Jackman, wrote to Senator Henry M. Jackson complaining about conditions at Cook's, Wind River and Underwood. Conditions were deplorable at Cook's, then home to sixty people, Jackman said. The water system was a one-half-inch steel pipe to a community faucet. Each household had a pail and tin dipper for drinking water. There was a row of outhouses, but no laundry or bath facilities. Local Indians needed to be involved in solving their problems of fish drying and living quarters, he said. The county official also told Jackson that any structures would have to meet county design standards. He suggested tepees at a local Girl Scout camp as a model.

Jackson passed the complaint along to the Indian Health Service for investigation. At the same time, Chambers returned to UCLA and wrote to Commissioner of Indian Affairs Bruce on behalf of twenty-one residents of the in-lieu sites. Chambers scoffed at BIA's justification for banning permanent residence on the sites because of a lack of water and sanitary facilities. Such inadequacy, Chambers said, is a direct consequence of thirty years of failure by the United States government to honor its promises to the Indians. He said the government should provide the needed facilities, not remove the Indians. He asked Bruce to support an appropriation of $211,000 to provide water and sewer service to the sites. Chambers' figure was the BIA estimate of the costs of installing standard sanitation facilities. The breakdown: Wind River, $51,000; Little White Salmon (Cook's), $3,000; Big White Salmon (Underwood), $39,000; Lone Pine, $58,000. Contingencies made the total $211,200.

The IHS report for Senator Jackson in April 1971 confirmed the need. Although the need was obvious, there was some apprehension about unintended consequences. Schlick told other BIA officials in July 1971 he feared that improving the sites would put the agency under pressure to evict the Indians living there. Schlick also was exploring the possibility of turning the sites over to the tribes and shedding BIA's responsibility. The evidence of problems continued to mount. Across the river, in October, the Port of Cascade Locks notified BIA it was canceling its maintenance contract for the in-lieu site there. The port cited as reasons for the cancellation both the "mess," including an abandoned car, and an Indian's charge that the port manager unreasonably destroyed a fishing platform.

Hansen and Jackson came through with the money needed to fix things in 1971. BIA obtained $211,000 to build water and sewer systems on the four sites that did not have them, plus $24,000 for one year's maintenance of all five sites. The Department of the Interior recommended that the money finance bringing the sites up to National Park Service standards. So little effort was made to achieve that goal that it was two decades before the Corps learned that the National Park Service has no such agency-wide standards. Use of the construction money was restricted to building rest rooms, water and sewer systems, and other waste disposal systems. There was no hint of using the money to build homes. There was talk of buying land for sites at Lyle Point in Washington and at Rowena in Oregon, now the sailboarding Malibu of the Columbia Gorge because of its excellent access to the river. But the Corps wanted to swap the land for the current sites, not add land. The Indians wanted to hold what they had. Treaty Indians of the Columbia River Inc. promptly took credit for getting the site improvement money. Leo Alexander, the organization's spokesman, told a November meeting of tribal members that Treaty Indians' influence resulted in the construction money and a yearly maintenance fund. He may have been right; Chambers represented Treaty Indians and he attracted Representative Hansen's interest.

Despite the availability of the money, nothing was built immediately. The Corps, which was to do the work, waited for the outcome of its plan to raise the pool level and change the contours, if not the size, of the sites. Treaty Indians, comprised mostly of residents of Cook's Landing, immediately began pressing BIA to use the money to improve the homes on the sites. Alexander said the group was submitting an application for money to build houses on the sites. Nothing came of that effort. In fact, residence on the sites became increasingly controversial. The tribal governments at Warm Springs and Yakama told BIA, they wanted the money used only for camping, boat launching, fish processing, and other facilities used by all tribal fishermen. At the time, about twenty-six families lived on or near the sites year-round, while 255 fishermen used the sites only periodically.

While the Corps delayed work, even some local government officials—generally no friend to the Indians—grew critical of the agency's failure to fulfill its promises to the fishing people. In March 1972, Kenneth L. Bowcutt, the chairman of the Skamania County Commission, told the BIA's in-lieu site committee there was little evidence of the Engineers' work. "Except for pit toilets, tin constructed smokehouses (wrong material and wrong construction) and a hand operated well pump at the Cook's site there has been no real evidence of integrity of intent demonstrated by the Army Corps of Engineers," he said. His remarks did not prod the Corps into action.

It took the Corps and BIA almost as long to negotiate an agreement over the construction as it did for the Corps and Umatilla tribes to reach agreement to mitigate damage from the pool fluctuations. The "memorandum of agreement" between the two agencies looks almost like a treaty, and is far more detailed than any of the Corps' documented agreements with the Indians to that time. In it, the Corps agreed to provide thirty days' notice before tearing down any structure to make way for a new one. And it agreed to build new water and sanitary facilities, fish cleaning stations, and fish drying facilities at Wind River and Little White Salmon. It would also build fish drying and cleaning facilities at Big White Salmon, Cascade Locks, and Lone Pine. The water system would be expanded, and sanitary facilities provided at Big White Salmon. Cascade Locks would be hooked up to the city sewer system. At Lone Pine, the water system would be expanded, and new sanitary facilities would be built and connected to a planned city sewer main. The work was to be finished within six months after the Corps completed work related to the "peaking" plan.

Some of the work got done; some did not. The Dalles abandoned its sewer project, and the Oregon Department of Environmental Quality tightened its regulations, ruling that the drain field at Lone Pine was inadequate for septic tanks. So Lone Pine did not get its sewer or water. The Oregon State Police office and Seufert's old cannery next to the site both had restrooms and water. Ada Frank, who lived on the Lone Pine site each March through August for thirty years, remembers vividly that there were no restrooms. "We had to use the service station nearby. We'd go in early in the morning." Officials also decided Cook's and Underwood were too small for sewer systems. They still have none.

In October 1973, Kenneth W. Hadley of BIA's area office in Portland told Schlick that Marion Lewis and about fifteen members of his family had lived in a metal drying shed at Lone Pine for ten or twelve years. The family could not pay for private housing, he said. However, Lewis would be entitled to collect $1,979 for the improvements he made to the shed he had converted into a home. But Schlick said Lewis's home and the other drying sheds would have to go to make way for the new facilities the Corps was going to put on the site. BIA acknowledged a moral obligation to help the Lewis family find other housing, but Lewis wanted his children to remain in the school district. Clara Sohappy, a widow with five children, also wanted to keep her children in their current schools near Cook's, where the family lived in a metal drying shed. Both sites would have to be cleared by November 1, Hadley said. The Lewis family eventually moved to The Dalles. In all, records show the Corps paid for buildings owned by twenty people on all the sites except Cascade Locks.

Fish drying in the fall of 1974 delayed work on the new facilities, and the Corps had to wait until December 1974 to raise the pool level because Congress had not authorized the project. The higher level left the refurbished sites unscathed. In May 1975 the Corps and BIA staged a ceremony recognizing completion of the sanitary facilities. By October, a BIA inspection turned up plumbing problems at three sites, although the agency said there was nothing "of major concern." There were other problems, however. Non-Indians began using some of the sites for camping and picnicking. Garbage cans were stolen from Big White Salmon.

Efforts continued through the next few years to get money for further improvements, including purchasing additional sites. The Corps made its request for additional money even before it had used the 1971 appropriation. In early 1974, the Corps, Department of the Interior, and Office of Management and Budget agreed on legislation that would supply $1.2 million to improve the existing sites and $579,000 to buy new sites. In sending the proposal from Interior to the Corps, Interior Undersecretary John Whittaker described the history of the sites as "a 34-year record of some action but mostly disputation, apathy and delay." Apathy remained evident. The Secretary of the Army sent the request for the legislation to the Speaker of the House. It arrived two months after Congress had passed the Army's appropriation. The Corps and Interior tried again in 1976. But Congress provided no money, and proposals to get money from Bonneville Power Administration on the basis that the sites were part of the Bonneville Dam project proved fruitless. An assistant secretary of the Interior made still another effort in 1979. "Our lack of follow up on this matter is more abhorrent because of the other fishing conflicts and restrictions which these tribes have been made to suffer in recent years," wrote Forrest J. Gerscal. Nothing was done.

# 9

# AN UNEASY TRUCE

*The Indian fisheries seem never to have been looked upon
by the state as genuinely legitimate fisheries.*

—American Friends Service Committee,
*Uncommon Controversy*

Non-Indian fishermen erupted with anger, confusion and retaliation after
U.S. District Court Judge George Boldt of Seattle ruled in 1974 that
Northwest Indians were entitled to half the salmon and steelhead. Jack
Donaldson, who became Oregon director of fisheries in 1976, remembers
the situation as "near warfare." That was on the Columbia River. On Puget
Sound the situation was worse. Washington appealed Boldt's ruling. But it
was almost five years later that the United States Supreme Court issued the
final word approving half the fish for the tribes. Meanwhile, Oregon officially
bowed to Boldt's ruling, which Belloni extended to the Columbia River in
1975. Washington, however, led by its aggressively anti-Indian attorney
general, Slade Gorton, engaged in a series of maneuvers, including a statewide
ballot measure, to avoid complying. To carry out his order Boldt was forced
to establish an advisory group and take over management of the fishery.
Non-Indian commercial fishermen on Puget Sound ignored the court's rules
and Washington refused to enforce them. Armed confrontations occurred
on Puget Sound, and state law enforcement officials regularly clubbed and
arrested Indian fishermen. The U.S. Circuit Court of Appeals described
Washington state's actions as "the most concerted official and private efforts
to frustrate a decree of a federal court witnessed in this century," except for
some desegregation cases. Boldt's ruling, which quantified Judge Belloni's

ruling in Oregon five years earlier, touched off events that eventually brought Congress to order fulfillment of the 1939 in-lieu site promise.

The National Marine Fisheries Service added to the tumult over Boldt with a report called "The Economic Impact of the Boldt Decision." The report, challenged by the Interior Department as distorted and inaccurate, suggested that non-Indian fishing income was severely reduced largely because of the Boldt decision. The U.S. Civil Rights Commission, in a 1981 reported titled "Indian Tribes: A Continuing Quest for Survival," said even the fishing groups most vocally opposing the Boldt decision knew other causes were more responsible for the commercial fishing industry's economic problems. Dams and logging reduced the fish runs, and a Canadian fishing fleet took more than 50 percent of Columbia River salmon and a larger share of the Puget Sound runs. Although there was no increase in the number of fish, Washington's commercial fishing fleet had more than doubled in size in the ten years preceding the Boldt decision, leading to reduced catches for some fishermen, while others prospered. But the Marine Fisheries report made it easier to blame the Indians. Making matters worse for the fish and fishermen, Columbia River fish runs declined in the late 1970s after construction of four Snake River dams that the Corps of Engineers completed in 1975. There were fewer fish, and the Indians were entitled to a lot more of them. At the time of the Boldt decision, Indian fishers accounted for no more than 10 to 14 percent of the total Northwest catch. White commercial fishermen in an overbuilt fleet feared loss of income. White sports fishermen, who concentrated on steelhead, believed that any capture of steelhead outside the recreation fishery was akin to sacrilege.

The Boldt decision coincided with a nationwide backlash against tribal legal gains, according to the Civil Rights Commission. In its 1981 report, the commission said Boldt's ruling was probably the most controversial of a series of court decisions upholding Indian treaty rights. The states had so whittled away the tribes' treaty rights that they no longer translated into fish for the Indians, Boldt said. He recognized the tribes' authority to manage their own fisheries without state interference, as the Indians did at Celilo Falls for centuries. Elsewhere, management had been the exclusive province of the states, dominated by commercial and sports fishing interests. Those politically powerful groups were not about to surrender any portion of their influence or income to Indians. Indian fishing rights were a threat to the fish resource, they said. There were several reasons, rooted in history and geography, that Washington was more intransigent than Oregon in combating tribal fishing. When Oregon's first white settlers arrived in the Willamette Valley, there were few Indians remaining there; most had died from disease. The largest remaining tribes were in areas the whites did not yet covet. Washington's Indian population, however, was still very much in evidence around Puget Sound when settlers arrived. The tribes remained and went on fishing as the white population grew. In Oregon, by the 1960s the only Indian fishing of any consequence was on the Columbia River forty miles and more upstream from the major population center of Portland. Non-Indian commercial fishing after 1957 was confined to the Columbia below Portland, and to the coast, where there was no Indian commercial fishing. In Washington, two dozen tribes retained rights to fish in Puget Sound and the streams around it within the state's major population center. They fished the same waters as did whites. Along the Washington coast, another center of white commercial and sports fishing, other tribes continued to fish. Proximity brought conflict. The economic and political clout of the well-organized white fishermen made it easy for Washington politicians to take anti-Indian positions. Although Indians often refer to Gorton, now a United States senator, as a modern day General Custer, he is only the most visibly virulent of anti-Indian politicians in the state. In the late 1970s two Washington congressmen, Republican John E. Cunningham and Democrat Lloyd Meeds, introduced legislation designed to severely restrict or abolish tribal fishing rights. None of the legislation so much as got out of House committees. But the proposals were indicative of public opinion in Washington.

Because the population and conflict were centered on Puget Sound, Washington gave a lower priority to the Columbia River, recalls Jack Donaldson, the former Oregon fisheries director. During Donaldson's ten-year tenure, Washington had five fisheries directors. Washington's governor frequently made the agency head a political appointment. Oregon's commission normally selected a biologist. Donaldson believes also that the different status of the attorney general in the two states made a difference. In Oregon, an assistant attorney general worked for the agency. In Washington, "the director, staff and biologists would all say 'this is the way' and Jim Johnson [the assistant attorney general managing the fisheries case] would say 'no.' It was awful," recalls Sidney I. Lezak, who was United States attorney in Oregon during the period. "Jim Johnson doubted the treaties meant anything." In 1979, Johnson complained to the BIA about "numerous and nearly continuous violations" of federal fishing regulations at the in-lieu sites. The Department of the Interior defended the Indians. In an icily worded reply to Johnson, John D. Hough, Interior's Western Field Office director in Portland, said Johnson had provided no examples of violations. Interior's regional solicitor was not aware that the state had ever reported violations on any of the in-lieu sites. Hough said if Johnson could tell him what law or regulations were being violated he could make a better response. The Department policy, of course, was to enforce its own regulations, Hough said. But he added, "Unsubstantiated accusations cannot, however, be the basis for enforcement action." Johnson's accusations and attitude about treaties followed the line that Johnson's then-boss, Gorton, has taken through most of his four-decade political career. Oregon has not had political leaders of such extreme anti-Indian views. Washington Indians did count as friends the two longtime Democratic senators, Henry Jackson and Warren Magnuson. However, even those supposed friends asked Interior Secretary Cecil Andrus to consider "less than full implementation of the Boldt decision" in 1978. Oregon tribes generally found support from both Senators Wayne Morse, a Democrat, and Mark Hatfield, a Republican, and Representative Al Ullman, a Democrat, during the 1960s and 1970s.

Although there was less violence along the Columbia than on Puget Sound, tension was high along the river too. Non-Indian fishermen and others supplemented official state efforts to control Indian fishing by attacking Indian fishermen, stealing or destroying their nets, and blocking their access to the river after the Belloni ruling. Then, just as tensions were easing, animosity flared with increased intensity after the Boldt decision. There was real fear of physical harm, recalls N. Kathryn Brigham, who joined the Umatilla Fish and Wildlife Committee in the mid-1970s. Brigham is a fisher; so are her husband, sons, and a daughter. Brigham got involved in the politics of fish just after the Boldt ruling. She recalls meetings where non-Indian fishermen carried signs saying, "Save the salmon; can an Indian." "Down with treaties." "Treaties are old." One meeting in Portland she remembers: "The place was full. There were no [other] Indian fishermen. We got booed when we testified. No one applauded. I was afraid. So I didn't speak my mind. One woman said, 'You guys are taking food out of our mouths.' My son and I started to get into it, but my husband said we are greatly outnumbered. We sat down." But it angered Brigham that her people's centuries of dependence on the salmon could be so blithely dismissed by someone whose people had arrived on the Columbia no more than 130 years before.

Brigham learned about fish and politics from her grandfather, Sam Kash Kash, a Umatilla leader for fifty years. By the time he died in 1980, Kash Kash had launched his granddaughter on a career as an intertribal fisheries leader. Kash Kash, who rose from interpreter for tribal elders to chief and chairman, left his granddaughter with many lessons. Brigham remembers his patience and humor. "A sense of humor keeps us from being bitter . . . One of the things Grandfather stressed is that you can't change people. Accept them if you can." She said, "One time I asked him about the Corps— why did we trust the Corps? He said there was no reason not to. They were the federal government. They didn't protest our treaty. So we trusted them— and shouldn't have." By 1976, Kash Kash thought his granddaughter was ready for leadership. Although she and her husband, Robert, lived off the reservation at Cascade Locks, the aging leader backed her for a vacant position on the tribal fish and wildlife committee. Percy Brigham, a veteran fisherman and sometime fish committee member, supported Robert Brigham, his son, for the job. The post required attending a lot of meetings. Robert Brigham wanted to fish; he withdrew from the race. Kathryn Brigham got the committee job and went on to serve on the Columbia River Inter-Tribal Fish Commission, help negotiate the U.S.-Canada Salmon Treaty, and win election to the Umatilla Board of Trustees. As she got involved, the fishing issue was at the height of contention.

The Belloni and Boldt rulings had another, more far-reaching, effect than violence. They brought belated and reluctant admission that the Indians must have a say in management of the fisheries on the Columbia and elsewhere in the Northwest. In their 1972 request for an injunction, the Indians said they wanted a piece of the process for setting seasons and conservation goals. Belloni told the states and tribes to work out a management plan for the river. Boldt, in his later ruling, specifically recognized tribal authority in fish management and limited state police powers in regulating treaty fishing. By forcing the states to look more closely at their policies, the Boldt decision may have saved the Washington state fishing industry, the Associated Press reported in 1982. The decision halted years of over-fishing that had depleted runs, and the ruling forced changes in management that put a biologist on every river. To allow the Indians a fair share, the state reduced non-Indian commercial harvests. The commercial fishing fleet that had grown so rapidly it threatened to destroy the fish runs shrank back to less menacing proportions. The Indians' catch did not grow as much as the non-Indian fishing shrank, leaving enough fish for a sustained harvest. The tribes already were struggling toward their own fisheries management. The Yakama Nation one year in the early 1970s decided to fish in the spring despite state prohibitions. Yakama invited other tribes to join. Kash Kash refused on behalf of the Umatilla on grounds his tribe had not been given time to consider the issue and approve the regulations. Those who fished wound up in state courts once more. The states continued setting seasons and regulations without consulting the Indians, creating continued conflict. Tribal fishermen balked, for instance, in 1975 when the states announced in August just before the fall season began that an eight-inch mesh net would be required instead of the previously approved seven-inch mesh. Kathryn Brigham remembers, "We didn't have the gear and we couldn't get it on such short notice. There was a really big debate on the process. We said you have got to give us some leeway. We knew it was crunch time." The change was delayed.

With Belloni's push, the two states and the tribes had reluctantly begun to work on a management plan for the river. Jack Donaldson spent his second day as Oregon fisheries director in federal court over U.S. v. Oregon. "This is nonsense," he thought. States and tribes were negotiating, but Donaldson said many state officials, especially in Washington, didn't want to deal with the Indians. Even Oregon's fish commissioners opposed talks with tribal representatives, but Donaldson, who believed the Indians had to become co-managers or the fish runs would be destroyed, had the support of Governor Bob Straub and later Governor Vic Atiyeh. Donaldson contends, "The court left no choice. Either we joined to manage the fish or the court would do it." The tribes found the process difficult, recalls Roy Sampsel, who was the first director of the Columbia River Inter-Tribal Fish Commission. "The time frame was terrible. The tribes needed money. They weren't organized to deal with the issues. They had no outside advocates for their off-reservation fisheries . . . . The BIA was not an advocate. I'm not sure they knew how to do it." Burnie Bohn, the longtime Oregon fisheries official, says the situation was difficult also from the state's view. "There was no focal point for tribal participation. The tribes were not organized. They did not have their own staff." The Indians had to rely on the Fish and Wildlife Service and Bureau of Indian Affairs for the scientific facts they used to propose management plans. The BIA got involved, but its only

*Percy Brigham, a Umatilla fisherman, scoops in fish at his platform below Cascade Locks. Photograph was probably taken in the 1980s. Courtesy Columbia River Inter-Tribal Fish Commission.*

scientist available to the tribes was not a fisheries biologist but a botanist. Planning efforts became "a big hodgepodge of disorder."

Meanwhile, Bonneville Power Administration, the federal agency that sells the electricity produced by the government's dams, was working with states to alleviate damage that the dams had caused to the fish runs. The 1937 act that created BPA gave it considerable authority to take action related to producing or distributing electricity. It had taken up salmon much as it had taken up preservation of the Columbia Gorge in its first power sales contracts, requiring buyers to agree not to despoil the Gorge. Donald Paul Hodel, now a private energy and natural resources consultant, was then the chief of the Bonneville Power Administration. The states were going ahead without any Indian involvement. BPA, however, dealt with the tribes on several issues. Hodel realized that the Indians' treaty standing, so recently affirmed by Judges Belloni and Boldt, gave them a chance to make demands that could have a major effect on BPA's power rates. He offered to fund tribal participation in the fish mitigation meetings. Hodel recalls that state fisheries officials opposed drawing Indians into the discussions. "Their basic position was they didn't want the Indians at the table. I persisted and we had a number of fairly heated meetings. I said you can't do business without the Indians and they had to accept them. It seemed to me if there was any hope of resolving these issues we had to have everybody at the table." The tribes went to the table but, without their own scientists, it was like having no dishes or utensils. Still, the BPA process, along with the river negotiations, did get the states talking directly to the tribes outside the court umbrella. In both processes the states, like the Corps of Engineers, found it difficult to deal with Indians. Like the engineers, the states wanted one spokesman expressing the "Indian point of view." Instead, they got dozens of Indians expressing a variety of views, some of them contradictory. Involving the tribes in fisheries management eventually reduced the number of Indian voices.

By late 1976, the tribes began to hire a few biologists and fisheries experts. They were gaining in the negotiations toward a river management plan. That year, the Yakama Nation convened a conference that resulted in a coalition that would have been unimaginable a few years earlier. The Columbia Basin Fisheries Alliance included commercial gillnetters and trollers from the lower river, sports fishermen, river packers and guides, wildlife organizations, and the tribes. The group's purpose was to restore the salmon runs, a goal in which it failed miserably before it quietly dropped out of sight.

Through this period, the four tribes with Columbia River treaty rights participated in river planning through their individual fish commissions. The Nez Perce, with headquarters in Lapwai, Idaho, were included on the basis of winning a piece of the Celilo Falls settlement in the 1950s. Also engaged in river planning, of course, were the Umatilla, Warm Springs, and Yakama. Tom Hampson, who was a planner for the Umatilla Tribes in the 1970s, remembers Sam Kash Kash, the tribal chairman, telling stories about arguments between the tribes when he returned from meetings. Kash Kash recognized that some kind of unity or coordination among the tribes was critical. Other tribal leaders had reached the same conclusion. One day, Hampson and Michael Farrow, now Umatilla's natural resources director, were sitting in Kash Kash's office when the chairman told them to get on a plane for Portland. They were to spend the next week working with the fish commissions of the four tribes to come up with a plan for the tribes to work together. In two or three days they had an outline, turned it over to the commissions, and went home. Eugene Greene Sr. was a Warm Springs Fish Commission member who worked on the draft constitution and bylaws. "Getting the four tribes to agree was difficult," Greene recalls. "We did it paragraph by paragraph and word by word. Each tribe did not trust any other tribe." He later served as chairman of the commission. A much-decorated veteran of Army infantry service in Korea during the Korean War, Greene studied fisheries at Peninsula College in Port Angeles, Washington. He began his career with the Warm Springs tribes as a fisheries enforcement officer in 1969. He now heads that department, which has grown to include a staff of scientists as well as fisheries managers and enforcement officers.

Despite the mutual distrust, the commissioners came up with a constitution for the Columbia River Inter-Tribal Fish Commission. The organization formally came into existence in February 1977 just as the tribes and states agreed on a river management plan. Where the tribes could agree they would speak with a single voice and they would speak from a basis of knowledge; CRITFC would have its own scientists. Initially, the states and federal agencies were not impressed. Tim Wapato, a Colville tribal member and an early director of CRITFC, recalls, "When it first started in 1977, most of the people in the fisheries agencies kind of thought it was cute in a condescending way that we had our own biologists. Not much attention was really paid to what was said or proposed by the tribes through CRITFC." That changed rapidly as CRITFC obtained a staff of experts who were regularly called on to advise the court in the ongoing U.S. v. Oregon case. Within a few years, state and federal agencies were calling CRITFC for information. Jean Edwards, a University of California-Davis graduate who went to work for CRITFC as a fisheries biologist in 1978, was impressed with the organization's approach to fisheries issues. Where the emphasis elsewhere had been on allocating harvests, the tribes recognized the importance of science and conservation, and their links to the native culture. They wanted to preserve habitat and protect fish. Ecosystem management is considered a new vogue in fisheries. Edwards says that in the 1970s the tribes were the only ones who articulated the concept clearly. Ted Strong, the former executive director of CRITFC, explains the commission's approach:

> In the region we are a voice that is supposed to provide harmony with other voices speaking in behalf of the salmon and salmon environment. Historically, that voice in this region was the natural melody that came from the Native Americans and that native voice blended with the sound of the water falls, the rushing rivers, the birds and the animals as they sang their songs of thanksgiving. Our

native voices also gave thanks. With the development of the
Columbia River, many of the voices of nature have fallen silent and
only the clamor and the voices of confusion that insult the ears are
heard today . . . . Science is trying very hard to take its place in fish
management and science and nature haven't yet learned to sing
together.

So as a technical and coordinating agency for the four Columbia
River treaty tribes our job is to learn science and strive for the
integration of science and culture with respect to salmon
management.

The tribes assess plans for salmon recovery on the basis of natural
environmental standards, the status of salmon's original home. By that
standard most plans are found wanting. But the tribes' approach won them
respect, even from their old adversaries, the state fisheries agencies.

The initial management plan complying with Judge Belloni's order was
not much, mostly allocating the harvest of various runs between users. There
was nothing about habitat protection or other aspects of fish protection.
But it was a beginning. Burnie Bohn recalls, "It was the first order on the
river, It worked . . . . Everyone wanted order, not the limbo that used to
exist." The court-sponsored management plan, BPA, and CRITFC had
given the tribes a voice in the fisheries. But those processes also had the
effect of shutting out the river people, whose interests often were not the
same as those of the tribal governments. Individual Indians often found
themselves caught in the various bureaucracies. One of those who did—
and fought them all at every step—was Mary Settler, who raised her five
children on the in-lieu sites. Settler's speciality was selling the salmon that
members of her family and other Indian fishing people caught. Sometimes,
when the river people were hungry, she sold their salmon for them out of
season. Eventually, that landed her in prison. But she was hard to catch.
Mary Settler is a vigorous woman now in her sixties, little more than five
feet tall and a trifle plump. She speaks softly, but is not one to be pushed
around. She is absolutely devoted to the protection of her people's right to
fish. She and her then husband, Alvin, challenged their 1968 and 1967
arrests by Yakama tribal fisheries officers, taking their cases to the U.S.
Supreme Court. In 1974, the same year Boldt's ruling touched off the
Northwest fishing "wars," the Supreme Court upheld the Yakama Nation's
jurisdiction over tribal members' fishing regardless of where they fished.

But it limited the right of tribal officers to enforce the rules through arrests off the reservation. Mary Settler had been arrested on an in-lieu site, more than fifty miles from the Yakama Reservation. Ironically, one of the defendants in the civil cases was the chief judge of the Yakama Tribal Court, the post Alvin Settler now holds. Mary Settler escaped a jail sentence in the 1960s, but the state of Oregon got her in 1979. She admitted selling more than twelve tons of salmon and steelhead that had been caught out of season, and spent five months jailed in Portland, and thirteen months in the Oregon state women's prison. She remained feisty in prison, refusing to attend classes to earn her GED. Injury in a kitchen accident won her an early release. Her son, Randy, who was a junior at Portland State University when his mother went to prison, says she has reason to be suspicious of schools. She was taken from her family when she was five or six years old, placed in school first at Warm Springs and then at the Indian school Chemawa near Salem. She was not allowed to go home for seven years. After her release from prison in 1980, Mary Settler went back to the river. The state got her again, along with sons Randy and Carl, in a sting operation in 1983. But the Oregon Supreme Court reversed their convictions on grounds the state had not proved a conservation necessity for its closed season, and the U.S. Supreme Court refused to hear the state's appeal. The Settler family still fishes.

Even river people such as Mary Settler, who saw invidious discrimination against them, remained aloof from the militant American Indian Movement except for a brief flirtation after Washington state so vigorously defied the Belloni and Boldt decisions. Northwest Indians were doing too well in court to join a national Indian rights group that drew sympathy, support, and intense opposition by taking over government property at Alcatraz and Wounded Knee, S.D. With the federal government on their side in most of the fishing cases, Northwest Indians won judgment after judgment. Only about the issue of permanent homes on the in-lieu sites was the government opposing the Indians. And the Indians themselves disagreed on that. Besides, the river people were traditionally peaceful. War was not a major part of their original life style. When the Warm Springs fought, it was to help the U.S. Army. Even the assertive Yakama engaged in war against the United States only after whites violated their treaty a few months after its signing. The Northwest tribes learned early to use courts and negotiation instead of violence. In the 1970s they also began to use science.

Eventually, as it expanded its role along the river, CRITFC also took on the in-lieu sites. The Celilo Fish Committee was long gone, and with it the role that the river people had played in the fishing sites through the 1960s. During the late 1970s, the in-lieu sites were subordinated to the battle over fishing rights. It was not that the sites were forgotten, explains Yakama attorney Tim Weaver. It was that it was more important that there be fish to catch when they did have the sites. Soon after CRITFC formed, President Jimmy Carter, at the request of the Washington congressional delegation, established a presidential task force to make recommendations for resolving the Northwest fish fight. The Civil Rights Commission's 1981 report is critical of Carter's approach. The commission suggested that the federal government, after the Supreme Court upheld Boldt, could have sent agents to enforce the court's orders. Instead of strict enforcement, however, the Administration chose a process that could have deprived the tribes of some of their court-won rights. By doing so, said the Commission, "the United States failed to act as trustee, operated with a substantial conflict of interest and subjected the tribes to a political process in which the tribal position was weakened." The Commission said far greater commitment and cooperation between the executive and legislative branches are required for effective enforcement of tribal rights. In the following three years CRITFC and its Washington counterpart, the Northwest Indian Fish Commission, played a major role in shaping what became the Salmon and Steelhead Conservation and Enhancement Act of 1980. The new law set up a permanent advisory committee that included tribal representation to create management plans for the Columbia River and Puget Sound. It provided money—$32 million for the Columbia River region—for fisheries enhancement projects. And it established a program to buy out non-Indian commercial fishing licenses. The measure would settle nothing.

# 10

# CONVICTION AND EVICTION

*I suspect that if Sohappy's ancestors had it to do over again,
they would have told Lewis and Clark, "Keep moving,
stranger. This fish is not for sale."*

—Thomas Patrick Keefe Jr.,
David Sohappy's attorney.

White people put seventeen dams between salmon and their Columbia
and Snake river spawning grounds. White people took river water to irrigate
their farms and returned it laden with fish-killing fertilizer and pesticides.
White people, mostly, logged the forests, grazed cattle on the plains, and
built riverside factories, sending silt and pollution into the rivers. White
fishermen in the Pacific Ocean caught more than half the Columbia River
salmon. So when the river's salmon runs hit a twenty-year low in 1980,
white fishermen and white governments naturally blamed the Indians. Their
proof, proclaimed throughout the region, was the disappearance in 1981 of
40,000 Chinook salmon between Bonneville Dam and McNary Dam, the
Indians' fishing grounds. Those fish were taken by Indian poachers, said
fisheries enforcement officials. Indians were stealing the fish, endangering
the runs. Not until two years later, four days after a federal court convicted
three Indian fishermen, did the fisheries officials concede very quietly that
no one had caught those "stolen" fish. Instead, most had spawned in streams
between Bonneville and McNary. And an aluminum plant just upriver from
The Dalles Dam had spilled fluorides into the river, confusing those fish it
didn't kill. Federal fisheries officials bragged that their arrest of dozens of
Indians reduced illegal fishing to virtually nothing in 1982. Later they

admitted that fish losses between the dams were about the same that year as in 1980 and 1981, when they were blaming Indian fishers for illegally taking the salmon.

The fisheries officials used the "stolen" 40,000 fish to justify a fourteen-month, several hundred thousand-dollar sting operation that became known as Salmonscam. However, the investigation began before the fish disappeared and before Congress passed the law the Indian fishermen were charged with violating. Salmonscam in turn was interwoven with efforts to evict residents from the in-lieu sites and with persistent state efforts to control Indian fishing. These events disrupted the lives of Columbia River Indians, decimated their livelihood, and for some, meant tragedy. Both Salmonscam and the later eviction of in-lieu site residents focused on David Sohappy and his family, members of the Yakama Nation. By 1980 David Sohappy had been a fisheries gadfly to federal, state and tribal authorities for more than fifteen years. A leader of the Feather religion, he followed the ways of his Wanapum ancestors. To state and federal fisheries officials Sohappy was a notorious poacher. To fellow river residents he was a traditional Indian. To the government of the Yakama Indian Nation he was an uncomfortable problem: he threatened the tribe's recently won status as a co-manager of the Columbia fishery and challenged its willingness to defend its members' treaty rights.

As a toddler, Sohappy had visited his grandmother occasionally at the mouth of the Little White Salmon River, where the grandmother's sister had a home. David's great-aunt was one of the river Indians whose homes were drowned by Bonneville Dam. The river mouth was one of the originally chosen in-lieu sites, but Cook's Landing was substituted and Drano Lake at the river mouth became a favorite sports fishing spot for non-Indians. "The Corps of Engineers promised the people that lived there year around that they would replace the homes that were flooded out," Sohappy told a congressional hearing in 1988. "To this day they never did live up to their word."

In upholding the Boldt decision in 1979, the U.S. Supreme Court ruled that the Indians were entitled to a moderate living, no more. Both state and tribal rules allowed Indians to fish for ceremonial and subsistence purposes with few restrictions. Sohappy insisted that he fished only for ceremonies and for subsistence, supporting an extended family of forty people and supplying salmon for the ceremonies of several longhouses. His living standard could only generously be called moderate. Selling fish was part of the subsistence, he said. Or, as his wife, Myra, explained: "You can't plop a salmon down when you need gas for the car." Sohappy ignored state-set seasons and tribal-set seasons with equal defiance. State and federal fisheries agents confiscated the Sohappys' nets. David got more nets. He lost track of the number of nets that state, federal, and tribal enforcement officers seized, but Myra thought the loss exceeded two hundred. He kept on fishing. David Sohappy's success in court with Sohappy v. Smith in 1969 hardly made him popular with the non-Indian fisheries officials who had hounded him for so long. The states and white fishermen had reasons to crush David Sohappy; he had challenged their dominance of the fishery and won. His relationship to the tribes, particularly the Yakama Nation, where he was enrolled, was more complicated. Although he was a major factor in winning judicial recognition of the tribes' treaty rights, he also challenged the tribes' management of the fishery. His 1968 lawsuit came just as tribal and Interior Department attorneys were persuading local prosecutors they could not get convictions of treaty fishers. Also the suit slipped into court just ahead of U.S. v. Oregon, which was designed to establish more clearly the tribal authority over Indian fisheries. Tribal officials lost no love on David Sohappy. And some tribal fishing people resented the permanent residences on the in-lieu sites.

The Supreme Court's action upholding the Boldt decision in 1979 left Washington state's influential fishermen, both commercial and recreational, frustrated and angry. Another federal court ruling in January 1981 extended the Indians' 50 percent entitlement to hatchery-produced fish, and further polarized feelings. But Congress soon gave the non-Indians a way to strike back. The Supreme Court provided the opening in 1978 by ruling that tribes could not enforce laws against non-tribal members for crimes committed on reservations. That left tribes unable to enforce their fishing regulations against non-Indians at traditional tribal fisheries even on the reservations. To fill that gap, Congress amended an early 1900s fish and wildlife protection law, the Lacey Act, to make violation of state or tribal fisheries laws federal felonies. So tribal and state violations that were misdemeanors punishable with fines or short jail terms became federal felonies carrying prison terms of up to five years. Congress explained to the tribes that the new law would allow federal agents to enforce tribal fishing regulations against non-Indians on reservations. Unquestionably, the law filled a law enforcement gap. However, its real purpose—reducing Indian fishing—can be deduced from the law's history. Washington Attorney

General Slade Gorton, who led the long fight to keep his state from complying with the Boldt decision, was elected to the U.S. Senate in 1980. Gorton began his term in January 1981, and soon sponsored the Lacey Act amendment. In March 1981, the Washington Department of Fisheries asked the National Marine Fisheries Service to begin its undercover operation "in anticipation of expected changes in the Lacey Act." The federal agency was only too happy to oblige, beginning the Salmonscam sting seven months before President Reagan signed the new law. And it may have been no coincidence that the Yakama Nation had recently filed suit to force the U.S. Department of Commerce to rein in ocean fishing to leave more salmon for the Columbia River. The fisheries service is an agency of the Commerce Department, which through the Pacific Fishery Management Council, promotes and regulates ocean commercial fishing. The fishing industry is a powerful constituency for the Department, and its interests are directly opposed to those of tribal fishers. Levi George, chairman of the Yakama fish committee, told a congressional hearing some years later, "The act was immediately turned against the very people it was supposedly intended to assist."

Randy Settler remembers the beginning of Salmonscam as a visit from Richard Severtson, the National Marine Fisheries Service undercover agent. Settler recalls that the agent came to the Settler home with "two cases of beer and a drunken Indian," whom Severtson had been plying with drinks at a nearby tavern. Within ten minutes, Severtson, using an alias, flashed a roll of $100 bills and said he wanted to buy illegally caught fish. Settler's brother Carl spotted Severtson as an agent and ordered him out of the house. Severtson moved on to the Sohappy home at Cook's Landing a few miles down the road. David Sohappy sold him ten fish. Severtson and his fellow agents wanted more. Other fishermen, hurting for money, brought their fish to Sohappy to sell for them. The agents asked for more. Then the agents quit coming, leaving Sohappy, who had no supply of ice, with several tons of fish to rot. Randy Settler moved in with his truck and ice to salvage the fish. A buyer turned him in. While Severtson and other agents were luring Sohappy into selling fish in Washington, they set up a fish buying station at Celilo, Oregon, and hired Bruce Jim, a river Indian, to run it on commission.

On June 17, 1982, thirteen carloads of heavily-armed agents swooped down on Cook's Landing in the early morning dark. Guns drawn, a helicopter overhead, they rousted families from their beds and searched the homes. Their major haul: a chest containing David Sohappy's collection of legal papers. David Sohappy was fifty-seven years old. He would spend the last nine years of his life defending his fishing and his home. Oregon, Washington and the federal government charged seventy-two members of the Yakama, Warm Springs and Umatilla tribes with illegally catching or selling fish. Eventually, thirteen of nineteen Indians were convicted of felonies or pleaded guilty in federal court; three others pleaded guilty to misdemeanors. Myra Sohappy and two others were acquitted. In Oregon state courts, only one conviction survived appeal of thirteen people charged. The few charges filed in Washington state involved only fish sales to non-Indians. No one was convicted of conspiracy, the major charge leveled by the National Marine Fisheries Service. The federal trials were moved to Los Angeles on grounds that anti-Indian feeling over fisheries was so high in Washington and Oregon that the defendants could not get a fair trial in either state. On June 6, 1983, U.S. District Court Judge Jack Tanner of Tacoma, Washington, sentenced David Sohappy Sr. to five years in prison for selling 153 salmon and twenty-five steelhead totaling 2,218 pounds for $4,675. The judge added five years probation for selling 132 salmon and seven steelhead weighing 2,184 pounds for $5,010. Tanner sentenced Sohappy's son, David Jr., twenty-four, to five years in prison for selling eight salmon and seven steelhead weighing 167 pounds for $400 and added five years probation for nine salmon and four steelhead weighing 146 pounds for $465. Tanner sentenced Wilbur Slockish Jr. to three years for sixty-three fish sold for $1,592, Leroy Yocash to two years for seventy-eight fish sold for $2,170 and Mathew McConville to one year for twenty-one fish sold for $565. The judge also imposed one-year prison terms on four other convicted Indians, and a five-year sentence on Bruce Jim for seven counts in which the amount of fish and money were unclear. All of those sentenced to prison appealed. Soon after the arrests, the Columbia River Inter-Tribal Fish Commission, made up of the four river tribes, pointed out to the public some disparities in the governments' concern. The Indians were accused of damaging the runs by illegally taking 2,300 fish from the upriver spring chinook run while ocean fishers legally took 129,000 salmon from the same run.

Virginia Beavert, then secretary of the Yakama General Council, went to two early court hearings to show support for the accused fishermen and their wives. "The women looked so pitiful," she recalls. "They had no representation, no attorney. I talked to the [Tribal] Council. I said these are about fishing rights. This is our treaty rights issue. We got a man to go defend them." But tribal government itself stayed out of the case. Beavert urged Sohappy and his family to go into Tribal Court and plead guilty, removing the issue from federal courts. Sohappy refused, she says. The Yakama tribe should have stood with David Sohappy, believes Lavina Washines, one of the river people who later served on the Tribal Council. "Instead, it intervened against him. That's when we lost our fishing rights." The tribe was rebuffed right after the arrests, when it asked that some of the cases be tried in its own court. It did not again assert its jurisdiction until four years later after Sohappy and four other Yakama tribal members had lost their appeals and were scheduled to report to federal prison. By then, Washines and several others who supported the river people had been elected to the Tribal Council. But it was too late. After the Sohappys, Wilbur Slockish, Mathew McConville, and LeRoy Yocash were acquitted in Tribal Court, they were whisked off to federal prisons scattered around the country. The Warm Springs tribes made an early attempt to get their accused members transferred to Tribal Court, but were denied and dropped the matter. Several cases were moved from Oregon state courts to the Umatilla Tribal Court.

Salmonscam put a national spotlight on Indian fishing rights and the in-lieu sites. It called public and congressional attention to the long-unfulfilled promise of fishing sites. The National Lawyers Guild established the Columbia River Defense Project to defend the embattled fishermen. Myra Sohappy, in traditional Native American buckskin and European lace stockings, went before the United Nations in Switzerland. Amnesty International got involved. And David Sohappy went to federal prison, where twenty months of incarceration led to a stroke and worsening of his diabetes. While Sohappy and his son, David Jr., were fighting five-year prison sentences for violating the Lacey Act, the government was pursuing civil fines, totaling $150,000, but no jail terms, against non-Indians charged with marketing 297 tons of illegally caught salmon worth $796,000. By contrast, the entire Salmonscam net hauled in fifty-three tons of salmon and seventy-two people, fewer than a fourth of whom were convicted. A dozen of those received jail terms. Myra Sohappy once calculated that the charges came down to about two fish a month per defendant over the fourteen-month period of the $350,000 investigation.

The effects of Salmonscam hovered over the river community for years. In September 1984 Oregon Circuit Court Judge John Jelderks prohibited one convicted fisherman, Warner Jim, a tribal elder and religious leader, from being on the river without his probation officer's written permission. In a heavy-handed attempt at humor, Jelderks issued a gratuitous slur on the Indians' religion: "This means no ceremonial fishing, no water skiing, no swimming." Salmon are at the heart of the Native American religion and ceremonial fishing is vital to it. As an elder and religious leader, Jim taught the fishing art to young tribal men. To equate ceremonial fishing with water skiing showed either complete lack of understanding of the river people or total contempt for their religion. Warner Jim's brother, Howard Jim, chief of the Wy'ams, fared better. Also charged in Salmonscam, Howard Jim went to court in his beaded white buckskins and carried an eagle feather as he defended his fishing to an all-white jury. The dignified old man was acquitted. With appeals and sentences, Salmonscam cases dragged on through 1988.

Bureau of Indian Affairs officials claim there was no relationship between the criminal investigation called Salmonscam and the agency's efforts to evict the residents of the in-lieu sites. But the two projects were concurrent, and both focused on the residents of Cook's Landing, specifically the Sohappys. The BIA had made halfhearted efforts to remove the residents since 1969. Its efforts became more serious in the 1980s with pressure from outside BIA to get rid of the Indian "camp." As early as 1971, Skamania County complained to Senator Henry Jackson, the powerful Washington Democrat who was chairman of the Senate Interior Committee. Describing conditions at the Cook's Landing site as "deplorable," Ray Jackman, chairman of the county's Park and Recreation Board, was seeking improvement of the sites, but his letter focussed attention on living conditions there. More than a decade later, Wayne C. Lewis, chairman of the Columbia River Fisheries Council law enforcement committee, began the drumbeat for eviction with a low-key letter to Gerald F. Rodgers, a special BIA enforcement officer. The Council was made up of fisheries officials from Oregon, Washington, and Idaho, the U.S. Fish and Wildlife Service, National Marine Fisheries Service and the Columbia River Inter-Tribal Fish Commission. Lewis expressed concern "about BIA's apparent condonation of the present status of Cooks' Landing, in what to many of us appears as a completely obvious disregard of the law by those individuals residing" there year around. Lewis was the National Marine Fisheries Service enforcement agent who directed the Salmonscam operation that imprisoned Indian fishermen. His letter was written April 16, 1982, a year after his undercover operation began, and just two months before the mass raid on

Cook's Landing. Officials paid more attention to Cook's than to Underwood or Lone Pine because more fishing families lived at Cook's and they had made themselves highly visible by challenging state regulations—and winning.

The Corps of Engineers, which had obtained the sites and built the few facilities on them, no longer had jurisdiction over the sites. But it too got involved. In March of 1982 the Corps demolished five Indian fishing platforms next to the Lone Pine in-lieu site just downriver from The Dalles Dam, which the Corps operates. The Yakama Nation protested and BIA arranged a meeting in which the tribe asked the Corps both to explain its action and to replace the platforms. Colonel Terrance Connell of the Corps told the Indians the platforms were so close to the visitors' center at the dam that they were a threat to public safety. "Children may find the platforms an attraction," he said. The Indians complained that the platforms had been there for six years but were removed without warning. Connell finally agreed to replace one platform, and said he'd go along with construction of temporary platforms. Marion Lewis owned one of the destroyed platforms. He remembers it took three years to get the Corps to pay for it. Although the Indians were exercising a treaty right upheld by federal courts, the Corps drew up a proposed use permit for the fishing platforms. The BIA refused to sign it on grounds it was too restrictive and did not allow Indian fishermen free access to their platforms.

Stanley Speaks arrived in Portland as the BIA's new Northwest Area director in August 1982, two months after the Marine Fisheries Service raid on Cook's Landing. A Chickasaw from the Southwest, Speaks came to the Northwest from Andarko, Oklahoma, where fishing was not part of a director's portfolio. The in-lieu sites were Speaks's introduction to the Columbia River. Although the sites were just one of a number of problems the new director faced, he plunged into the issue by making a tour of the Columbia River. Speaks describes his reaction: "Under our management, they were not being managed very well. I recognized they were going to need some repairs. We hadn't been keeping up the facilities. We needed to dispose of old equipment, old tents, old cars— especially at Cook's. That was the major one . . . . We started working with our staff, our office, and the solicitor's office for better management procedures, better law enforcement in certain areas. One of the things, it would be easier to manage the facilities without people living there. It was impossible to manage the sites when a few people were living there and everyone had the opportunity under the law to be able to gain access to the river. It was difficult to manage properly with a few people living on the sites. That was not reasonable at all."

While Speaks was laying out his plans, residents of Cook's and other Yakama and Warm Springs Indians were being indicted on the various Salmonscam charges. Without so much as a nod to the fact that the families already had plenty of problems, Speaks embarked on his program. "We started the process to clean them up—remove old vehicles, old shacks, bring the sites up to a more manageable standard. We proceeded to ask the people there living on the in-lieu sites to leave so that could happen." But he wasn't acting fast enough to suit state and federal fisheries enforcement officials. The new president of the Fisheries Council's law enforcement committee, Maurita Smyth, wrote to Interior Secretary James Watt May 6, 1983, asking him to eliminate the permanent dwellings "as quickly as possible." Smyth was the Columbia River Inter-Tribal Fish Commission's representative on the law enforcement committee. She, too, focused her attention on Cook's Landing. She painted a vivid picture of "life threatening" encounters between the Cook's residents and law enforcement officers. The residents continue to engage in illegal commercial fishing activities and thwart safe access to the site for "lawful tribal members." Despite requests, the BIA in Portland had not removed the residents, Smyth complained. "Inaction by the BIA creates a gross impediment to the efficient implementation of the enforcement needs of the Columbia River Fisheries Management Plan," she wrote. Then she added ominously, "The likelihood of violent conflict with law enforcement personnel increases daily." Her letter was written three weeks after David Sohappy Sr., his son, David Jr., and Bruce Jim, a Warm Springs Indian, were convicted of Salmonscam charges in Los Angeles. Her dire predictions of armed conflict echoed the federal attorney who asked that the convicted men be denied release on bond until sentencing on grounds there might be an armed uprising at Cook's. No conflict, armed or otherwise, occurred. David Sohappy's religion spurns violence as it does alcohol. Fear of violence at Cook's was a recurring theme with law enforcement officers, but there are no reports that show any use of weapons there or need for them.

Smyth fired off her complaint to the four U.S. senators from Oregon and Washington and to five of the two states' thirteen House members. Response from the senators was almost immediate. In a letter initiated by Senator Slade Gorton, Washington's veteran Indian fighter, the four senators demanded that Watt push his BIA into action. Again, the only site mentioned was Cook's, although there were permanent residences also at Underwood and Lone Pine and possibly other sites at the same time. There was no mention that the government had promised the Indians four hundred acres of sites forty-four years earlier, and so far had supplied only forty acres. Calling Cook's "the last remaining focal point for illegal fishing activity on the Columbia River," the senators accused BIA of standing in the way of law enforcement efforts by failing to oust the residents. In addition to Gorton, Republicans Mark Hatfield and Bob Packwood of Oregon and Democrat Henry M. Jackson of Washington signed the letter. By this time Myra Sohappy had been acquitted of fish-selling charges and returned home, where son Andy continued to follow the family tradition by keeping a net in the water every day. Some days he caught one or two fish, some days none. Speaks made a prompt but measured response to the senators. In a masterly understatement, he noted, ". . . unfortunately, the problem does not lend itself to easy solution." He outlined a four-step plan, but wisely did not limit himself to a timetable. Federal attorneys were working on proper notices telling the residents that they would have to move, he said. He wanted to be sure that the approach was proper and legal in hopes of avoiding "a national confrontation or a long legal battle." But he said the Interior Department's regional solicitor already was warning her superiors that the issue might not be resolved without court action.

Two days later, the regional solicitor in Portland, Gina Guy, wrote the department's top attorney in Washington, D.C., with a "Request for Litigation—Ejectment from Federal Property." She too described the situation at Cook's in dire terms. The Fish and Wildlife Service regional director was concerned for the safety of his agents. There were reports firearms were being amassed there. There also were reports that non-Indians had been frequenting the area and harassing the residents in attempts to provoke an incident. Guy described the settlement at Cook's as "a rather unique combination of ramshackle structures, trailers, and lean-tos." One individual, she said, had built a combination grocery store and fish supply outlet on the site. Some of the residents had tapped into the water and electrical lines that BIA had installed to serve its facilities there. The situation was complicated by the tribes' view that the sites were Indian trust lands, not federal lands, and by the fact that some of the homes were partly on the Burlington Northern Railroad right of way. Guy went briefly into the history of the sites, mentioning that they were promised to the Indians to replace sites flooded by Bonneville Dam. She, too, didn't mention that the government promised four hundred acres and delivered less than forty.

Soon after he responded to the senators, Speaks dispatched a uniformed BIA law enforcement officer to Stevenson, Washington, to help defuse increasing tension between law enforcement officials and residents of the in-lieu sites. Handwritten notes in BIA files record a telephone conversation June 15, 1983, involving Speaks, special BIA officer Gerald F. Rodgers, Skamania County Sheriff Bill Closner and his chief deputy, Ray Blaisdel, and an unidentified BIA agent. Speaks asks what sort of trouble Closner has had involving the sites. The sheriff replies, "Several conflicts. Cook's cousins fighting each other. One game warden in trouble, people throwing rocks at the Game Department." Blaisdel adds that there had been "shooting over fisheries peoples' heads." Speaks asks if the troubles are Indian vs. non-Indian. Closner replies that Indians are not getting fair treatment at the local boat launch, which is used by tourists. Closner calls Cook's "a hell of a mess" and "a can of worms." He feels he needs a court order to assist with the demand that the residents vacate Cook's. Then he asks "DV," the assigned officer, "Do you have a bullet proof vest?" "I'm fully packed," DV replies. Closner responds, "I've a feeling we're going to see a lot of each other. There was history done with the investigation [Salmonscam] and you'll probably make history with this one too." Speaks tells Closner that BIA will get the federal courts to act. "It's going to take some time." "I like your style," Closner says.

Eight months later, March 16, 1984, Speaks issued his eviction notices. He gave the residents until April 19 to remove all their personal property. The official reason: their residences violated the BIA's 1969 rule prohibiting permanent dwellings on the sites. The BIA offered to help the people find other homes, but said it would ask the United States attorney to taken legal action if they did not leave. Although the order affected all five sites, attention focused on Cook's and Underwood. The *Oregonian* newspaper in Portland quoted unidentified BIA sources that the evictions resulted from complaints that other members of the treaty tribes were being denied use of the sites. Some tribal fishers were unhappy with permanent homes on the sites, although the residents contended they never interfered with others' use of docks, sheds or space. Belatedly, in 1989, Philip W. Olney, chairman of the Yakama General Council, told Speaks he was not aware of any impediment to fishing caused by homes at Cook's or Underwood. He said he knew of no Yakama leader who had complained about the homes, and he personally wished the government would allow the residents to stay. Jack L. Schwartz, a Portland attorney who represented the site residents, had another explanation for the evictions at the time: they were retaliation for the government's limited success with the Salmonscam prosecutions. And, he said, the government was bowing to white sports fishermen and other non-Indians who wanted to "clean up" the river shores by removing Indians. Certainly, the politically powerful recreation fishing organizations had long fought against what it considered "special privileges" for Indians. Chief Johnny Jackson of the Cascade Band, who still lives on the Underwood site, has his own explanation: white fishermen, windsurfers, and cruise boats, all million-dollar operations, although windsurfing, or sailboarding, and cruises were just beginning development in the early 1980s. The BIA and Schwartz also disagreed on the number of people affected. BIA said "a handful." Schwartz said about fifty people lived on the five sites.

One family moved in response to the eviction notices. The others, Jackson and the Sohappys among them, stayed and appealed to higher BIA authority. Jackson should have had an irrefutable case. His family had lived at the mouth of the White Salmon River before Bonneville Dam was built. His relatives' homes were on what became the Underwood in-lieu site. Jackson said he had been told to move a year earlier but had ignored the notice. He planned to ignore this one too. He described himself as a caretaker for the Underwood site, watching over the drying sheds, boats, and nets left there by other fishermen, and keeping the site clean. A watchman was needed, he said. "We have had our boats burned, set on fire by non-Indians. One trailer house was there and it was vandalized—nothing taken, just vandalized. It was fairly new and afterward looked like junk." Jackson had moved away from the site for a time, but returned to deter just such damage. He was not about to leave.

In his appeal, he said if he did move, the white people would say the Indians had abandoned the site and would take it over for recreation and dump their trash there as they had before he moved back. They look at it as Indian country and feel they can dump their trash on it, he said. "We are not going to abandon what is ours from the beginning," Jackson told BIA in his appeal. "Our forefathers used this area and lived and fished here. It was passed down from generation to generation and we are part of that land and river. We are not foreign. We did not come from nowhere else." David Sohappy, in his appeal, explained his activities at Cook's. "We dry fish for our services, take to ceremonials, name givings, fish of all kinds. In our reservations, Yakima, Warm Springs, Umatilla, Colville, Lapwai, Idaho, we supply fish to all these places. Sometimes senior citizens come down for fish, either free of charge or trade something for fish." His grandmother, he said, died waiting for her home to be replaced. "It was promised to the people—that was their understanding." As for crowding out other tribal members, Sohappy said, ". . . no one is turned away, that house we use as a religious place, meet on Sundays ever since my Dad officiated there in 1965, until he died. We hold services there . . . . To us it is like a longhouse." Myra Sohappy proclaimed, "I live like an Indian and I will stay an Indian. I am proud of my heritage."

The statements were written at a meeting April 5, 1984, called by Roger Jim, chairman of the Yakama Tribal Council. In addition to the Sohappys and Jackson, Lawrence Goudy, Delbert Olney, Hadley John, and Nelson Moses, all sometime residents of in-lieu sites, attended the meeting. The appeal was sent to Speaks by Hiram E. Olney, the superintendent of the Yakama Indian Agency, who noted that Jim "has agreed with these people." Speaks agreed to hold off further action until the appeals had worked their way through the BIA bureaucracy. That bought the families two years.

Meanwhile, the appeals of the nine Salmonscam defendants sentenced to federal prisons were moving through the judicial system. On September 4, 1985, the U.S. Ninth Circuit Court of Appeals turned them down. They appealed to the U.S. Supreme Court. With the Salmonscam defendants still free and the in-lieu site residents still at home, the number of Chinook salmon crossing both Bonneville Dam and The Dalles Dam rose in 1984, 1985, and 1986.

Jack L. Schwartz was a struggling young Portland attorney with a 1960s activist conscience when the Salmonscam cases began. He was just the sort to represent strapped-for-cash Indians suddenly dumped into the high-powered federal and state justice systems. Schwartz soon got the National Lawyers Guild involved. When the Indians' case moved from criminal fishing to civil eviction, Schwartz and the Guild stuck with them. They were as dogged in drawing public attention—world wide—to the Indians' plight as they were at courtroom battles. Considering the enmity so many white fishermen expressed for the Indians, the in-lieu site residents got surprising support from their neighbors along the river. The White Salmon, Washington, *Enterprise* speculated April 19, 1984, that the evictions resulted from the government's losing so many of the Salmonscam cases. "The Feds can take little pride in these proceedings," the paper said. Elaine Cogan, writing in *The Oregonian* of Portland, April 17, was more blunt. "The feds lost four of five fishing cases. In the eyes of many . . . this is another way to gain the same end—removing them from the river."

The BIA wasn't listening to either the Indians or their neighbors. On November 16, 1984, Theodore C. Krenzke, the acting deputy assistant secretary of the Interior for Indian affairs, said Speaks was right. So the Indians took their case to the Interior Board of Indian Appeals. That didn't work either. On April 4, 1986, Jerry Muskrat, an administrative law judge for the appeals board, also said Speaks was right. The site residents had argued that the BIA had no authority to exclude permanent residences. They said the rule stating the ban violated both the 1855 treaty and the 1945 law that established the sites. Then, they said in a clearly secondary argument, the agency had misinterpreted its own rule. Nowhere along the way had the Indians been allowed to present any evidence. Muskrat said he had no authority to change any BIA rules or determine whether a rule was valid; so he refused to hear any arguments on that issue. But he did decide that the BIA had correctly interpreted its own rule barring permanent homes on the sites. A frustrated Schwartz commented, "If the highest board in the Interior Department can't say whether their own regulations are valid or not, they shouldn't use them." Speaks said he hoped the Indians would comply with Muskrat's decision and move out. The Indians, however, were not about to go quietly. David Sohappy Sr., Myra Sohappy, their son David Jr., Johnny Jackson, and six other in-lieu site residents filed suit in U. S. District Court. The Chiefs and Council of the Columbia River Indians, an organization of Indians who lived along the river, joined them as plaintiffs, and Gary M. Berne, another young Portland lawyer, joined Schwartz to take on the federal government on behalf of a dozen very poor clients. The lawsuit claimed that the evictions violated both the 1855 treaty and the 1939 and later agreements to acquire and construct facilities on in-lieu sites. It also claimed that eviction would take the residents' property without compensation, that BIA had no authority to evict them and that, by allowing them to remain for decades, it had lost whatever right it might have had to evict them. The residents asked the court to declare the no-permanent-residence rule invalid, and to order the government to comply with the agreements to provide in-lieu sites. Like Salmonscam, the eviction controversy drew public attention to the government's failure to keep its promise to the Indians.

Two weeks after filing the suit, David Sohappy and his son got another blow. The U. S. Supreme Court refused to hear the appeal of their 1983 convictions. The Sohappys and the other seven convicted fishermen were ordered to report to prison August 8, 1986. At that point, the Yakama Indian Nation suddenly got involved. Among other things, tribal elections since 1982 had put several people from the river or sympathetic to the fishermen on the council. For another, the sentences meted out to the Indians were far more harsh than non-Indians had received since then for the illegal sale of far more fish. Generally, the non-Indians drew fines, not jail time. It looked to tribal officials as if their members were being singled out for unfair treatment. But most important was the argument that by allowing tribal members to be sentenced in federal court for violating tribal law, the tribe was abdicating its sovereignty, ever a touchy point with the tribes. The 1934 Wheeler-Howard Act that established the framework for tribal governments specifically gave tribal courts jurisdiction over most on-reservation crimes. The Supreme Court ruling in 1974 said that tribal authority extended to off-reservation fishing sites. In addition, the 1855 treaties implied that the tribes would remain sovereign on their reservations, and sovereignty includes the right to establish laws and judge and punish violators. So the Yakama Tribal Council on August 6 passed a resolution asserting its jurisdiction over both the tribal members and their fishing offenses. The three Warm Springs and one Umatilla convicted in federal Salmonscam cases reported to federal court as ordered. The Yakamas instead reported to Tribal Court for arraignment, touching off a year-long tribal-federal tug of war. Tribal Court released the men and ordered all five to stay on the reservation until their trial. The federal government did not accede gracefully to the Yakama Nation's late assertion of its jurisdiction over its fishermen. U.S. District Court issued warrants for their arrest August 12. A few days later, Tribal Court Judge Ne'Sha Jackson revoked the fishermen's bonds and ordered them jailed while awaiting trial.

The two Sohappys gave up and went to jail August 22 after federal agents raided their home at Cook's twice in a week looking for them. Father and son said they feared someone would get hurt if the raids continued. Mathew McConville joined them five days later after officers went to his home in Wapato three times. But Wilbur Slockish and Leroy Yocash vanished into the 1.3 million-acre reservation. Yocash sent an audio tape to the International Indian Treaty Council, which passed it along to the Tribal Court. Yocash said the two men would appear for their trial and would remain on the reservation until then. Although the U.S. Marshals Service officially continued to search for the two, it said it had no agents on the reservation. In Seattle, Assistant U.S. Attorney Stephen Schroeder, who prosecuted the federal cases, said the government would let the Yakama Nation try the men, then take them into custody after they served any tribal sentences. He said they would get no credit for time served in a tribal jail. The BIA's area director, Stanley Speaks, took an equally harsh view of the tribal proceedings. In a letter providing background for a BIA response to an inquiry from the White House, Speaks criticized the Yakama Nation's fisheries enforcement record and said its steps to try the men in Tribal Court "demonstrates a lack of good faith in the tribe's concern to obey state law, maintain credibility and integrity of their own tribal regulations . . . ."

Some tribal officials were more than a little reluctant to grasp the political hot potato. Tribal Judge David Ward got rid of the issue September 11 by dismissing the tribal charges. That led to the unusual spectacle of a defense attorney supporting efforts to get charges reinstated against his clients. By that time, Seattle attorney Thomas Patrick Keefe Jr., a former aide to Washington's Senator Warren Magnuson, had begun representing McConville and the two Sohappys. Ward ordered the men released on condition they post $1,000 bonds and stay on the reservation during the prosecutor's appeal of the dismissal. But tribal Police Chief Davis Washines said the federal detainers required that he turn the men over to federal authorities. He had his officers whisk them off to the county jail in the city of Yakima, Washington, a federal holding facility. By the next morning they were on their way to Tacoma, and before the tribal appeal could be heard they were in the El Reno Federal Prison near Oklahoma City en route to Sandstone Federal Prison in Minnesota. Both are medium-security prisons filled with drug dealers, robbers and a few killers. Neither had any other prisoners convicted of selling fish. Amnesty International opened an investigation. The Yakama Appeals Court reinstated the charges against the five men on October 6. The Department of Justice first agreed November 24 to return them, but reneged, saying their return might spark violence between Indians and the FBI. Federal authorities did not release the men to the tribe until February 14, 1987, just as Myra Sohappy was telling their story to the United Nations Commission on Human Rights in Geneva, Switzerland. Although the UN never took any official action, Myra Sohappy was a hit. She drew the international publicity that was as much an aim of the visit as UN action.

By the time he returned to the Yakama jail for tribal trial, David Sohappy, who was sixty-two and diabetic, had lost thirty pounds. "I can't eat the junk food they feed me," he complained to Myra. To a man whose lifetime diet had been salmon, roots, and berries, the high fat and sugar content of prison food was deadly. He regained five pounds after his attorney, Keefe, complained to the Sandstone warden. The prison also had confiscated as "contraband" the eagle feather that is as essential to Sohappy's religion as the rosary is to Catholics. At the end of a two-week trial in April 1987, a tribal jury returned unanimous verdicts of innocent on all counts for all five men. The next day the Tribal Council asked President Reagan to pardon the men for the federal charges. There was no response, and on June 4 the tribe turned all five back to federal authorities. David Sohappy returned to Sandstone two thousand miles from his family and his beloved Columbia River. David Jr. also went to Sandstone, where he was put in a cell with a man serving three life sentences for murder. "I was really scared of him," the younger Sohappy said of his cellmate. Both Sohappys, along with the other three Yakama men, eventually were transferred to the Geiger Center at Spokane, Washington, which at least is in visiting distance of their families. With the eviction lawsuit in progress, David Sohappy knew Myra, their six children and the fourteen grandchildren had a place to stay—for a while.

But David Sohappy suffered a series of medical problems in prison, culminating with an incapacitating stroke. His diabetes worsened under prison conditions. At Sandstone, a blood vessel burst in his eye. After he returned to Washington state, a physician discovered early signs of glaucoma, and urged that he see an ophthamologist. Keefe, writing a month after the doctor's recommendation, asked the Bureau of Prisons to provide the needed medical care. A few days later, Keefe asked prison officials to grant both Sohappys a three-day furlough to allow David Sr. to conduct a memorial for his predecessor as leader of the Feather Religion. The officials turned that request down on grounds the Sohappys could not be trusted to return. In an angry reply, Keefe noted that both Sohappys had returned from weekend furloughs. The stroke occurred later that month. Again basing his request on a doctor's recommendation, Keefe sought an immediate medical furlough for Sohappy Sr. in October. Prison officials waited two weeks to respond and the answer was No. Keefe protested, accusing corrections official J.E. Sugrue of deliberate or gross negligence. He reminded Sugrue that for more than a month he also had ignored medical advice to provide Sohappy with treatment for the eye problem. In addition, Sohappy had fallen as a result of the stroke-related disability, Keefe said. The prison official's response, a month later, was to ship Sohappy and his son to a federal prison medical facility near San Diego, farther from home and family.

That fall the site residents lost the first round in their court battle to remain in their homes. U.S. Magistrate George Juba recommended eviction. Judge Helen Fry confirmed the recommendation in December. The Indians appealed. The next blow came when the U.S. Parole Commission set minimum sentences for the Sohappys that far exceeded norms for the amount of money involved in their cases. Thomas W. Hillier II, the U.S. public defender, who first represented the fishermen, cried foul, saying the minimum was the time set for a conspiracy conviction—of which the Sohappys had been acquitted. Hillier and the federal attorney who prosecuted them, Assistant U.S. Attorney Stephen C. Schroeder, had sent a joint letter to the commissioners pointing out that it would be unconstitutional to base a minimum sentence on the conspiracy charge. The commission said it never got the letter, and set a minimum sentence of thirty months for David Sr. and twenty-four months for David Jr. Hillier said federal guidelines indicated the minimums should have been less than twenty months for the father, and even less for the son. If the commission had applied recently adopted new guidelines, he said, each would have had a six-month minimum. The Yakama Nation asked President Reagan to commute the sentences. Senator Mark Hatfield of Oregon wrote a letter supporting commutation.

Keefe took the Sohappys' case to friends who were senior staff members of the Senate Indian Affairs Committee. Patricia Zell and Alan Parker of the Indian committee had worked on the Indian Civil Rights Commission report on Northwest fishing, and retained ties to the Northwest. It was easy for them to interest Senators Daniel Inouye, the Hawaii Democrat who headed the Senate Select Committee on Indian Affairs, and Daniel J. Evans, the Washington Republican who was the committee's vice chairman. The Hawaii senator has what then Evans aide Joe Mentor Jr. called "a real genuine feeling for native peoples." Democrat Henry M. Jackson, who signed the evict-the-site-residents letter in 1983, had died later that year and Evans replaced him in the Senate. Evans believed the fishing case was one that should have been handled by the Yakama Nation, not the federal government. Inouye and Evans took up the Indians' cause. Evans assigned aide Mentor to get Sohappy out of federal prison. Mentor recalls the case as amazing. Evans called the White House. The Parole Commission got involved. Mentor flew to Spokane and, with Keefe, worked out a statement for the Sohappys to sign so that the Justice Department could argue to Judge Tanner that the Indians were no longer a threat. The two lawyers took the statement to the imprisoned Indians at Geiger. David Sohappy Sr., showing the effects of his stroke, was disoriented and confused. But he signed.

By then, it was late evening. Mentor returned to Washington. The next day he called U.S. Attorney Gene S. Anderson in Seattle and told him Evans would like him to present an order asking for early release of the Sohappys. Anderson said if the senator wanted that he could make the call himself. Evans, who was in the next room, took over the telephone call, dressed down the attorney and threatened to go over his head to Justice Department officials in Washington. Anderson did ask Judge Tanner on March 3, 1988, to reduce the Sohappys' sentences to time served. The next day the two senators issued press releases saying they hoped Tanner would act quickly in accordance with the Justice Department's recommendation. Tanner had acted even more quickly than they hoped. He rejected the request without a hearing the day before their announcement, within hours after it was filed. That was a shocker, Mentor recalled. Inouye and Evans were sharply and publicly critical. Calling the sentences extremely harsh, Evans said he couldn't understand Tanner's intransigence. The government's motion seeking the Sohappys' release said the men had been fairly convicted and the sentences Tanner imposed justified. But, it said, the sentences had made their point: the government will firmly enforce its fishery conservation laws. Father and son had now agreed to abide by laws applicable to Yakama tribal members under their treaty, the motion stated. And David Sohappy Sr. was suffering residual disability—probably permanent—from his stroke. "A compassionate review suggests that he be discharged into the care of his family." Tanner made no comment in denying the request. The Sohappys had been in federal and tribal jails nineteen months.

Mentor remains puzzled about why the federal agencies made such a big thing of Sohappy. He recalls the issue as "totally out of control," but he cannot say whether the case had an impact on the in-lieu sites. Nevertheless the two issues converged in April 1988, when Evans and Inouye turned the Senate spotlight on David Sohappy's plight and all the issues surrounding it.

David Sohappy missed the hearing. He was still in prison at Spokane, but he sent an eloquent statement that became part of the Senate record.

*One of the photos that won the case. From the files of Gary Berne.*

Soon afterward, May 18, 1988, David Sohappy Sr. was released on parole. David Jr., was freed the next day. They went home to await the outcome of their suit challenging their eviction. David Sr. had lost much of his vigor in prison. Only sixty-three, he seemed older. Forbidden to fish by terms of his release from federal prison, he remained at Cook's Landing with his family, his activities reduced by failing health as much as by parole restrictions. Myra, however, feisty as ever, told their story to anyone who would listen, and took care of the fish for the sons who went on fishing. David Jr., facing the same restrictions as his father, got a job near, but not on, the river. The son began substituting for his father in some public appearances. He started studying to follow in his father's footsteps as a religious leader.

A year later, on May 1, 1989, the U.S. Ninth Circuit Court of Appeals listened to the now familiar arguments over the Bureau of Indian Affairs' effort to evict the permanent residents of the Cook's and Underwood in-lieu sites. Judge Alex Kozinski asked Angus E. Crane, representing the Department of the Interior, whether a new law providing additional sites would change the secretary of the Interior's view on permanent residences. Crane said he hadn't discussed that issue with his boss, Secretary Manuel Lujan Jr. Kozinski said he found that amazing. The Indians' attorney, Gary Berne, said the government in the 1930s, 1940s, and 1950s had told the

Indians, "We will replace the land; we will replace the buildings." Then, said Berne, "They didn't do that." In 1990, the Court of Appeals finally ruled that the Bureau of Indian Affairs had exceeded its authority when it ordered the Sohappys, Johnny Jackson and others out of their in-lieu site homes. By allowing the families to remain for up to four decades without taking steps to remove them, the BIA implied their right to remain, the court said in a 3-2 ruling. The only question left to fully establish their right to have permanent homes there was whether these had been homesites before Bonneville Dam was built. Meanwhile, with the government threatening to appeal to the Supreme Court, Senator Brock Adams, a Washington Democrat, pushed through an attachment to the Interior Appropriations Bill barring the government from spending any money to oust the in-lieu site residents. That guaranteed the residents they could remain.

The final chapter came September 5, 1991. Gary Berne, the Indians' lawyer, still smiles when he remembers the scene in Magistrate George Juba's court in Portland: "They say a picture is worth a thousand words. We showed them pictures of the sites with wooden houses on them, obviously permanent buildings. He didn't take any more testimony. Case closed." But Juba's final ruling that day was too late for David Sohappy. He died five months earlier at the age of sixty-six, a victim of diabetes, stroke, and federal prison. Myra remained at Cook's for a few more years until she too suffered a stroke and moved to the Yakama Reservation to live with a daughter. But her heart remained at the river on a barren point of land where the wind tells the fishermen when the salmon are running. Various Sohappy sons and daughters remain at Cook's. Johnny Jackson lives at Underwood. And Gary Frank adds yearly to his home at Lone Pine.

# 11

# A NEW START

*The ongoing fight for "in-lieu" access should be an embarrassment for all Americans of conscience.*

—Yakama Nation comments on
Corps of Engineers Systems Operation Review, 1994

Salmonscam and evictions consumed most of the tribes' and BIA's attention during the 1980s. Even so, they kept trying to get the Corps of Engineers to fulfill its 1939 in-lieu site promise. Late in the decade, all three issues came together before a United State senate committee, thrust there by David Sohappy's highly-publicized problems. But the tribes faced many frustrations before the Senate finally addressed the issue.

As Salmonscam was getting under way in 1981, the commissioner of Indian affairs made another effort to get both additional sites and improvements for the existing sites. The legislation he submitted was identical to the agency's 1979 proposal, and Congress similarly failed to act on it. But BIA apparently was optimistic for a while. It arranged a boat trip, much like the 1937 voyage, to have Indians point out possible new fishing or camping sites. This time, April 29, 1982, the guide was Nelson Wallulatum, grown from tag-a-long little boy to chief of the Wasco. The delegation included Delbert Frank Sr., who spent his childhood at Celilo and his early adult life fishing. Frank had become chairman of the Warm Springs Tribal Council. Other members included Juanita Bourland, the Warm Springs council secretary, and river residents Bessie Quaempts and Adeline Morrison. The BIA took pictures, just as Kenneth Simmons had arranged on the 1937 trip. Les McConnell of BIA took notes.

Chief Wallulatum provided a commentary on the river of his childhood and the river now. Before the dams, he said, the river in early spring was so high that Celilo Falls was just a large outcropping of rocks. When settlers first arrived, in the 1850s to 1880s, the Indians were more worried about retaining land to camp on and pasture their horses than in permanent living quarters. At the mouth of the Klickitat River, Lyle, Washington, he said the people who lived up that stream spoke a different language and became part of the Yakama Nation. Across the river, he pointed out land on the Oregon shore that the Warm Springs tribes had tried to buy, but it was sold to others while the tribes were arranging to have it put in trust. A few miles east, at river mile 190, he said many Indian artifacts had been found there before the dams. Also near The Dalles Dam, he pointed out Big Eddy, which had been a good sturgeon-fishing spot. Nearby were several salmon-fishing areas, now under water. He pointed out remnants of houses and shacks from communities that had moved first in the 1880s under pressure of white settlement, then when Bonneville and The Dalles dams were built. He did not point out the industrial area and the Corps of Engineers park that had been built on what originally was promised as a two-hundred-acre in-lieu site for the Indians. Just upstream from The Dalles Dam, at river mile 197, was the island where seals had pups. The boat passed under the railroad bridge at 11:45 a.m., and a few minutes later, at river mile 201, the chief told the party they were over the flooded falls. "There is a wide calm river current barely discernable," McConnell noted. The boat pulled ashore at Salmonhead Beach, once part of the Indians' Celilo community, now a Corps of Engineers public park and boat launch. In early days, Wallulatum said, the fishing platforms were only on the shore at Celilo Falls. As more people moved to Celilo Falls to fish, some built their platforms on rocks at mid-channel. By the 1940s, after Bonneville had flooded the Indians' fishing grounds up to The Dalles, the falls were crowded.

The boat trip was instructive, but the bill that inspired it did not even get a vote in Congress. So in 1985, when a real estate agent offered to sell the BIA seventy-eight acres on the Washington shore for $130,000, the agency said it had no funds or authority to make the purchase. In 1987, however, the BIA made some additional efforts to improve the in-lieu sites, despite fending off strong attacks on the national scene. Among those suggesting that the bureau be abolished was its director, Ross Swimmer. "Don't terminate the tribes," he said. "Terminate the BIA." Northwest tribes said it was Swimmer, not BIA or the tribes, that should go away. Jack

Schwartz, an attorney representing the in-lieu site residents, used the controversy to argue that the BIA "has attempted to destroy the Columbia River Indian community." Despite the hullabaloo, the BIA met with the Yakama Nation in April to discuss refurbishing the Wind River site boat ramp. The river had become so filled with silt that it was too shallow for boat launching. As a result, Indian fishermen had virtually abandoned the site. BIA suggested that the Corps of Engineers could dredge the river. The Corps estimated the cost at $1 million, and said it would require two years and authorization from Congress.

Salmon runs rebounded in the mid and late 1980s to levels not seen since before the dams. Increased numbers of fish eased the conflict between Indians fishing for their livelihood and others laying claim to the fish. But the improved prospects drew more tribal fishers back to the river. The number of recreational boaters and fishermen grew more than the number of fish. And the Gorge, noted for its winds, became the sailboarding capital of the world. That brought an influx of seasonal residents and a business boom to riverside communities. Congestion and conflict at river access points resulted. Indian fishermen, already coping with commercial and pleasure boats entangling their nets, had to deal with a whole new group, most of them from outside the Northwest. The newcomers sped through nets, sometimes pulling loose the buoys marking Indian fishing sites on the water. Sailboarders grumbled that the nets interfered with their travel; Indians said the boarders interfered with their fishing. In 1985, the Port of Cascade Locks complained to the BIA that Indians launching their fishing boats from the public ramp were causing severe traffic congestion and restricting river access for non-Indians. The port's launch was near the Cascade Locks in-lieu site that had been the subject of controversy in the 1950s. The site, a tiny 1.6 acres instead of the originally proposed eight acres, had no place suitable for a boat launch. In fact, neither Oregon site had a boat launch, forcing the Indians to use public ramps.

The influx of people and development threatened more than the Indians. It also threatened the scenic quality of the Gorge, a spectacular gash through the Cascade Mountains. A variety of groups pushed Congress for protective legislation. One proposal would have made the U.S. Department of Agriculture through the Forest Service responsible for the in-lieu sites. The BIA offered a substitute proposal that included a provision allowing it to buy more in-lieu sites. The tribes applauded the move to control development in the Gorge, led by Republican Senators Daniel J. Evans of

Washington and Mark O. Hatfield of Oregon, but the various bills proposed to protect the Gorge raised the tribes' fears too. If the Columbia was protected from future development, would the development move up the tributaries where the remaining salmon spawned? The land-use planning that was envisioned seemed to exclude the tribes. Would scenic land acquisitions include tribal land and individual Indian allotments? And what about the hope of additional in-lieu sites? The Yakama Nation told Evans it supported the concept of his Gorge protection bill "and its intention to slow growth in the Gorge and to protect the areas where the Yakama Nation and its members exercise our most important treaty secured rights." In the past, the tribal statement said, the Yakama Nation has had little voice in development. "As a consequence, we have seen our grave and village sites destroyed, our fishing places flooded and developed for non-Indian uses thereby rendering them valueless, and have seen the destruction of spawning habitat for our fish . . . ." In late 1984, the Yakama Nation asked Evans to include more in-lieu sites in the Gorge protection bill. Evans feared that would complicate the Gorge measure, which already was extremely controversial and subjected to major compromises. But he promised the Indians, if they would support the Gorge protection, he would begin work on a bill to get their additional fishing sites as soon as the Gorge Bill passed.

Congress passed the Columbia River Gorge National Scenic Area Act in 1986. Although Indian fishing sites were not a part of the new law, the congressional report accompanying the measure recognized a need for more sites. It also recognized that the available shore land was finite. The report stated: "It is the intent of Congress that previous agreements with Tribes be fulfilled and that this legislation not prejudice the ability of Congress to accomplish what was promised 47 years ago. Recreation plans must recognize the need for additional sites and provide for them in the planning process, following the recommendations by the appropriate tribes."

Evans kept his word to the Indians. Right after the Gorge Bill passed, he told aide Joe Mentor Jr. to look into the in-lieu sites. Mentor, now a Seattle attorney, believes, "Evans never really had any doubt that it should have been addressed. The Corps never offered any good reason why it had not provided the sites. My recollection is that Evans's approach was that it was going to happen. It was a question of finding appropriate surplus land to be made into sites." Mentor moved from Evans's personal staff to become director of the Republican staff of the Senate Select Committee on Indian Affairs. The Republicans lost control of the Senate in the 1986 elections, but Evans became the ranking minority member of the Indian Committee. The chairman, Senator Daniel Inouye, an Hawaii Democrat, wanted a bipartisan committee. He changed Evans's title to vice chairman and combined the two parties' staffs. There were plenty of national issues for the committee, but Evans used his opportunity to take care of some specific issues for Washington and Oregon. In those he worked closely with Senator Mark Hatfield, Oregon's venerable GOP senator whom the Indians considered a friend.

At the same time, the BIA also began discussing the possibility of finding new Indian fishing sites. The new Gorge legislation allowed it to talk both to the Corps and to the Forest Service, which had been designated federal manager of the Scenic Area. Early in 1988, the BIA gave the Corps a map of possible sites picked by the Indians. It included a list of eight key requirements for sites, such as vehicle access from public roads, boat access from the river, and a source of drinking water. The Corps said it would have to make environmental impact statements if it acquired any new lands because all the possible sites were within the Scenic Area, near a railroad, and near the river. That might be avoided if the Corps transferred lands it already owned to the BIA.

While these talks were going on, the states and tribes were submitting a new comprehensive fisheries management plan to the U.S. District Court in Portland. Judge Walter E. Craig, who had taken over the case from Belloni, had ordered them to improve on the initial sketchy plan adopted in 1977. The new plan, approved in March 1988, covered management, enforcement, and fisheries enhancement, It recognized the tribes' primary responsibility to enforce regulations on their members. The plan would not end conflict on the river, but it put tribal and state governments on amicable speaking terms and recognized the tribes as full co-managers of the river.

By the spring of 1988, the Senate committee staff had throughly researched the site issue and Evans was ready to give the matter a public airing. At the same time, the recent failure of Evans's efforts to win the Sohappys' release put their plight on the committee's agenda. Evans combined convictions, evictions, and unfilled promises into a single hearing by the Select Committee on Indian Affairs April 19, 1988. With Evans presiding—because Sohappy was a citizen of Evans's state—the select committee hauled in representatives of the Army Corps of Engineers, the Bureau of Indian Affairs, the Department of the Interior, the U.S. Fish and Wildlife Service, and the National Marine Fisheries Service. Spokesmen for the Yakama, Warm Springs, Umatilla, and Nez Perce tribes appeared. So did Johnny Jackson, Howard Jim, Edythe McCloud, and Mary Jim Chapman, all from Indian river families. David Sohappy set the tone for the hearing with a poignant written statement sent from Spokane, where he was still imprisoned:

> My old grandfather Smohalla said, "It is a bad word that comes from Washington, It is a bad law and I cannot obey it . . . ." This Lacey Act was a bad law for the Indians on the Columbia River, and I hope the United States Senate Indian Affairs Committee will help to keep it from being used to hurt other Indians.
>
> Ever since they got this Lacey Act conviction on me, the same agencies have been trying to get me and my family kicked out of our home at Cook's Landing. They claim we are dangerous, but the most dangerous thing they found in their raid was my old trunk filled with constitutional law books. They call us greedy, but our house has a dirt floor, wood-burning stove, and only a few salmon in the drying shed which they took and sold . . . .
>
> All these years of arguing with the state, and sometimes with my own tribe, don't mean much if I have to be remembered as a criminal and a dangerous poacher. I want to set the record straight, so that the people who care about the truth will know what happened to David Sohappy for trying to keep his religion, and for trying to live as the old people lived. I want my children and their children to know that I did not get equal justice under law and that the state and federal agents who conspired to put me away will someday have to answer for what they did. My struggle has been for all the Indian people who have rights along the Columbia River, for our children, and for the natural salmon in our river.

Leaders of the Yakama Nation, Warm Springs Confederated Tribes, and Nez Perce Tribe scolded the agencies for Salmonscam and its attack on their tribal governments. Levi George, the Yakama fish, wildlife and law and order committee chairman, said the law was "misinterpreted, misapplied and used as a tool to undermine tribal sovereignty and to create disharmony among our people and government." And he called it "curious" that the National Marine Fisheries Service used an interpretation of the act to harshly punish tribal fishermen just when the tribe was suing the federal agency to reduce ocean fish harvests. Allen V. Pinkham of the Nez Perce Tribal

Executive Committee said the federal fisheries agencies not only had turned the Lacey Act against tribal fishermen but his tribe was unaware of any attempts by either the Marine Fisheries Service or Fish and Wildlife Service to help the tribes enforce tribal laws against non-Indians. That assistance was the rationale the agencies had used to obtain tribal acquiescence in the 1981 amendments. Delbert Frank Sr., vice chairman of the Warm Springs Tribal Council, accused the fisheries service of undermining tribal programs by taking over the enforcement. The tribe is fully capable of deciding whether its laws have been violated, he said. Bruce Jim, the last of the three Warm Springs tribal members serving time in federal prison, had been released only the month before.

George of Yakama set the stage for the site portion of the hearing. Dams turned the Columbia into "a series of still water lakes," he said. "Under these lakes lies the heritage of the Yakama people. Gone are our traditional villages, camp sites, drying sheds, rapids and falls and usual and accustomed fishing places, covered by these lakes in the name of progress. Also gone are many promises made to us by the white man during the building of the dams, including promises that fish ladders at the dams would fully protect our salmon, that our fisheries would not be lost through progress and that our fishing places, at least in part, would be replaced . . . ." Delbert Frank said new in-lieu sites would not restore the river to its pre-dam condition or restore the fish runs. "Additional in-lieu sites will, however, make it a little easier for the Indian people to adapt to the tremendous changes that have taken place along the river," he said.

After the Indians' testimony, Evans turned his attention to the government officials. The senator did his best to get some of those agents—or their bosses—to explain the failure to provide four hundred acres of in-lieu sites. He said the 1939 agreement "represents solemn commitment by the Federal Government to the Indian tribes along the river to compensate them for their fishing sites taken as a result of the construction of the great main stem hydroelectric dams." He added, "I believe it is time for us to honor this commitment, and I will make every effort to achieve this end."

To explain itself, the Army sent Morgan Rees, deputy secretary for civil works policy, planning and legislative affairs. Rees went through the history of the sites and said the Army had only recently become aware that the Indians needed more access and facilities. He said the Army was trying to identify sites, including some suggested by the BIA, that it could let the Indians use subject to a master plan for the river that was in the works. But his basic message was, "From a purely technical/legal perspective, we believe the Corps has met its legal obligations to provide in-lieu sites." His statement did not satisfy Evans. The senator asked, "Do you have a question about the validity of the agreement and the facts as they apparently have been set forth here today that there was an agreement of 400 acres of in-lieu sites, and about 41 acres have now been transferred, which leaves approximately 359 yet to go?"

Rees responded, "There is no disagreement about the initial agreement of approximately 400 acres and the subsequent provision of about 40 acres." He said the cash settlement for Celilo with construction of The Dalles Dam and the fact that the Corps had spent all the money appropriated for the Bonneville sites meant "the Corps' authority to do more had been exhausted."

The two sparred over the 1972 agreement settling the Umatilla Tribes' suit against the Corps. The Corps had promised then to seek money for more sites. Evans asked what the Corps had done after its 1974 request to Congress was rejected. Rees said he found no record of any other efforts. But, he added hastily, "We are certainly receptive to that at this time."

*Evans*: Would it be a reasonable thing to say that you are receptive to the proposal because of the hearing today?

*Rees*: We are receptive to the proposal because our office was unaware of this issue until we were notified of the hearing.

*Evans*: I guess it just faded into the distance and other—

*Rees*: I guess so.

Evans referred to Rees's mention of the master plan, and quoted the Army official's statement: These studies should indicate whether additional sites for tribal fishing are feasible, taking into consideration recreational and navigational use of the Columbia River.

*Evans*: Are you saying that there is some question in your mind as to whether the agreement is subject to recreational and navigational priorities?

*Rees*: There are some project purposes involved in the dams along the river that we are required to hold through the authorization of those projects, and there are some areas within those projects that are designated for recreation and navigation use, so that any consideration of in-lieu sites must take into consideration the existing uses of those federal projects in terms of the congressional authorization for those uses. That is not to say that would provide an absolute obstacle to any solution to the need for in-lieu sites.

*Evans*: Let me put it in another very blunt way. If you got to the point where there were simply no other sites available—and you could not acquire 400 acres as the 1939 agreement proposed except to take a portion of some recreational site that is already currently set aside for recreation, do you think that would be appropriate?

*Rees*: It would certainly be possible.

*Evans*: That wasn't my question. Would it be appropriate?

Rees again dissembled.

Four more times Evans asked whether the Corps would at least recommend that the agreement be fulfilled if it meant using sites designated for recreation. The fifth time, he said, "Maybe I have to design a question that is a little more explicit, and I will submit it in writing, and we'll get an explicit answer in writing then."

*Rees*: We'd be pleased to do that.

But the Army's written response months later was, "Because of the multiple use nature of these sites, it is not possible at this time to make any commitment as to the use of these sites for additional in-lieu fishing sites." And the Corps conceded that it had not compensated Indians in money or in kind for any sites flooded by the John Day Dam. The response, by C. Eugene Reinke, the Corps' North Pacific Division counsel, said the Corps had no records that the Indians made any claims. Documents indicated there may have been Indian fishing sites on the John Day pool but they had been abandoned for lack of fish, the Corps said. Reinke found problems of ownership and conflicting use with all but four of the thirty sites suggested by BIA. And anything the Corps did about sites would be subject to its "Corps Master Planning Process."

Evans's hearing had made its case, however: the Army had made a promise; the Army had not kept that promise. When Colonel Charles E. Cowan, commander of the Corps' Portland District, reported to the division in September he was more positive. He wrote that he could speed up the master planning process and include a study of proposed in-lieu sites for

$465,000. That way, the Corps could recommend legislation in fiscal 1989, as it had promised to do in 1972. Meanwhile, working with Hatfield's office and the Columbia River Inter-Tribal Fish Commission, Mentor and his staff put together a bill. Jeff Curtis, who worked on the bill for CRITFC, recalls that Evans "kind of finessed" the issue of obtaining sites outside the Bonneville pool. "He picked the acreage number from the original agreement rather than the site number . . . . The fact is there was a need for sites up and down the river." There also, as Mentor pointed out, were no sites left on the Bonneville pool by this time. "The question became how far up river we would need to go to provide suitable fishing sites." The staff started by asking the Corps for lands it considered surplus. In building the dams, the Corps had acquired flowage easements over land on the Bonneville pool but acquired outright most shore land on The Dalles and John Day pools. The Senate staffers traveled up and down the river with people from CRITFC and tribal elders looking for potential sites. Curtis believes the states were not involved. "I don't think the states saw it coming. It was not a high visibility issue."

Curtis recalls some arguing over whether the measure should provide for housing. Some tribal members wanted it included. Tribal elders did not. Evans did not want to deal with the housing issue. Let the tribes resolve that one. Mentor said, however, that four hundred acres seemed like a lot of space for dip net fishing, the only method the Indians used when the 1939 agreement was made. The assumption was that the space was intended for housing.

Evans had decided not to seek reelection in 1988 and was preparing to leave the Senate at the end of the year. He wanted the legislation approved before he left. And time was running out. In September, he found his opportunity. During a work session of the Indian Affairs Committee he attached an amendment that would fulfill the 1939 agreement and the Corps' 1970s promise. There was little opposition. Gorton, the Indians' strongest enemy, was gone, having lost to Democrat Brock Adams in the 1986 election. Adams had hired Keefe, Sohappy's attorney, as an aide. Hatfield, despite signing the 1983 letter to Interior Secretary Watt complaining about the Washington shore in-lieu sites, had long been a friend of Oregon tribes. The combined prestige and popularity of Evans and Hatfield eased the bill's passage. Most people didn't care. Evans really wanted the bill. And nobody messed with Hatfield. The bill sailed through both houses of Congress and President Ronald Reagan signed it November

1, 1988, a few days before Congress adjourned and Evans ended his Senate service. It came just in time; Gorton was elected to the seat Evans was vacating and returned to the Senate in January 1989.

The bill ordered some immediate actions and made some long term commitments. It ordered the Corps to provide new in-lieu sites totaling 360 acres, finally fulfilling the 400-acre promise. It authorized spending up to $2 million. Among the provisions:

—Federal agencies that owned land along the river were to administer it as Indian fishing sites.

—The Corps of Engineers must identify all land for sale adjacent to the Bonneville pool and acquire at least six sites there.

—The Corps was to improve all the sites, old and new, to National Park Service standards for improved camp grounds.

—The Corps was to build a boat ramp at the Cascade Locks site and dredge the river at the Wind River site.

—Cost of the sites and improvements were charged to the Columbia River dam projects that had drowned the original Indian sites,

—The Secretary of Interior was given right of first refusal on any Columbia River shore lands that another federal agency made available.

The bill identified twenty-three specific sites that should be turned into Indian fishing sites. Two of the sites on the Washington shore, North Dalles and Maryhill, were not immediately available because the federal government didn't own them. Eight other sites would impact public use areas such as boat ramps, river access roads, parking areas and restrooms.

Congress had passed the bill; the issue then became how to put it into effect. The measure set no timetable for acquiring the land or making the improvements. But Mentor had told the Bingen-White Salmon Enterprise in the spring, "We have told the Corps that this isn't a project that's going to languish for even six months. We want to start on this right now. There is no question that (the government) had an obligation to do this and the Corps as much as admitted it. They realized that somebody had dropped the ball on this." Senator Brock Adams of Washington was more realistic about the Corps. He noted, "It is known that a multi-year program will be necessary." That turned out to be a major understatement.

The tribes recognized that buying more sites on the Bonneville pool would be difficult. Sparsely populated in 1945 when the first money for in-lieu sites was appropriated, the western end of the Columbia Gorge by 1989 had little vacant land left with access to the river. Complicating site acquisition was the management plan for the Columbia River Gorge Scenic Area, then being developed. The problem was far more complex than it would have been in the 1940s.

To deal with the Corps, the tribes created a task force made up mostly of leading elders who had long been involved with fish and land issues. Included were Nelson Wallulatum and Delbert Frank of Warm Springs, Levi George and Wilferd Yallup of Yakama, Jay Minthorn and N. Kathryn Brigham of Umatilla, Pete Hayes and Allen Pinkham of Nez Perce. The Corps assigned a park ranger. The Indians asked him what he knew about the in-lieu sites and the new law and whether he could speak for the Corps. The ranger said, in effect: Nothing and No. The Indians told the Corps: Send us someone with more knowledge and authority. The Corps sent George Miller, a rising young civilian planner.

Even so, for the first four years of their meetings distrust between the tribes and the Corps was so high that they required a transcriber to attend each meeting, and the next session consisted largely of reading the transcription and clarifying comments. There was no communication, just each member stating his position and asking the others to respect his integrity. In the beginning, Corps officials balked at consulting with the tribes although the policy of the Reagan Administration required consultation on projects affecting Indians. "The attitude was: We won the war; why do we have to do this?" Miller recalls. He had to explain more than once that there hadn't been any war. The tribal representatives suspected the Corps of using public statements to stall Indian acquisition of the sites. They pointed to an October 1989 news story in which the Corps' Dick Webster was quoted as saying the agency was working on a multi-year plan that would keep the contested sites in joint use by tribal fishers and non-Indians. At the time, the Corps had not met with the tribal task force for more than three months. Nor had it discussed with tribal delegates long-term joint use of the new sites. Tribal representatives also were frustrated with what they viewed as Corps foot-dragging. "It is difficult to accelerate the Corps' planning process," one CRITFC report stated, "because they can always point to someone else who is causing the delay." The Portland District pointed to Corps headquarters in Washington. Headquarters told the tribes to deal with the Portland District. And both blamed Congress for lack of funds.

Mentor is convinced that attitudes against Indian fishing long played a major role in the Corps' failure to pursue fulfillment of its agreement with the Indians. "The Corps felt that Indian presence along the river in significant numbers should be discouraged." Putting the new law into effect required the Corps and tribal representatives to spend a lot of time meeting together. Curtis, the CRITFC staff member assigned to the sites, recalls, "The negotiations were hysterical. The Corps was totally unused to dealing with Native Americans." His descriptions tally with Colonel Theron D. Weaver's complaints about Indian "pow wows" fifty years before. Current Corps employees explain that the Corps has few minorities within its military or civilian ranks, and therefore Corps officials tend to be both uncomfortable and insensitive with non-Caucasians.

The tribal task force, Corps, and BIA met in December, a few weeks after President Reagan signed the bill. The Corps said it had a little planning money but none to put the law into effect that fiscal year. However, the Army expected to have a draft plan ready by mid-January and offered to show it to the tribes. But when the tribal and Corps representatives met in January, the Portland District of the Corps was still waiting for the Washington headquarters to finish reviewing the plan. Army staff members said numerous problems with the new sites might require some boundary adjustments. And they said they wanted BIA to serve as a liaison with the tribes. They indicated they had met with BIA officials without tribal representatives, an insult to the tribes. The task force wrote District Engineer Colonel Charles E. Cowan formally informing him of the appointment of the task force members and telling him the tribes wanted to deal directly with the Army. Later, the tribes complained to Stanley Speaks, the area BIA director, about a planned meeting between the two federal agencies without tribal representatives. The agencies agreed to meet with the tribal group April 12. But two weeks before the meeting, the Corps backed out. It said Washington headquarters was still reviewing the plan for putting the new law into effect. A task force delegation went to Washington. The Corps issued a news release about its "implementation process" for the sites April 21. The tribes learned about it when reporters called for comment. Corps officials rescheduled their meeting with the tribal task force first for the last week in April, then the first week in May, then the second week in May. Task force delegates went to Washington again. Meetings there with high ranking Corps officials and congressional staff members got results again. The Corps did not cancel the next scheduled meeting with the task force May 19. Before the meeting, the tribal task force members agreed they needed to counteract the negative press coverage that followed the Corps' April 21 press release. They also decided they should work with the Columbia Gorge Commission and local governments and would try to prod the Corps into making some progress on its plans. When the two groups met, they laid plans for a joint press conference on May 25, 1989—half a century after the initial agreement.

The press conference was just before the Memorial Day weekend, when the river is normally filled with recreation boats. Colonel Cowan announced that the eight designated sites already developed for public use would be shared by Indians and non-Indians for the rest of the year. After that the Corps and Bureau of Indian Affairs would negotiate site use each year until the Corps finished its work and turned the sites over for exclusive Indian use as required by the new law. He hinted at delays, saying that exclusive Indian use was "the long term objective" of the law. Cowan also suggested there might be boundary changes in the sites that would preserve the public use. He said the Corps would hold a half dozen public meetings to describe the law and hear comments. He said the law did not include any provision for additional public access to the river. Delbert Frank Sr., vice-chairman of the Warm Springs Tribal Council, explained, "The sites described in the new legislation are places our people have fished for generations, not for sport or recreation, but for survival." Frank added, "As the recreational season gets under way and the sockeye come upriver, those of us who work and play on the river need to be especially respectful of one another."

The public didn't wait for the Corps' meeting to react. A week later, on Thursday, June 1, both outdoor columnists for *The Oregonian* reported opposition to setting the sites aside for Indian fishermen. "The question of public access is howling like a Gorge wind on a 130-mile stretch of the Columbia River between Bonneville and McNary dams," wrote Tom McAllister. Oregon state's Marine Board, Department of Fish and Wildlife, Parks Division, and State Police had agreed on a six-point statement, McAllister said. Key elements included improved river access for both tribal fishermen and recreational river users. The state agencies said they wanted to participate in the Corps' final plan and urged local "public reviews." McAllister also offered some samples of non-tribal opinion. Hobart Manns of Gresham complained, "River access points are already overcrowded and now they'd be taking away our boat ramp at Rufus and building another for the Indian fishermen a few miles upriver at Preacher's Eddy." John Thomas, president of the White Salmon River Steelheaders who shared the Underwood site with the tribes by informal agreement, said, "We've co-existed all this time with our Indian friends." If the steelheaders were forced out, they would face a sometimes dangerous five-mile run from the nearest launch point to the mouth of the White Salmon River, he said. The other columnist, Bill Monroe, reported that tribal leaders said they would lobby for replacement of the recreation sites the tribes were taking over. He also quoted Levi George of the Yakama Nation and Frank as saying they believed conflicts between tribal and recreation fishermen had eased in recent years. The tribes were, however, worried about the growing number of windsurfers, who they said paid no attention to existing use of facilities, blocked boat ramps, and sometimes cut nets. Monroe's column did not include a favorite story among the tribes. George, a longtime fisherman, was putting his boat into the water at a public ramp when a windsurfer demanded to know what he was doing. George explained. The windsurfer told George to leave because "we were here first." George shook his head. "No," he said. "I was here a long time before you."

The tribal task force and Corps met three times more in June and July, much of the time arguing over whether the Corps could restrict the Indians' treaty fishing rights on Corps land outside the newly designated access sites. At the last of those meeting, the Corps finally came up with its timetable for putting the 1988 law into effect. First, the Army would conduct a two-year planning study. Then it would take a year to make a design study of the proposed facilities—drying sheds, showers, rest rooms. The earliest construction could begin was 1994. Construction would take five to ten years. Depending, of course, on the Corps' budget process and appropriations.

The Corps began its series of public meetings August 2 in The Dalles. Others were held at Goldendale, Washington; Boardman, Oregon; and Richland, Washington. Jeff Curtis recalls "awful public hearings—truly horrible." He said, "The one in Goldendale was pretty ugly. There was a lot of 'Why give the Indians anything?' It was racist and ugly. The Corps did not keep a handle on it. . . . I felt physically threatened. . . . It reminded me of growing up in Louisiana in the bad days of racism."

Carol Craig, a Yakama tribal member and then on the CRITFC public relations staff, took notes of the Goldendale meeting. A sample:

> *Carolyn Rinta*: Are there going to be daily inspections for sanitation at these smelly sites? Well, Klickitat County will find itself with a problem on their hands. I don't want my children near these sites.

> *(First name not recorded) Toomey*: We've seen state parks like Celilo and everyone knows that everything the Indian touches turns into a garbage dump. If we have to have co-habitation it will be like a garbage dump with their intimidation and coercion.

> *Jay Ray Hall*: They have built more in-lieu sites but nothing for the sports fishermen and we've used these sites for many, many years.

The tone at the Goldendale hearing was the most venomous, but the others included plenty of complaints about the new law too. At The Dalles, Mark Weston of The Dalles accused the Indian fishers of taking over the river. Two Indian fishermen said some of the conflicts with sportsmen arose because tribal fishermen require a long time to load and unload gear and unload fish. Nez Perce tribal member Loretta Halfmoon said windsurfers, Corps employees and others had harassed members of her family at fishing sites. At the final meeting, *The Oregonian* reported, "Angry sport fishermen have sharply criticized the federal government for designating 23 Columbia River fishing-access sites for Indian fishermen only." "I don't understand why we can't use them equally," said James A. Bates of Kennewick, Washington. George Miller responded for the Corps that the intent of the law was to separate commercial and sport fishermen, who required different amounts of space and time at docks and ramps. Kathryn Brigham, a Umatilla tribal member serving on the In-Lieu Site Task Force, tried to dampen conflict, saying, "The tribes want to work with you to meet your needs and our needs." The Columbia River Inter-Tribal Fish Commission issued a fact sheet in an effort to answer questions raised by the sports fishermen. One recurring plaint: Why did the tribes rather than sports fishermen get these new sites? The answer: The government paid the costs of moving many homes and businesses flooded by the dams without a fifty-year wait. In addition, there is a federal fund derived from taxes on fishing tackle and motor boat fuel that provides money for fisheries enhancement, including boating access for sports fishers. The fund, known as Wallop-Breaux, goes to states on the basis of state area and number of fishing licenses. In 1998, Washington got $6,071,831 in Wallop-Breaux funds and Oregon collected $6,330,898.

Opposition came outside the meetings too. Letters to the editor, editorials and legislation all showed little tolerance for Indian fishing or understanding of the country's treaty obligations. Representative Sid Morrison, a Washington Republican whose district covered the sites on the Washington shore, introduced a bill that would prohibit turning any sites over to the Indians unless replacements were obtained for non-Indians. The bill did not become law. Later, Morrison helped work out compromises that defused some of the public anger. The Dalles *Weekly Reminder* showed the least grasp of history or the status of Indians and their treaties and the most strident of racist views in an editorial April 27, 1989. It warned that the conflict over river access "could erupt into a heated, perhaps bloody confrontation between Native Americans and non-Native Americans," It called federal policies toward Indians "an attitude of guilt" that "goes beyond logical understanding." After all, it said, the government hadn't "handed out reservations" to other ethnic groups who immigrated to North America. It called for an end to government programs for Indians and asked Indians to restrain their fishing. Fortunately, other voices were more reasoned, mostly calling for tolerance and understanding on both sides.

After the series of public meetings, the tribal task force met with Boardman and Morrow County officials to discuss the two access sites at Boardman and agreed to consider an alternate to one site. Boardman officials were concerned because one site was where the city's marina planned to expand, and where a future well would be drilled to allow the city to grow. When John Day Dam was built, the Corps of Engineers paid to relocate the entire town—at the same time it was stonewalling the Indians on a few acres of in-lieu sites. Task force members met with the Columbia River Gorge Commission. The Corps did not attend the sessions with Boardman officials nor did it meet with the task force. In October, the Indians went back to Washington, this time to tell the congressional delegation about its concerns. They were not pleased with the length of time—six years after passage of the bill—before construction would start. And it was frustrated in its attempts to work with the Corps. In an effort to spell out their working relationship, the task force had proposed a memorandum of agreement and sent it to the Corps in May. It had not received a reply in October. The Corps' foot-dragging on the sites can probably be partly explained by its being out of its element. The Corps usually does big projects, such as dams, not little projects such as restrooms and fish-drying sheds. And the agency was reluctant to admit that it had failed to carry out a promise.

Finally, however, after the task force's second visit to Washington, some of its higher administrators realized the tribes had some political clout, and decided the Corps should act. The Corps representatives met with the tribal task force and BIA on December 14. Corps delegates said the agency's Washington headquarters had sent policy guidance on the approach to the fishing sites in mid-October, and the District was reviewing it. It would get back to the tribes. The policy guidance included such items as agreeing to "a coordinated approach to plans for facility development, public information and selection of acquisition sites." The Corps would go through a planning process and would involve the public. Construction would be "phased in." Corps and task force quarreled again over Corps plans to impose management restrictions on its open lands along the river.

There also were disagreements between the tribes. The Warm Springs and Yakama questioned the presence of the Nez Perce among the participants. That decision was made by Congress, not the Corps, but the Corps was not above exploiting the intertribal animosity to avoid action.

Joe Mentor, who drew up the legislation for Senator Dan Evans in 1988, was astounded nine years later when he learned that the Indians did not yet have the legislated sites. This was not what Senator Evans had in mind, Mentor said. "It had gone on long enough. We expected the tribes would start using the new sites within a year or two. Senator Evans' intention was to move quickly . . . . If we'd had any idea, we could have exempted them from an EIS." But the environmental impact statement, which required more than two years to write, was only one of the procedural roadblocks that delayed site construction. The organization that built Bonneville Dam from bedrock to power producer in less than five years took seven just to break ground to build boat ramps and fish drying sheds on the first of the twenty-three new sites. It planned to take seven more to finish the rest.

# 12

# A SHOVELFUL OF MUD

*We did not inherit this earth or its natural resources from our ancestors; we are only borrowing them from our children's children; therefore, we are duty bound and obligated to protect them and use them wisely until such time as they get here and then they will have the same obligations.*

—Eugene Greene Sr., former chairman,
Columbia River Inter-Tribal Fish Commission,
in introducing CRITFC salmon recovery plan

Taking in-lieu sites from concept to construction after the 1988 legislation was like running an obstacle course in slow motion. It was as if nothing had changed since 1939; fishing sites for Indians were low on the priority list. To be fair, there were more obstacles for construction in the 1990s than there were in the 1930s when the Army Corps of Engineers built Bonneville Dam and promised the river people it would replace their flooded fishing sites. In the 1930s, the Corps blocked the raging Cascades, moved railroads and highways and anything else in the way almost without constraint. And in the 1990s the Indians themselves created some of the obstacles. But the delays caused by the tribes' insistence on checking sites for graves and other remnants of their ancestors and on Indian preference in contracting and employment could have been minimal. The Corps used most of the time between legislation and construction to study each site in exquisite detail and to look for alternatives wherever the legislation gave tribal fishers rights in Corps parks along the river shore. Wherever a legislated tribal site overlapped an existing recreation site, the Corps sought another place for the Indian fishers or a change in the site boundaries. It eliminated two sites that turned out to be privately owned land. Of the twenty-one remaining, it wanted to abandon one, move another, and change the boundaries of nineteen. Conflicting recreation parks, of course, all came after the dams and long after the promise to the Indians. Many of the parks are on traditional Indian fishing sites and some, such as Celilo, were once Indian villages.

While the Corps studied and studied and studied and the tribes prodded for action, the river people kept fishing. And, after a brief resurgence in the mid-1980s, the fish runs were dwindling once more. This time they fell to the point that in 1992 several Snake River runs were placed on the endangered species list, Sockeye as endangered and spring, summer and fall Chinook as threatened, or likely to become endangered. The tribes were fighting two battles—one to get the sites built, the other to restore the fish runs so there would be fish to catch when the sites were completed.

The first part of the Corps' new in-lieu site program looked relatively easy—rehabilitating three of the existing sites and building a new one on eight acres of Corps-owned land at the north end of Bonneville Dam. There was little opposition from non-Indians, no land to acquire, only design, contract and build. But even that part of the work was delayed. When the Corps put fish drying sheds and sanitary facilities on the original in-lieu sites in the 1950s, it got tribal approval of the locations but not of anything else. The Corps made the plans, hired the contractors, and told the fishing people: Here they are. Army engineers intended to carry on the same way in the 1990s. However, the tribes demanded a voice, and changes in laws and politics provided them one. When the Corps showed its initial reluctance to coordinate site development with the tribes and laid out its timetable of eight to fourteen years, the tribes suggested alternatives. They drafted a memorandum of understanding that included a phased approach to speed the work. They won support from some key members of Congress, but only after agreeing to boundary adjustments on some sites to avoid inconveniencing recreation fishers and boaters.

The Corps agreed that a phased program would work but did not respond to other parts of the tribal memorandum until 1991, when it presented the tribes with a much modified agreement and said it would do no more on the sites unless the tribes accepted it. Reluctantly, three of the four agreed. So three years after the legislation, the Corps began planning the first sites.

The Corps' take-it-or-leave-it attitude did nothing to build the tribes' confidence in the Army. George J. Miller, the Corps' civilian project manager for the sites, was the man in the middle. He recalls that when he first proposed that the Corps consult with the tribes as it developed plans, all four Corps section heads in Washington disapproved. He finally persuaded the highest levels of Corps officials that the sites were "mitigation" for effects of the dams, which is exactly what the 1988 law says they are. That definition seemed to legitimize working with the tribes. In addition, after tribal leaders made several trips to Washington to meet with their congressional delegations, the Corps realized the tribes now had some political clout. They could no longer be ignored. Howard Arnett, tribal attorney for the Warm Springs, recalls similar experiences. "We had to tell them the history of the legislation and the background over and over again. Their first reaction was, 'Huh?' . . . We keep having to remind them these are not Corps parks."

Other battles were more serious and more protracted. One was over Indian preference in contracting and employment. The other was over the handling of cultural resources—evidences of early tribal occupation—that might be uncovered on the sites. After the Corps finished its multi-year studies and was writing its six-pound report, the tribes invoked the law giving preference to Native Americans in both contracting and employment on Indian projects. That doesn't apply to the Army Corps of Engineers, said the engineers. Federal regulations require it to accept the lowest bid. To bolster its resistance, the Corps' dredged up a law dating back to the Indian wars that required tribes to get BIA approval before signing any contract. The law was still in effect, but by the 1990s, BIA contract approval was almost automatic. After six months of discussion, the Portland District of the Corps asked its Washington headquarters for a waiver from federal rules so it could give special consideration to Indian subcontractors and the hiring of Indian workmen. That was not good enough, the tribes said. As the Corps knew, they meant prime contractors, possibly with the tribes themselves taking on that role. Also, the tribes said submitting a request that ignored the tribes' proposal to include prime contractors was a breach of faith hinging on ethical misconduct. They went to the next level of the Corps, the North Pacific Division commander, General Ernest J. Harrell. Local Corps authorities could amend their request, Harrell told the tribes, but that might take two more years for approval. The more modest request, then being considered at the Corps' highest level in Washington, probably would be approved, he said. That was in April 1994. At that point the

Corps planned to call for bids in May of 1994. It did not. But before several other issues were resolved and it did call for bids a year later, the Corps had agreed to Indian preference on the first phase contract.

The battle over cultural resources, always an emotionally charged issue for the tribes, turned into an intertribal quarrel as well as a dispute with the Corps. Tribes wanted their own cultural staff people involved to assure sensitive handling of human remains, funerary objects or other cultural artifacts and traces of villages. So many villages once dotted the Columbia's shores that almost anywhere a bulldozer scooped, it disturbed bones and relics. Discussions began in 1991. The following year, the Corps issued a draft proposal that the tribes found unacceptable. They said it failed to comply with either federal historic preservation requirements or the Native American Graves Protection and Repatriation Act. Because work was not imminent, neither tribes nor Corps focused on the issue until 1994. Then the Umatilla Tribes' objection centered on the Corps' statement that if human remains were found, "data recovery becomes a focal point in project planning." That meant that archaeologists would be brought in to remove the remains and any associated articles and they would be reburied elsewhere. "The idea of exhuming human remains to develop an access site is not appropriate," said Paul Minthorn, a Umatilla member of the In-lieu Site Task Force, the intertribal committee keeping watch on the project. Tribal policy would be to move the project to a different location. After all, he said, they were talking about boat ramps, bathrooms and drying sheds— minor developments not crucial to treaty rights or cultural preservation. The graves of their ancestors are sacred. Many Indians are bitter about the cavalier way in which state and federal governments have sometimes treated Indian graves. One Warm Springs elder, now deceased, always crossed the Columbia to travel on the Washington side on trips to the Umatilla Reservation to avoid Interstate 84 on the Oregon side of the river. Part of the Oregon freeway crosses a native graveyard.

During a recess in a meeting where the issue was being discussed, the Umatilla delegates wrote a new proposal. The meeting erupted in shouting. A Yakama delegate objected to upriver tribes—Umatilla and Nez Perce— meddling in cultural resources in Yakama territory. All four phase one sites are in the areas ceded to the United States by the Yakama and Warm Springs tribes. But Umatilla and Nez Perce delegates responded that their governing bodies would decide the issues its delegates will discuss and with whom. The agreement on cultural resources would cover both phase one and phase two, which includes areas ceded by Umatilla and Nez Perce tribes. Tempers cooled, and Donald G. Sampson, chairman of the Umatilla Board of Trustees, later wrote a conciliatory letter to his fellow chairmen. He said his tribes had no intention of making claims to burial sites or any other sites important to downstream tribes. Umatilla would defer to Warm Springs and Yakama in decisions in their areas, he said. Agreement among the tribes was vital. Delay in reaching an understanding with the Corps could stall the project a year.

One by one, through frequent, long and contentious meetings, the obstacles were overcome. But when Corps and tribes were on the verge of agreement, an inter-agency squabble threatened to derail the project. All three major pieces of in-lieu site legislation dating back to 1945 stated that the Corps was to acquire and build improvements on the sites, then turn them over to BIA for the use and benefit of the Indians. But in the early 1990s, the BIA balked—as it had in the 1950s—at taking responsibility for the sites. It did not have the money or staff to maintain fishing grounds, it said. The Corps was building them; the Corps should keep them up. The 1988 legislation said the costs of the new sites should be treated as part of the project costs for each of the Corps-built dams that had flooded Indian fishing sites. BIA said that meant the Corps had to pay for maintaining them too. The Corps, however, only wanted to finish the work and end its involvement with tribes. Citing BIA's "terrible track record" on the existing sites, the Corps also said it did not want its new work allowed to deteriorate so that it would all have to be done again. The tribes sided with the BIA. They feared that, if the always cash-strapped BIA were responsible, money for the upkeep would come from other tribal programs. That meant the tribes would have to pay for the maintenance, or they would all fall into disrepair as the original ones had. The tribes also believed the money should come from dam operation budgets because the government had made hundreds of millions of dollars profit from the dams that destroyed the Indian fishing sites, homes, and livelihoods. The four dams that spanned the tribes' lower Columbia fishing grounds were built as multi-purpose projects. That is, the economic justification for construction of each dam was based on two or more presumed benefits—power production, navigation, flood control, irrigation, and recreation. Those economic benefits include sale of 6,040 megawatts of electricity a year, navigation facilities that move nine million tons of a cargo a year, irrigation of more than 200,000 acres, and lakes that provide 4.5 million recreation user days each year. But the tribes—and environmental groups—contend those benefits are all heavily subsidized. They say aluminum plants and irrigation farmers buy electricity at prices far below cost, that barge operators' fuel taxes fall far short of paying for their passage through Columbia locks, and that users of riverside parks get a free ride. The Indians contend that those subsidized benefits came at the expense of their fishing sites and the fish. They argued that, if the construction and maintenance of boat ramps for recreation fishers can be counted into the costs of dam building, then construction and upkeep of fishing sites for Indians have an equally legitimate claim as a project cost. The Indians' commercial fishing after all contributes to the region's economy. Eventually, the Corps agreed.

The issue came to a head in December 1993. Army officials said they would do no work on the first phase until the BIA agreed it would accept the sites as soon as they were completed. Only one new site was involved, Bonneville Area Office at the north end of Bonneville Dam. All the other phase one work was at original in-lieu sites that BIA had so reluctantly accepted in the 1960s. Exasperated tribal leaders went to Washington. They didn't tell the Corps they were coming. But when they arrived at Corps headquarters they told the receptionist they had come to meet with high-ranking officials. The receptionist said the meeting had already started and ushered them into a room where a session about other issues was in progress. Some participants, thinking the Indians were on the agenda, gave them their seats at the table. For an hour and half the tribal leaders lectured startled Army brass on Indian treaties and the Corps' responsibilities under those treaties and the law. The Corps officers were impressed but not enough to take any action.

The tribal leaders then called on Ada Deer, the assistant secretary of the Interior for Indian affairs. Two previous bills had promised to provide the sites, they said. They did not want this one to fail as the others had. Deer had set a goal for her administration of clearing up just such matters that had been hanging for decades. She assigned Dr. Catherine Vandemoer, BIA water-rights specialist, to resolve the impasse. And, in a repeat of conferences more than fifty years earlier, Deer herself met with the John Zirschky, assistant secretary of the Army for civil works, and attorneys for both agencies. They decided a formal memorandum of agreement between the agencies would be the best way to work out the differences. The tribes, of course, insisted on being involved. Vandemoer recalls the first meeting she attended in Portland to work on the agreement: Army officers in dress uniforms, their attorneys in suits and neckties, and twenty tribal members in casual clothes or traditional regalia. The Army, going first, had a formal and rigid agenda. Vandemoer went next, threw out the Army agenda and suggested small working groups to facilitate discussion. "The Army was flabbergasted," she recalls. Army and tribal approaches were entirely different. But "It worked." Army, BIA and tribes agreed that BIA would take responsibility for the operation and maintenance. The Army would obtain an appropriation to finance the upkeep. BIA would invest the money in treasury bonds to provide permanent financing for repairs and maintenance. Then BIA decided it didn't have authority to accept the money. That meant getting Congressional authorization, another delay. So the memorandum of agreement was not signed until June 1995, a year after the Corps had planned to award its first contract. Even then, it almost failed. A few minutes before the signing ceremony, Zirschky had second thoughts. George Miller remembers an angry argument. Sign or walk away from the Army's commitment, Miller said. It was not a prudent course for a civil servant, but Miller had come to believe in the project and that the Corps must fulfill its promise. On another occasion he became impatient with the rigid cost/benefit economic justification that the Corps uses to decide whether to recommend building dams and dikes. He took a policy review staff member to Cook's Landing and showed him the rotting outhouse. "How can I economically justify whether to build a one-holer or a two-holer?" he demanded.

The assignment has not been an easy one for Miller. Work with the tribes has continued so long that he has gone from young bachelor to married father of two. On the eve of his fortieth birthday he remarked ruefully, "I've spent more family holidays with Fred Ike [longtime Yakama member of the task force] than I have with my wife."

Finally, all the disputes between Corps and tribes and between Corps and BIA seemed to have been resolved. Congress had passed the necessary amendments, and the Corps was ready to call for bids on the first phase, the modest rehabilitation of the existing Lone Pine, Cascade Locks and Underwood sites and building the new Bonneville site.

As the Corps finally prepared to call for bids, Yakama tribal member Delbert Wheeler, the owner of a reservation-based logging company, incorporated Wheeler Construction in May 1995 and went after the contract. He knew it would be a battle. It was not his first. Nor was winning the contract his first victory. Wheeler got his first illegal fishing citation from the state of Washington when he was twelve years old. He has battled white prejudice and white opposition to Indian treaty rights ever since. And he has faced the battles that plague reservations across the country: poverty-bred lethargy, rampant drug and alcohol abuse, lack of jobs. Wheeler's Wasco roots are firmly on the Columbia River at Wishkum, east of The Dalles Dam. Dams drove his grandfather, Furman Wheeler Sr., to an in-lieu site, where he fished for years while the tribes and Corps negotiated. The Wheeler family allotment, one of the original Vancouver allotments issued a century ago, is under water. "It's listed as a number," Wheeler says. "It doesn't exist." Family members were involved in the fishing conflicts of the 1970s and 1980s. Furman Wheeler Sr. eventually moved to the Yakama Reservation, where he worked for the federal Bureau of Reclamation and reared his grandson. Delbert Wheeler dropped out of school after the eighth grade and went to work in the woods.

He credits a white man, Jim Stewart, with teaching him the logging business and giving him a chance. Stewart's friendship caused Wheeler to extend traditional Indian respect for elders to all elders "no matter what color." In 1981, at the age of twenty-two, Wheeler struck out on his own. His first independent job was cutting a cord of firewood that he hauled on a flatbed truck. He raised $14,000, bought a logging truck and bid on cutting timber in the Yakama tribal forest. He was the first Indian logger on the reservation, and the whites who found logging Indian timber profitable disdained the young Yakama. He says they tried to shut him out of the work. Wheeler resented the discrimination. He says only that he "took physical stands" and "did jail time for creating a disturbance." But he began getting contracts. "Non-Indians felt they owned this reservation," he recalls. "The BIA kept shutting us down . . . . mills tried to pay us less than they did others. It was just like fishing." Wheeler persevered. Now, he is sole proprietor of a successful reservation-based logging company and president of the fledgling construction firm that bears his name. His logging company has 110 employees, nearly all Yakama tribal members. Wheeler lives at White Swan on the reservation in a tidy ranch-style home filled with high-quality furniture and appliances. His goal is to create jobs that will give fellow tribal members self-respect and a chance at the American dream that has so often eluded Native Americans. "I believe in the American dream," Wheeler says.

In Delbert Wheeler two cultures meld. He speaks the Caucasian business language with confidence and knowledge But he retains and honors his tribal traditions and religion. Handsome, forceful, self-assured, he can hold his own with Army engineers. He has done so without losing his traditional concern for family, band, and tribe that is reflected in the benefits he pays and the concern he shows for his employees' lives as well as work. The company is drug and alcohol free. Employees with addictions have a choice: company-paid rehabilitation or leave. In 1991, forty-three employees went through treatment. The employees get life insurance, paid vacations, and company backing to buy cars and homes financed through banks.

When Wheeler decided to branch out into construction, among those he recruited to help lead the new company was Terry Goudy Tecumseh, another Wasco from a prominent fishing family. Tecumseh, herself a treaty fisher woman, spent twenty-three years with the Bureau of Indian Affairs working in personnel, forestry, and contracts. She took on the job of writing Wheeler Construction's proposal to rehabilitate the sites at Lone Pine, Cascade Locks, and Underwood, and build the new site called Bonneville Office. She had a week and a half to two weeks to do the paper work. Sometimes working twenty-three to twenty-four hours a day, she met the deadline. Then a major obstacle appeared. Furman Wheeler Sr. and Furman Wheeler Jr., Delbert Wheeler's grandfather and uncle, had agreed to provide the financial backing for the project. Shortly before the bids were due, both died. Their estates went into probate, and Delbert Wheeler was left without the financing he needed to win a contract. He went to Colville Tribal Services Corp., a construction company owned by the Colville Confederated Tribes in north central Washington, and offered to work with it in an effort to swing the contract to an Indian-owned company. Colville authorities agreed, the Wheeler-Colville combination won the $2.97-million contract, and the Colville firm waived its interest to allow Wheeler full responsibility.

First, Wheeler hired fishermen because most can no longer make a living on the river. The decimated runs have forced a reduction in fishing days to two or three weeks a year. Half the new employees had never worked in construction. Wheeler trained them. He feels he accomplished much in hiring tribal members. "Today they can look at themselves and be proud of their work." Employing their members in the construction was a major goal of all four tribes. "Equity is the real issue for our people." Indians lost much in both property and opportunities when the dams flooded the river banks. But "Indians were not offered maintenance or park jobs to employ people on the river where they belonged." Unemployment is high on the reservations and pay rates are low. Wheeler hopes to help change that. "This joint effort for the American Indian in a self-help, self-determination, self-development program and project is the opportunity to build and refurbish the Columbia River in-lieu site areas," Wheeler said in a company brochure. "I believe this to be the greatest hope for Indian progress which lies in the emergence of Indian leadership and initiative in solving Indian problems with projects such as this one."

Hiring an Indian contractor was only one measure of difference from the original in-lieu site construction in the 1950s. Before he began work, Wheeler spent many days, including Saturdays and Sundays, at longhouses and with elders along the river asking what they wanted at each site. In contrast to the earlier work, this time the Corps asked the Indians how to build a drying shed. It took a while to persuade some of the older women to come in and advise the Corps' Gail Lovell while she drew the shed designs. It was not an easy task to meld traditional Indian construction into Corps of Engineers specifications. Nor was it always easy to get the Indians to agree on specifics of construction. But the collaboration resulted in handsome pine buildings with louvered windows and wide doors that allow the Columbia River winds to dry the salmon. The Indians finally agreed to the Corps' demand to set the sheds on concrete pads, but at least this time there was space for a fire so they could smoke the fish if they wished. At Lone Pine, Wheeler used the concrete slabs from the original drying sheds, avoiding the possibility of new disturbances on ground that could contain sacred relics. Terry Tecumseh, however, remains resentful about the process. The drawings may have been done by Corps draftsmen but the designs were those of the Indians. The Corps people were paid for their work; the Indians were not. Tecumseh says they should have had a consulting fee.

An Indian contractor made differences elsewhere in the construction too. Wheeler considered the Corps' dock designs inadequate for heavy fish-laden boats in the strong Columbia current, He built them stronger, and he redesigned the pump system serving the restrooms. At Cascade Locks, the first site Wheeler worked on, no archeologist had examined the area for graves or cultural remnants. "In the first scoop of dirt, we had bones," Wheeler recalled with a shudder. Worked halted. The ground was studied and little more found. Wheeler Construction did not charge the Corps for the delay, nor did it charge for the design changes at the Bonneville site. In some areas, the Corps, in its usual pattern, planned to drill and blast to level ground for construction. Wheeler persuaded officials to let him cover a sacred site with dirt, leaving the original ground undisturbed. At Lone Pine a fight broke out over digging into sacred ground. Wheeler absorbed the cost where his methods cost more. "It is our sacred place," he explained.

The Corps' engineers were openly skeptical of the ability of a tribal company to do proper work. Wheeler believes the contract was designed so that an Indian company would fail. He didn't. The contract was completed on time, at cost. Wheeler says his working relationship with the Corps became professional and excellent about seven months into the project. But if he won over the Corps, he then faced criticism from the tribes. Expectations for jobs were high. Reservation rumors put the number of jobs at a hundred or more. Instead, there were eleven. All the tribes hoped to put members to work on the sites. Wheeler's crew included one non-Indian and one Umatilla tribal member; the rest were from Yakama.

The second phase of construction is bigger and requires more people. Wheeler went after that contract too. He lost to a lower bidder, a company owned by Fred Cooper, a member of the tiny Shoalwater Bay Tribe from the southern coast of Washington. Wheeler challenged the bid award, but turned philosophical after the Claims Court rejected his appeal. "We've gone on to other things," he said. The construction company has several road projects and work on a mill.

However, like many other Indians, he fears that he has built something that will not long remain in Indian hands. If the 150-year effort to get Indians off the river succeeds or if salmon runs dwindle too low for fishing, these tribal members fear that Wheeler's work will wind up as more rest stops and picnic places for others. Sixty years of delay feeds such suspicion.

But ground-breaking for the new Bonneville site finally brought tangible evidence of progress toward keeping the promise. Tribal leaders turned the first shovelful of dirt on the rain-soaked riverbank November 17, 1995, seven years after President Reagan signed the law ordering the Corps to get the sites and improve them. The Corps trotted out its best public relations to mark the event. It hired buses to take participants and spectators from the south shore across the dam to the site on the north shore. Col. Tim Wood, the Corps' Portland District engineer, joined Nelson Wallulatum from Warm Springs, representatives of the three other tribes and Johnny Jackson from the river people in turning shovelsful of mud. Yakima Valley Veterans, some of them Yakama tribal members, provided a color guard. The Minthorn family drummers from Umatilla supplied music. Everybody sat down to a salmon lunch prepared by tribal members in a meeting room in the Corps' office complex at Bonneville Dam. "Many of my ancestors died waiting for this day," said Johnny Jackson, chief of the Cascade Band. With no unforeseen delays, the fishing people would have all their sites—thirty-one totaling around three hundred acres—by the year 2002. It's not the promised four hundred acres, but after sixty-four years, it's as close as they're going to get.

While Delbert Wheeler was putting an Indian stamp on site construction, another Yakama was winning a long battle to save another fishing place upstream. Margaret Saluskin hadn't planned to follow in the footsteps of her grandfather, Alex Saluskin. In fact, she barely knew the wise old Yakama tribal chairman. But when tribal tradition and sacred ground were threatened, she found a talent for leadership she didn't know she possessed. She battled a private developer, county and state officials, and sometimes her tribe to save the spot of land for the river people. In large measure, she won.

Lyle Point was an overlooked anomaly on the Washington shore of the Bonneville Dam pool. The point and the town from which it takes its name lie toward the east, or dry, end of the Columbia River Gorge. For years, as communities downriver boomed with the rise of sailboarding, Lyle remained a mere dot on the highway untouched by growth. But development marched steadily eastward. Land-hungry newcomers with money to spare discovered, as financier Sam Hill had eighty years before, that the rugged grass and shrub-covered slopes had a beauty of their own. Hill, attracted by the sparse grandeur of the eastern gorge, built a castle named Maryhill for his wife on a bluff nine hundred feet above the river, miles from any neighbor. Mary Hill refused even to visit the place, preferring to sparkle in society in cities. Hill planned the castle as the center of a seven thousand-acre farm to be worked by European immigrants. For some years it was a farm, and some of the river people worked its vegetable crops. As a child, Howard Jim, now the venerable chief at Celilo, earned three cents a bunch preparing the farm's onions for market. Eventually, Hill's castle became a fine small museum with excellent collections of Rodin sculptures and Klickitat Indian baskets, and no gardens.

Lyle, twenty-five miles downstream from Maryhill, huddles close to the river beneath majestic hills. On the river side of the town, between the last three-block row of small, mostly shabby houses and the windswept riverbank, lies Lyle Point, covered with brush and grass, dotted by clusters of pine and pocked with basalt outcroppings. The Burlington Northern-Santa Fe Railroad runs along the town side of the point. Indians have fished there from time beyond memory. Part of the land they consider sacred. Lyle Point would seem to have been an ideal in-lieu site from the beginning. It is near the upper end of the Bonneville pool. It covers about three-quarters of a mile of river front, with terrain that provides platform fishing spots, a boat launching site, and good gill net fishing just offshore.

But except for a request from Treaty Indians of the Columbia in 1974, nowhere in any record of site negotiations is there mention of Lyle Point. Treaty Indians, the organization of river residents involved in challenging the raising of the river level in the early 1970s, listed Lyle among four sites it wanted the Corps to add to the five original in-lieu sites. The Treaty Indians' request also included Le Page Park at the mouth of the John Day River, Oregon; a site near a sawmill in the Cascade Locks vicinity; and land near Willow Creek on the Oregon shore between John Day and McNary dams. The group's 1974 list was submitted in response to the Corps' promise to seek additional sites as partial settlement of the Umatilla tribes' 1972 lawsuit over raising the Bonneville pool. It is the only pre-1988 list that incldes sites outside the Bonneville pool. There is only other one hint that Lyle Point might have been considered before 1988. A single letter from a Corps official in 1954 mentions a potential site upriver from the mouth of the Klickitat River. Whether the writer meant upriver on the Klickitat or on the Columbia is not clear. The Klickitat empties into the Columbia near the western end of Lyle Point. The letter says the writer fears Washington state would object to the location because it is near a state fish hatchery. There is no evidence that the Indians proposed it as one of the original six sites or as a substitute when the Big Eddy site, eleven miles upstream, was lost to The Dalles Dam. Burlington Northern-Santa Fe Railroad owned the land as successor to Northern Pacific, the successor to the Spokane, Portland and Seattle Railway that first built track to Vancouver along the north shore of the Columbia. The fishing people had access to the land as a usual and accustomed fishing site. There was little conflict. No one else wanted it.

As development marched upriver into the dry country, however, Lyle Point changed from land no one wanted to prime development property. As a designated urban area, Lyle was exempt from the Columbia Gorge Act restrictions that controlled development in other communities. In 1990 the railroad sold the forty-acre point to Columbia Gorge Investors Limited

Partnership, a Massachusetts company headed by Henry Spencer of Hood River, Oregon. Despite protests from the Yakama Indian Nation and the Bureau of Indian Affairs, the Klickitat County Commissioners changed the land use designation of the point from urban/industrial to community. Hiram E. Olney, the BIA's superintendent of the Yakama Indian Agency, said he feared conflicts between the new owners and the tribal fishermen, whose right to use the "usual and accustomed place" was protected by treaty. "We are opposed to any redesignation or future development which would impair access or lead to conflicts when Yakima fishermen exercise this right," he said. He asked to be notified of any plans for development of Lyle Point. The Yakama Nation also protested, adding that it had not been notified of the proposal until too late to send representatives to the public hearing on the issue.

Indians continued to fish at Lyle Point, and the land remained unchanged. Then in 1993, the Klickitat county commissioners took the first step toward approving a major development. They declared the point a place of nonsignificance under environmental and cultural listings. The Yakama Nation appealed that decision. William Yallup, manager of the Yakama cultural resources program, told Klickitat County Planning Director Francine Havercroft that the tribes and Corps of Engineers had been talking to owner Henry Spencer about buying the land for an in-lieu site. But Spencer had been elusive, he said. "One day Mr. Spencer is a willing seller and the next day he is not," Yallup wrote. In any event, the Yakama Nation objected to development.

County officials ignored the protests and approved a thirty-three-unit gated housing development complete with lots up to 1.4 acres priced at $70,000 to $280,000, tennis courts, swimming pool, sail board launch, and a sail board speed course just offshore. The plan included closing several primitive roads that cris crossed the site to the river. However, tribal fishers could continue to use a hundred-foot strip of beach, which also would be used by the windsurfers and boaters from the development.

Margaret Saluskin was unaware of either Henry Spencer's plans or the county's approval. No activist, she had been wife, mother, fisher, and preserver of fish and culture. Her only involvement in tribal or other politics had been to urge speedier development of the in-lieu sites. In 1968, while still in her teens, she had married Douglas Palmer, a fisherman from Warm Springs. They had four children. Her life was her family and the river. In 1976, the Palmers moved to the river at Lyle to stay. Douglas Palmer was among the tribal fishermen caught in the Salmonscam net in 1981. He had a Warm Springs tribal permit to catch fish for the tribe's ceremonies. Tribal rules forbid sale of salmon caught under ceremonial permits. Government agents went to Palmer and told him they knew he needed money. They offered to buy some of his fish. "We took the money," Margaret Saluskin recalls. "We didn't know it was a sting operation. They came to us. It was nice to pay our bills." But "My children's father paid the price—one year in prison." The family stayed at Lyle. Parents and sons fished from five scaffolds on Lyle Point. "When we fish like we are taught, if we are balanced in our hearts and minds, the salmon will come to us," Margaret Saluskin explains. Enough came to provide food for the family and she began supplying fish for a calendar full of events—memorials, namegivings, weddings, medicine dance ceremonies, Sunday services. All these are important occasions in the lives of the tribal people, and salmon are the centerpiece of each ceremony. Elders began asking Margaret Saluskin for fish, and she provided.

Soon after the county gave Spencer's development the go-ahead, in 1993, she saw machinery working on Lyle Point. She told her family to stay away. Unaware of the impending development, she thought the workers must be clearing the land. Dry brush on the point sometimes caught fire. However, she was soon behind in providing fish for events on her calendar. She explains her concern: "I was afraid I'd let people down. Time passed and I could see they were not going away. It was more than landscaping. I called the tribe."

The developer had begun work on the streets and utilities for his subdivision. The battle began. As Margaret Saluskin saw it, "It became an issue and struggle for the Columbia River people because it interfered with our inherited fishing rights." Tribal fishers feared that the planned road closures would eliminate their access to boat launch and fishing spots. Even at best, it would deny them access to their sacred spots; at worst, it would cover those sites with the sacrilege of houses. And they knew what usually happened when they docked their commercial fishing boats at marinas used by recreation boaters. Noisy argument was the least of it and the Indians usually lost out. It takes longer to unload a net full of salmon than it does to get half a dozen boaters aboard a motor boat. And whites are notoriously impatient, especially when they are delayed by the messy, smelly process of unloading salmon. Fastidious picnickers object to fish nets spread to dry on the beach. And conflict between the fishermen and the sailboarders already was acrimonious. The area threatened to spawn a river battle, like those near White Salmon where a sail board tourney and a special Indian fishing season conflicted. Tribal fishermen were offered a rare opportunity to fish near Washington's Spring Creek hatchery when more fish tried to return than the hatchery could handle. As soon as the offer was made, tribal fishermen eagerly set out their nets. No one had told them a sail board tournament was about to begin and no one had told the sailboarders the Indian nets would be there. Back and forth across the nets sailed the boarders. Some of the crossings were accidental. Emotional fishermen and sailboarders clashed on shore. Later, Klickitat and Skamania County officials suggested that the Indian treaties had an illegal impact on the counties' economy. Eventually, tempers cooled.

In this climate of conflict, Margaret Saluskin set out to save Lyle Point. A diminutive woman with no experience in public relations, public speaking, or leadership, she knew only that the fishing people could not lose this place so vital to their livelihood and their traditions. Her often lonely battle would become the focus of her life for the next three years. Some supporters came and went; some went in different directions. Always, Margaret Saluskin focused on the land and the fish and the culture they represent. Some support came from the Yakama Nation. Tribal Council member Joanna Meninick offered advice and communication with tribal government. Johnny Jackson, still fresh from winning his battle to stay at Underwood, was an ally. Jackson shrewdly pointed out that rare bald eagles had only recently returned to the point and that a gated subdivision would probably drive them away again. The fishing people won the backing of the Columbia Gorge Audubon Society and Greenpeace, along with a number of non-Indian "wannabes" who apparently relished setting up tepees and defying developers. Their tepee village was visible to both river travelers and motorists on Interstate 84 across the river. Publicity was plentiful. The beauty of the tepee village thrilled Margaret Saluskin. "It was the way it was supposed to be." Her allies complied with tribal elders' request that there be no banners—just the peaceful village.

The Trust for Public Lands got involved. So did the Native American Rights Fund and the American Indian Movement. The Columbia Gorge Audubon Society filed suit in state court challenging the county commissioners' decision to close the point's primitive access roads. Contending the development would violate its treaty rights, the Yakama Nation then filed suit in federal court. The Warm Springs tribes joined the Yakama suit. Margaret Saluskin, Jackson, and friends took their case to the state Capitol at Olympia. About 130 people marched on the Capitol on a chill December day in 1993. She, Jackson, and a few others met with aides to Governor Mike Lowry, but the governor took no action. A judge threw out the part of the tribes' suit challenging the road closures, saying that issue belonged in state court. The rest of the suit stayed alive and the developer and tribal attorneys began to negotiate very slowly. By then the paved roads and underground utilities were in place. There development halted. The protestors' ten tepees and their occupants remained on the point.

Nearly a year after the stalemate began, nontribal members supporting the Indians and the Klickitat County Sheriff's Department engaged in a 1960s-style confrontation at Lyle Point. The incident began when ten Indians and several dozen nontribal members marched onto the property intending to stage a religious ceremony on the private property. Deputies tried to stop them. Several dozen shouting protestors surrounded the sheriff's van. Four people were arrested. When the protestors arrived the next day, some thirty deputies and tribal police were on hand. This time, the officers arrested two dozen people, all nontribal members. The tepees stayed. Another year went by.

When the tribes and the developers reached an agreement in July of 1995, it was a victory of sorts for Margaret Saluskin. The Columbia Gorge Limited Partnership agreed to sell two of its thirty-three lots to the Corps of Engineers for an in-lieu fishing site for $260,000, and five acres outside the development to the Yakama Nation. Neither piece of land included the sacred land Margaret Saluskin had fought for. The company also agreed not to construct the planned shoreline improvements for sailboarders, to establish boat loading and unloading points for the Indian fishers, and to insure tribal access to the shore. But in return, the Indians had to agree not to camp on the site—no more tepee village. The tribes also agreed not to occupy company land, and not to invite nonmembers of the Yakama and Warm Springs tribes to enter the property. Although the agreement came in July 1995, Judge Alan A. McDonald did not sign the court order approving it until the following March.

During the campaign, Margaret Saluskin's marriage to Douglas Palmer fell apart. By the time the Yakama Nation celebrated its $365,000 purchase of Lyle Point property in June 1997, she had married a handsome Sioux lawyer, Rory Snowarrow FlintKnife, then a member of the Yakama legal staff. Margaret Saluskin rode in the lead car in the parade commemorating the purchase. A year later there was no sign of construction on Lyle Point.

Margaret Saluskin was not totally satisfied with the settlement. She believes its ban on camping and drying fish on the point violates the rights affirmed in the U.S. Supreme Court's Winans decision early in the century and upheld several times since. She is happy that an in-lieu site will be developed there, but it is not enough. She still has dreams that the tribe will buy or Spencer will donate more of the point—someday maybe all of it. Meanwhile, with the success of her campaign, she has embarked on a larger project—assuring a supply of salmon for tribal elders and needy tribal members. Until Lyle Point, she had no experience with organizations of any kind. "Lyle opened my eyes to a whole different world." Now she is writing grant proposals to create a foundation. "We want to develop this into a useful spot where we can catch fish, process them and deliver them back to the native people." She embarked on her work after smoking, canning and drying salmon for her blind mother. "Why not for all elders?" she thought. Ewatea Sin It N'Chi-wana was born.

Among other phases of her project, she tries to get intertribal fish enforcement officers to give her the salmon they confiscate from violators. She wants to prepare the salmon properly for elders' use instead of risking its quality from indifferent handling. She even hopes for a tribe-sponsored commercial cannery. Her concern and her vision extend to the dwindling salmon runs and the diminishment of the river culture. "Every time we lose an elder we lose a piece of our culture." The ever-encroaching development in the Columbia Gorge pollutes the river and its fish, and pushes the river people from their roots. She sees Lyle Point as a place where the fish, the language, the culture, and the land can be revitalized. "We are the stewards. We are the caretakers," she says.

# 13

## BLAME TO SHARE

*Great nations, like great men, keep their word.*

—Chief Justice John Marshall, 1831

If the issue were not so serious, the in-lieu sites could be likened to a Tom and Jerry cartoon. Every time the cat seems to have the mouse trapped and is ready to pounce, Jerry turns the tables and wriggles away, leaving a frustrated Tom to try again. Every time the river people seem to have the in-lieu sites within their grasp, some bit of bureaucracy pushes completion farther into the future. Much changed in the first six decades of the Indians' struggle to see a promise kept. But too much remained the same. An In-Lieu Site Task Force meeting of tribal representatives, the Corps of Engineers and the BIA in 1997 echoed meetings in 1938 and 1946 and 1955 between tribal delegates and the government. Chief Nelson Wallulatum, whose memories go back to the first promises, was there as a Warm Springs member. Agencies offered more reasons things couldn't be done now than ways to accomplish them. Jay Minthorn of Umatilla, who has served on the task force from the beginning, finally erupted: "What the hell is going on here? We're back to day one."

What indeed?

By the 1990s the tribes and the Columbia River Inter-Tribal Fish Commission could match the government fisheries biologist for fisheries biologist, archaeologist for archaeologist and environmental document for environmental document. And in some cases, tribal bureaucracy rivaled government bureaucracy. In some cases too—as with the drying sheds— the Corps had learned to listen. Instead of the government providing technical advice to the Indians, the Indians began providing technical advice to the Corps. For example, the Confederated Tribes of the Umatilla Indian Reservation contracted with the Army to provide professional services to identify and protect cultural resources. But the process of obtaining sites still seemed endless. The relatively easy first phase of work under the 1988 legislation included building the Bonneville site near the north end of Bonneville Dam on land the government had long owned. It also included refurbishing the original sites of Cascade Locks, Lone Pine and Underwood. Still, that work was not completed until January 1997, more than eight years after Congress passed legislation ordering the Corps of Engineers to fulfill its promise. Even then, not everybody was happy. Chief Johnny Jackson, who lives at Underwood, surveyed the new asphalt parking lot with disgust. "You can't dry fish on asphalt," he said. He also complained that every site but Underwood would have showers. "The women like to have showers." But a fish cleaning station with running water stands at the edge of the asphalt, and there are restrooms. There is room for little else on the tiny site.

The second phase was more difficult. It included developing the new sites on The Dalles and John Day pools and buying additional sites on the Bonneville pool. First, the Corps discovered numerous boundary problems. The legislative map delineating the sites used aerial photographs marked with a ball point pen. As a Umatilla tribal report explained it, "unfortunately, many of the sites were in error either because the [whole] site was not owned by the COE [Corps of Engineers] or the site is under water or the site includes land not owned by the COE or is otherwise not feasible to construct such as a site on a steep incline." By the time the boundary juggling was done—shrinking some sites and expanding others— the total acreage for the new sites had shrunk to around 280 acres, far short of the legislated 360. With the forty acres of the earlier sites the tribes will wind up still nearly eighty acres short of the 1939 promise. After on-the-ground inspections and negotiations with states and localities, the Indians accepted the deal anyway as the best they were likely to get.

Site boundaries were not the only issue. Points of contention emerged in seemingly endless succession. During one 1994 meeting with the Corps, a tribal representative on the In-Lieu Site Task Force scribbled: "Project from Hell." Conservative Doc Hastings replaced moderate Sid Morrison as congressman from Washington's Fourth District in 1992. When Benton County commissioners "discovered" in 1995—four years after a public hearing in their county—that two sites would impinge on public riverside parks, Hastings threatened to reopen the whole issue. He proposed legislation to build new fishing parks for non-Indians displaced for Indian access and to make all the Indian sites joint use with the recreation fishermen. Recreation fishermen, angry at potential loss of some access to the river, argued that the in-lieu sites should be open to all fishermen. Jerry Meninick, vice chairman of the Yakama Tribal Council, notes wryly that the non-Indians think this is a fine idea when it refers to in-lieu sites. But they object strongly when joint use is suggested for Doug's Beach, a popular sailboarding spot on the Washington shore, or Crates Point, a recreation boat launch on the Oregon river bank. Separating Indian fishing and recreation was, of course, a major premise of the 1988 law. Hastings' proposal died.

The City of Boardman snatched one site in 1996, winning title to the unused portion of Boardman Marine Park, where the Corps had promised to put one of the Indians' access sites. Boardman's park district had leased the land from the Corps but negotiated a purchase, pushing the tribes to accept expansion of the nearby Faler Road access site as a replacement. Even before title to the property had been transferred, the city started developing a windsurfing park on the land that was to have been an Indian site. The Faler Road site includes part of the original Boardman, including remnants of the asphalt highway that ran through the town. There were other conflicts, some settled amicably. But there remained examples of the indifference to Indian treaty rights and antagonism toward Indian fishers that marked the in-lieu site issue from its beginning in the 1930s. Problems that were no obstacle to development of non-Indian facilities suddenly became obstacles to development for the Indians. Washington's State Parks and Recreation Commission agreed to a site next to Maryhill State Park. Like the park, the proposed site was on land the state leased from the Corps. The commission was a little more prickly about a site adjacent to its Crow Butte State Park upstream, agreeing to a changed location but hedging on sharing utilities. Speaking for the commission in a letter to the Corps in April 1995, David W. Heiser, environmental programs manager, wrote, "As to the conversion of other public-managed recreation sites being converted to Indian fishing sites, we have substantial reservations. It is our staff position that any existing recreational sites taken for sole use by Native Americans must be replaced (mitigated). To do less is to deprive non-Indians of an existing use area in a location that is already substantially lacking in water access facilities." Klickitat County objected to a fish cleaning area at the Roosevelt site on grounds it would overload the local sewer system. But Fred Ike, a Yakama member of the In-Lieu Site Task Force, points out that just over the edge of the bluff, the county created a massive regional landfill to collect garbage that eventually will send seepage into the river.

Several of the sites designated in the legislation included pieces of railroad right of way, where the Corps could not build Indian fishing facilities. In one case, Avery on the Washington shore at river mile 197, the Corps recommended expanding the site to include some land under water. Its rationale: when The Dalles pool is at its lowest operating level the tribal fishers can still reach the river from the site. The Corps planned to replace the existing boat ramp. Railroad right-of-way posed another problem. There is no question that the tribal fishermen have the right to cross the rails and railroad land to reach their fishing sites. But there is a question whether that right extends to the BIA to maintain the sites. Pine Creek can be reached only by crossing the railroad tracks and the BIA balked at accepting that site from the Corps until the access issue was settled. Finding practical sites for boat launching was one of the trickier problems. The engineers found, as they had forty years earlier, that a boat ramp was not feasible at Cascade Locks. Instead, to satisfy the legislation and the Indians' needs, a dock was built near the site. Dredging at the silted Wind River site made a new boat ramp there environmentally and financially impractical. Instead, a boat ramp and dock were planned for an added Wind River site across the river from the old little-used location, which would have new camping facilities built.

Despite the obstacles, in 1997, the Corps was ready to turn some sites and more than $1 million for the maintenance fund over to the BIA. But the Indian agency discovered it had neglected to get authority to invest the money in Treasury bonds as provided in its 1995 agreement with the Corps. The agency had to go back to Congress. The interest from the investment was to pay for maintenance of the sites; so caretaking work was delayed while the agencies tried to arrange the needed authority. They believed they had it resolved, but federal budget officials disagreed. Even so, not to be outdone by the Corps' extensive planning efforts, BIA hired a facilities director, built a maintenance building, and began drawing plans for equipment and a staff to keep the sites neat and clean. Attorney Laurie Jordan of CRITFC suggested quietly that it would be a lot less expensive to contract, probably with tribal members, to empty the garbage and clean the toilets. Tribal delegates seemed to support Jordan's idea. They feared the money would go to building and overhead with nothing left for paying the water and electric bills, repairing the plumbing, and doing the cleaning.

The Corps said the completed sites were no longer its responsibility. BIA said it hadn't accepted them yet. Fishermen used them, but no one was in charge and the electricity was turned off. Nearly a decade after the 1988 legislation, the BIA was just drawing up regulations for use of the sites. It avoided the issue for years, partly because it didn't want to get involved in inter- and intratribal disputes over whether permanent residences should be allowed on some sites. Also, BIA officials claimed, the tribes were slow to respond to its initial requests for suggestions. Both BIA and tribes got down to serious work on the rules in early 1996. One of the thornier issues was law enforcement. Would tribal police, the Columbia River Inter-Tribal Fish Commission, or state police be responsible? By mid-1998, there were still no rules and no decisions. Jay Minthorn commented disgustedly, "BIA hasn't done a darn thing . . . . They knew eight years ago they had to do this."

Handling of cultural and historic materials came up again. At a 1997 task force meeting Corps archaeologist Michael Martin complained that the tribes had delayed a memorandum of agreement on material found on the sites. He had, he said, sent a proposed document to the tribes. At this point Yakama's Joanna Meninick pointed out that some things have changed in sixty years. Now, she said, the tribes write the memoranda "and see if you sign."

Meninick's comment highlighted changes in the tribes' political, governmental and social position in the six decades since Bonneville Dam flooded the initial two dozen fishing sites. In the 1930s, the tribes were almost entirely dependent on the whims of the BIA officials who managed their reservations. Compensation for confiscated resources, such as the fishing places, was based almost entirely on whatever good will or guilt the government officials involved might feel. But in 1998, the tribes had the support of federal laws defining their rights, strong tribal governments, well-educated spokesmen, the ear of several influential members of Congress, and the services of some of the sharpest lawyers in the region. No longer supplicants, they dealt with governments from local to federal levels on a near-equal basis. The tribes also had learned—in most cases—to present a united front to the government. In the 1940s, each issue, when the Indians got a voice at all, went to each tribe separately. Now, they might still have their disagreements, but they could work together in CRITFC or the In-Lieu Site Task Force to reach consensus before confronting the government.

Another thing that changed in the sixty years between promise and progress is cost. The Corps could have spent $50,000 in 1945 and settled the whole issue. By 1995 the agency estimated project costs at more than $67 million, a whole lot more even if inflation over sixty years is taken into account. The Indians see that figure as a fraction of the subsidies the dams have provided to aluminum and pulp mills with low cost electricity, to farmers with cheap irrigation, to barge operators with locks at each dam, and to recreation boaters and fishers with free public parks and boat launches. And they are quick to point out that the mills and farms pour thousands of tons of pollutants into the river. The industrial and recreation users have changed the quality of the river water, affecting more than the fish. "I used to drink out of the river," says fisherman Randy Settler. "Now, the grime on the nets, I don't touch it."

In short, both the tribes and the government are dealing with a different world from the 1930s. When the government built Bonneville Dam, the Northwest was mostly sparsely-populated farming country outside the major cities. There was little industry. The Dalles, Oregon, for example, the largest city on the Bonneville pool, had 6,266 people in 1940; today its population is 11,325. Then, there was a serious question about whether there would be a use for all the electricity Bonneville and Grand Coulee dams would produce. Today, with more than a dozen additional dams on the Columbia River and its tributaries, power production barely keeps pace with consumption. Those rivers power much of the nation's aluminum and paper production. A booming electronics industry and recreation feed an ever-growing population. Where riverfront land was considered of little value in 1940 because it could not be farmed, it now brings premium prices as homesites and river access. Native Americans, who number only 145,000, are easily overlooked among the 8.8 million people in Oregon and Washington.

On the river itself, the biggest change in sixty years, of course, is the still-shrinking number of fish. By the time the 1988 legislation passed, salmon runs had declined on the Columbia for a second consecutive year. By 1990, the runs were little more than half their 1986 levels. By 1992, when the National Marine Fisheries Service listed three species of Columbia River salmon for Endangered Species Act protection, the Indians had long since abandoned their spring and summer chinook commercial seasons. They confined themselves to fishing those runs for ceremonial and personal subsistence use. Their only remaining commercial season was fall chinook, which included a threatened Snake River run. The 1994 spring chinook run was so small the tribes took barely enough to supply the first food ceremonies in their longhouses. In Indian country, environmental disaster curtails religious freedom. Restoring the fish, long a tribal priority, acquired new urgency. Tribes and the Columbia River Inter-Tribal Fish Commission were deeply involved in regional efforts to improve the runs. Frequently, the tribes found themselves at odds with most of the others at the fish planning table. The Indians focused on the fish; other political entities, mindful of the agriculture, transportation, and industrial users of the river, sought ways to increase fish runs without disturbing the dams. Tribes and environmental groups would seem to be natural allies in the save the salmon campaign, and to some extent they were. However, advocates for purely wild fish, such as Trout Unlimited, argued for an end to hatcheries on grounds hatchery fish weaken the wild strains. Tribes fought for their experimental hatchery programs, using first generation hatchery fish to supplement natural spawners. The states, which had advocated hatcheries for a century, began to look at the biological effects as well as pure numbers of fish. The squabbling with state fish agencies, the National Marine Fisheries Service, Pacific Northwest Power Planning Council, Pacific Fishery Management Council, and Pacific Salmon Commission spread tribal resources thin. And in 1997, the Power Planning Council, which doles out federal money for fish restoration, drastically reduced its funding for Indian fisheries programs. There has never been a specific allocation of salmon catches between ocean fisheries and river fisheries, nor has there been serious control of salmon taken as so-called "by catch" in ocean nets aimed at other fish. So ocean factory-style fishers continue to take Columbia River salmon. In the late 1990s, El Niño weather conditions further damaged the dwindling Columbia runs. El Niño is a wind and current shift that warms the North Pacific Ocean and creates a hostile climate for the cold-water salmon.

Continuing decline of the salmon exacerbated conflicts between Indian and non-Indian fishermen. More and more recreation fishers and boaters and sailboarders crowded along the shore and onto public docks. Indians would arrive at places where they had camped their entire lives to find the spot occupied by a sailboarder. "When the economic boom hit the Gorge is when the fighting started," observes Jay Minthorn, a Umatilla member of the In-Lieu Site Task Force. There were conflicts with sailboard races and fishing tournaments. Separate Indian sites were clearly needed to keep peace on the river.

Ironies abound in the site development. Nowhere is the contrast between treatment of the Native Americans and treatment of the new Americans more evident than at Celilo. This most historic of the Indian fishing sites lies ten miles east of The Dalles Dam. Indians had lived and fished at Celilo Falls from time immemorial. First the railroad, then the highway narrowed the Indians' land base. As white efforts to push Indians from the river shore accelerated, the government in 1927 put seven and a half acres of government land where the Indians lived into trust as a permanent Indian village. Later a "new" village was created south of the highway and railroad. The Dalles Dam, of course, drowned Celilo Falls and the "old" Celilo Village on the river shore. The unflooded area next to the old village, where Indians once camped for much of the year, is a well-kept Corps of Engineers park that stretches half a mile along the south bank of The Dalles Dam pool—which the Corps named Celilo Lake. Residents of the mostly dilapidated houses at Celilo Village, where the sewer system is broken and the water quality is suspect, look across the tracks and Interstate-84 to a park planted with grass and shade trees. There are picnic tables and concrete block restrooms, a camping area and a boat ramp. All this was built during the years the Corps could not find in-lieu sites to fulfill its 1939 promise to the Indians. Sixty years after the promise—forty-three years after Celilo Falls disappeared—the Corps began developing seven and a half acres just east of its Celilo Park as a treaty access site for the Indian fishers displaced so many decades ago. It will have a boat ramp and dock like its public counterpart/neighbor. There will be a camping area, a new well, toilets, and showers. And it will have fish cleaning and net repair stations and drying sheds built to Indian specifications. It will even have pretty plantings like its public neighbor. So why didn't the Indians get to keep a piece of their original village and have this site sooner? For one, this is on The Dalles pool, not Bonneville pool where the original agreement was struck. For another, the Indian fishers were too devastated by the loss of Celilo to want to remain there. They did not ask for the site. If they had, it was unlikely they would have gotten it. The Corps wanted the public park, and politics was not on the side of the Indians. In more recent years some Indian fishermen have launched their boats from the public area. As elsewhere, that has sometimes led to conflict with the hundreds of recreation fishers who swarm to the park from spring through fall.

Seven miles upstream on the Washington shore Maryhill State Park covers part of an ancient Indian village site. The Corps will build another of the new Indian access sites on ten acres next to the state park. Several of the new sites will have no development. They are too small for camping, the soil is too rocky to install toilets, and the adjacent water too shallow for boat launches. In 1968, after John Day Dam was completed, *The Oregonian* trumpeted: Corps Offers 75 Miles of Recreation. The accompanying news story described potential park sites on both sides of the river between John Day and McNary dams. The Corps wanted to build parks, then lease them to other agencies to operate. On that promise, the Corps was as good as its word. Washington has five riverfront parks between John Day and McNary dams. Oregon has four, counting a recreation area at John Day Dam. Between John Day and Bonneville there are six more parks in Oregon and four in Washington. That does not count city or county park-marinas in Hood River, The Dalles, Arlington, Irrigon, and Umatilla in Oregon and Bingen in Washington, plus an undeveloped sail board launch site and a newly acquired state park in Washington. That makes twenty-seven parks, an average of a park every ten miles on both sides of the river, all developed after the Corps' promised six sites to Indian fishers. Corps operated or leased parks alone total 952 acres, more than double the land it couldn't find for the Indian fishers. "I imagine if the shoe were on the other foot the government would send us a letter every day demanding payment," says Jerry Meninick, the Yakama vice chairman, who also is a former disk jockey and radio advertising salesman.

While the seemingly interminable process dragged on, the permanent Indian and Corps members of the task force established a mostly cordial relationship despite an occasional flare-up. George Miller, the civilian project officer, won the respect of most of the tribal leaders he works with. They give him credit for doing all he can to keep the Corps moving. They recognize that he has to deal with people in Washington who could not care less, explains Zane Jackson, who has served more than a quarter of a century on the Warm Springs Tribal Council.

Although fish numbers continue to fall and tribal members are moving more into other occupations, the sites remain important to all tribal members. The people who use the sites supply the salmon that remain vital to the tribes both as the center of religious ceremonies and a source of food. The issue has never been dormant so far as the tribes were concerned. Fish committees have dogged the issue, and a consistent item on tribal council agendas at frequent intervals has been a report on the in-lieu sites. The Indians speak in the long term—in generations. They remember grandparents or parents who were promised homes and electricity, and lament children whose fishing opportunities are severely limited. They owe allegiance to the seven generations that preceded them and work for the benefit of the seven generations that will come after them.

Five days a week Frank Gunnier works at an 8 to 5 job on the Yakama Indian Reservation. On the sixth and seventh day—when the salmon are running—he fishes. Gunnier is an example of the way Northwest tribal people have retained their traditions while adapting white technology. Gunnier makes his own dip nets. His grandfather used hemp, then switched to monofilament when that came along in the 1920s. Gunnier uses fine wire. While the net material is modern, the needles he uses to sew them are made from "seven" bark. Gunnier knows no other name for it. His father, Robert Gunnier, showed him the plant and taught him how to make the needles and sew the nets using different size needles for different size mesh. On spring nights the two Gunniers, father and son, stand at their fishing station near the mouth of the John Day River waiting for the salmon as countless others have done since long before Lewis and Clark floated past vibrant communities here. Frank Gunnier has a son. He will teach the boy to fish and to make nets as soon as he is old enough.

Jay Minthorn of Umatilla looks at the years of conflict and effort and sighs. "It should have been easy. But with the tribes nothing is simple." Later, he asks, "Why is it so hard for us?"

The reasons are many. All are probably rooted in a basic attitude of the European Americans who created the United States. Convinced that theirs was a superior culture, they assumed that everyone coming to the country would want to be like them, to be absorbed in the united whole—the melting pot idea. They assumed the same thing about the Native Americans. In addition, because the Indians were "heathens," that is, non-Christian, the newcomers believed the Native Americans should either be converted or eliminated. If the tribes had resources the newcomers wanted, elimination was preferable. To the European-Americans, farming was the proper use for land, once any trees had been removed for lumber. Because most of the Indians did not farm but used their land for hunting and gathering, the newcomers felt justified in taking the lands so that the country could be properly utilized. But the Native Americans had been here for millennia. Taking what they needed from their environment, they had created a lifestyle they found perfectly satisfactory. They lived with a continuing cycle of seasons, accepting some change if it came but not seeking it. European Americans built their lives on "progress," constant change that they believed made an increasingly better life. The Indians in the mid-1800s thought they had made a bargain that would allow them to keep their way of life while adapting what was useful from the newcomers. The fact that they wanted to retain their culture and their way of life both baffled and infuriated the European Americans and continues to do so. Lacking knowledge of history, the region's non-Indians see no reasons the Native Americans shouldn't shed their culture and assimilate into the melting pot. Those non-Indians who know about the treaties often consider them outdated. With those prevailing attitudes, keeping a promise made to comply with a treaty does not seem terribly important. People who would be chagrined if the United States broke a treaty with England, brush off treaties with Indian tribes as unimportant, although both were negotiated and signed with the same procedures, and both call on the integrity of the nation.

Some of the Indian people believe that the delays and broken promises are part of a concerted effort by the government to remove them from the Columbia River. However, Howard Arnett, an attorney for the Warm Springs, believes, "That attributes more forethought than the agencies are capable of." His view is that the problem was just so low on the Corps' priority list that the agency was not going to do anything unless Congress ordered it. "There was no way the Indians could make them do anything. They could always say they had no authority." The Corps did just that; frequently its officers said they lacked authority or funds or both. The tribes found the Corps so intractable that Arnett believes they probably would have found the whole process easier if they had been able to deal with the Fish and Wildlife Service or some other agency.

Even so, in the early years after World War II, the Corps appeared to make real efforts to keep its promise. However, it never explained why it committed as an in-lieu site a chunk of land that was destined to be a footing for The Dalles Dam, and it never suggested going beyond the Bonneville pool to look for sites. By the late 1950s, the Corps was trying to disentangle itself from the project. Corps employees explain that the sites did not fit the Army's categories of projects. They did not make up a big project like those the Corps usually does. The agency knew it had not fulfilled its obligation, but did not want to deal with that fact. Corps employees say there was a reluctance to admit it failed to carry out a mandate. The intense opposition by the states and non-Indian fishers to Indian fishing and new sites certainly made it easier for the Corps to let the problem fade. For most of those decades the tribes had only a few friends in Congress, while state officials and fishing interests had powerful political voices. With no one to push the Indians' case, there was no penalty for the Corps in avoiding the issue. And with its regular turnover of district and division commanders, it was easy for the Corps simply to forget the whole thing.

Tim Weaver, the Yakama attorney, faults the BIA. "The BIA probably has a lot of blame for not pushing the Corps. It was an administrative headache for them . . . . They didn't know how to deal with the sites." In the beginning "there were a number of years of benign neglect" on the part of BIA. The agency saw the sites as a budgetary issue; it was under funded and didn't want more headaches. According to its own records, BIA at best was only an on-and-off advocate for the sites. At times, especially the termination period of the 1950s and 1960s, it sabotaged the program. The rest of the time BIA was either preoccupied with other issues or impotent. Arnett explained much when he shrugged off BIA's 1997 failure to get authority to invest the money it received from the Corps. "It's just the Bureau. It can't get its act together."

Catherine Vandemoer, the water rights specialist in the office of the assistant interior secretary for Indian affairs, believes that doing nothing worked for both the Corps and BIA. "It was typical of things [in Indian country] before the 1980s . . . . The previous standard of business in Indian country was do nothing." Increasing sophistication of tribal governments in the 1980s gave them an increased voice. They had their own Ph.D.s, biologists, and engineers on staff, enabling them to respond to attacks and inquiries. They also have their own lobbyists in Washington, D.C. But Vandemoer notes that throughout the in-lieu site project, including today, the tribes clearly have limited resources and must focus on the most important issues. In the 1950s, it was the threat of terminating the tribe-federal tie. Through the 1960s, 1970s and 1980s it was, for Northwest tribes, protecting their treaty fishing rights. Now, it is restoring the fish runs.

William H. Burke, a Umatilla tribal official, explains the long delay in promise-keeping this way: "It is like a renter who is in arrears in his rent and will do anything to get away from paying." The landlords are the Indian people and government represents the newcomers who took the land and are more than a century behind in their rent.

Congress should share the blame. It authorized the Corps to replace the sites, but did not give it a specific appropriation, leaving the Corps to pull money from other projects more compatible with Army experience. Never, before 1988, did it demand an accounting from the Army for its progress in meeting its obligation or use of money appropriated in the 1960s and 1970s. Had a program for any other purpose been so shamefully delayed, Congress would have demanded an investigation and chastised Administration officials. There were no penalties for either Corps or BIA officials who ignored the in-lieu sites.

Although the delays were not over in 1998, prospects for completing the sites looked more promising. Miller of the Corps says one intangible result of the long process has been new understanding between the Corps and the tribes, the Corps and communities, and the tribes and communities. Jay Minthorn echoes Miller's assessment. He had spent more than half his twelve years on the Umatilla Board of Trustees tied up in site issues, mostly "butting heads with the Army." He adds, "I never thought I'd be sitting with the Corps, complimenting them instead of being at war . . . . There's been a big changeover . . . . It's a lot better."

As relations with the Corps of Engineers improved and acquisition of the long sought sites came nearer, an old threat to all the tribes arose, and the Yakama grew apprehensive again about the tribes' relations with the state of Washington. The old threat was Senator Slade Gorton. This time the career Indian fighter was making a direct attack on tribal sovereignty. Tribal governments, like state governments, are immune from lawsuits unless they agree to be sued. Gorton was pushing a bill to strip them of that government status. Gorton also used his position as chairman of the Interior subcommittee of the Appropriations Committee to reduce and redirect money for Indian programs. The tribes call his actions "termination by appropriation." If Congress goes along with Gorton, especially on the sovereign immunity issue, tribal leaders see it as an abrogation of their treaties. Asked Nathan Jim Sr. of Warm Springs, "Will he give back the land?" The tribes gave up their land in exchange for retaining their own societies on their reservations, and their hunting, fishing, and gathering rights off the reservations. If the government takes the rights it guaranteed, doesn't that mean the deal is off and the tribes get their land back? And if the government abrogates its Indian treaties—as the courts say Congress has a right to do—what does that say about the United States' word in international treaties? Chief Justice John Marshall said, in ruling on a case involving the Cherokee Nation in 1831, "Great nations, like great men, keep their word."

Gorton is recognized as an implacable enemy. Washington state's relations with tribes, long venomous, had become almost amicable under the governorship of Booth Gardner in the late 1980s and remained so under Mike Lowry, who took office in 1993. However, the Legislature forced a change in state fish and wildlife management, giving the Fish and Wildlife Commission, not the governor, authority to appoint the department director. The effects were not immediately felt in fishing. But for the first time in memory of the tribe's longtime attorney, Tim Weaver, state agents came onto the Yakama Reservation in 1997 and arrested a nontribal member for hunting under a tribal permit. The state had long recognized the tribe's game management, including licensing a few nontribal members to hunt on the reservation. Tribal officials feared the war with the state was beginning again.

If it was, the Yakama would be in court again, although as courts have grown more conservative in recent years the tribes have grown reluctant to place their treaties on the line. Tribal leaders prefer, where possible, to work things out. But if they found their rights constrained, they would be back. After all, the tribal people have survived a century and a half of changing policies designed to isolate them, destroy their culture, and eliminate them as a people. They are tenacious and they are patient. They have kept reminding the government that it made a promise sixty years ago. Chief Wallulatum has been involved for more than fifty of his seventy-three years, and his family's efforts to sustain the fisheries go much further back in time. "We always had someone talking about it," he says. "They were always opposing things like fish wheels. They didn't give up." Neither did Wallulatum and his generation of tribal leaders, nor will the new generation of tribal leaders.

"I wish the United States of America would simply keep its word, fulfill its promises, and give back to the Indian people what is rightfully theirs," says Ted Strong. Or, as an earlier Yakama leader, Chief Kamiaken, phrased it at the treaty talks in 1855, "Let them do as they have promised."

# EPILOGUE

The epilogue to the first edition of this book began with these words:

"The U.S. Army Corps of Engineers completed the first of its massive Columbia River dams, Bonneville, in just five years. The Bureau of Reclamation built Grand Coulee, then the biggest concrete project on Earth, in eight. Eleven years have passed since the United States renewed its promise to replace the fishing sites taken from Columbia River Indians in the 1930s. But the Corps of Engineers is not quite half way to fulfilling that 1988 commitment."

When I wrote those words, at the end of 1999, fifteen of the treaty-fishing access sites were finished or under construction; six were scheduled for construction in 2000. George J. Miller, the Corps' project manager, estimated that the ten remaining treaty-fishing access sites would be completed in 2004—or later, depending on congressional appropriations. Seven years later, the twenty-ninth of the thirty-one sites was on track for completion by September 30, 2006, and the Corps was close to acquiring the final two sites. In the meantime, the project had added a major new component, reconstruction of the Celilo Indian Village. Much sounded familiar in 2006, but much had changed in the previous half-dozen years.

Issues that plagued the project from the 1940s remain contentious and unresolved. Some of the fishing people continue to insist that the project also should include housing for Indian families displaced from river villages in the 1930s, 1950s, and 1960s as dam construction moved upstream. Restoring the salmon runs remains central to the long-running controversy over management of the Columbia and its tributaries. Other disputes, mostly minor in the larger context, have popped up over management, maintenance, and use of the sites. Even the aftermath of 9/11 affected the fishing sites. A number of the fishing platforms at the Lone Pine site are on the grounds of The Dalles Dam. After the World Trade Center and Pentagon attacks in 2001, access to the area around all the Columbia River dams was tightly restricted. At first, Corps personnel escorted the fishers to their platforms; later, the agency issued them card keys to open gates to the fishing areas.

However, there have been more positive developments than negative. Indian fishers are using the sites and, for the most part, find them suited to their needs. Maintenance improved markedly after the Columbia River Inter-tribal Fish Commission took over the work in 2003; as a bonus from that change, the maintenance jobs, including benefits, went to river people. The tribes have recorded some successes in supplementing the natural fish runs with their hatcheries, and they have done much work toward improving fish habitat on tributaries. The sharing of a few sites with non-Indians has benefitted the general public, apparently dampening some of the early public opposition to the treaty site program. As the fish commission and individual tribes have gained scientific expertise, other river interests listen to Indian concerns with more respect.

Tribal leaders appear optimistic both that their sites will be completed and that the fish will be back in numbers large enough for more extended fishing seasons. As he had noted seven years earlier, Jay Minthorn of the Umatilla Board of Trustees said, "We are patient people."

Miller, who began working on the fishing sites soon after Congress passed the 1988 legislation, hopes to finish the work, including Celilo Village, before he retires, in about 2013. In 2006 the target date was 2012. Miller was right in his 1999 prediction that the level of appropriations would affect the work schedule. Although Congress initially authorized spending $67 million for the construction, the actual funding was subject to annual appropriations. During one period Congress severely reduced the Corps' money for civilian work and removed its authority to reprogram funds from one project to another, slowing work on the treaty sites. With the fishing-site work almost completed in mid-2006 the Corps had spent $65 million, $2 million under its budget. Restoration of Celilo Village, with funding authorized separately, will add an estimated $12 million to $13 million and several years to the project.

In addition to lagging appropriations, finding land to fulfill the commitment to add two sites on the pool behind Bonneville Dam delayed the program. The Corps was confined to using surplus federal property or land purchased from a willing seller. There was plenty of federal land along The Dalles and John Day dam pools although finding a site that met the Indians' needs was not always easy. However, much of the shore of the Bonneville pool was in private hands and the demand for property after creation of the Columbia River Gorge National Scenic Area in 1987 put most potential sites on the Bonneville pool out of reach of the Treaty Access Fishing Site program. What was available wasn't suitable, Miller said. The acquisition budget of $2 million was stretched to the limit and finally doubled to $4 million.

Eventually, in 2006 the Corps, Union Pacific Railroad, and the state of Oregon agreed on a 25-acre site at Wyeth about 10 miles east of Bonneville Dam. The railroad no longer needed the land to creosote ties for its track. The state had long wanted the area for a park. The people of Cascade Locks had once suggested a nearby Wyeth site to the Corps in an effort to prevent the Army from building a site in their town, but the engineers had considered it so unsuitable they did not bother showing it to the Indians. For the new site there is to be a three-way transaction; the state will buy the land from UP and the Corps will buy a portion of it from the state. The new site lies between Interstate 84 and the river at an interchange leading to the community of Wyeth south of the freeway. The Corps plans to extend the interchange with a road north to the river, including a bridge over the railroad, the UP's main line. Once across the bridge, the road will divide, one branch leading to the treaty-fishing site, the other to a state park. Wyeth was the second site obtained for the Indians with cooperation from the state of Oregon. The Stanley Rock site 9 miles east of Hood River was acquired from the state and completed in 1999 on a piece of unused land adjacent to a state highway rest area, which remained in public use.

There are two possibilities for the final site, both on the Washington shore. When those last two sites are finished, the Corps still will fall 60 acres short of the 400 acres it promised the Indians in 1939. "We are looking for surplus land," Miller said. Any additional land would not be developed but could be places for fishers to camp during the fishing season and possibly to dry or smoke their fish. If the Indians who claim that they are still owed housing near the river win their point, those areas could provide home sites.

Although the acquisition and construction generally went smoothly after the initial public opposition, there have been some problems. Wind River, one of the five original in-lieu sites, was improved but siltation became so severe the boat ramp was unusable. Because dredging in the sensitive tributary estuary would damage the fish habitat, the Corps declined to keep the channel open and the site became usable only for seasonal camping. At the Celilo site, built on the shore of The Dalles Dam pool that drowned the ancient Celilo Village, construction crews did much of the needed

digging by hand to avoid disturbing cultural resources. At the Maryhill
site, contamination remaining from construction of the Highway 97 bridge
across the Columbia decades earlier required abatement.

The two treaty sites in the town of White Salmon, population 2,200,
on the Washington shore initially drew opposition from city officials.
They complained that the first site would take too much of its waterfront.
"The reality was, there was a willing seller," Miller said. The site, between
Burlington Northern Santa Fe Railroad tracks and the river, was developed,
but safety concerns grew when fish buyers crossed the tracks during the brief
commercial fishing seasons. The Indian fishers had asked earlier for a place
where they could process their fish. So the Corps acquired a second site at
White Salmon with plans to build an 80- by 100-foot facility on the 8 acres.
Town officials objected on grounds the Indian facility might interfere with
planned expansion of the city's nearby waste-treatment plant, inhibiting
the town's potential for growth. The city, tribes, and Corps negotiated an
agreement that put the Indian funds for waste treatment into the city's
expanded facility. The Indian plant got a higher level of waste treatment and
the city got the money it needed to expand its facility. By midyear 2006 the
blast freezer (for quick-freezing fish), refrigeration, freezer, and an ice maker
capable of producing 10 tons a day were in place. The new plant is part of an
aggressive effort by the fishing people to increase the value of their fish and
to intensify their marketing during the commercial seasons. As part of that
effort CRITFC is developing a safety code for fish handling and conducted
classes on marketing and the safe handling of fish. The commission published
a brochure outlining when and where the public can buy freshly caught
salmon along the river. Another project developed speciality fish products.
The new facility adds the possibility of selling frozen fish and may provide
custom processing for non-Indian fishers. Jon Matthews, who oversees the
project for CRITFC, said the plant will probably employ fifteen to twenty-
five people on a seasonal basis. Fishers along the river say the facility will
add value to their catch. The Bureau of Indian Affairs and the tribes will
operate and maintain the commercial facility.

The other treaty-access sites and the original in-lieu sites—except those
shared with the general public—are managed by the fish commission under
a contract with the BIA. The maintenance crew includes one member from
each of the four treaty tribes and a supervisor, who is Nez Perce. The crews
clean the restroom facilities, dump the trash and garbage, and maintain
landscaping. The issue of site management almost derailed the entire

project in the 1990s. The legislation called for the Corps to refurbish the five original in-lieu sites and construct the new treaty-fishing access sites, then turn them over to the BIA. The Corps, however, wanted assurance that the sites would not be allowed to deteriorate as the original sites had. The BIA had no guarantee of additional appropriations for maintenance work and wanted the Corps to provide the funds. The impasse resulted in a year-long delay in work on the sites. In 1995, the agencies agreed that the Corps would provide about $6.3 million to be invested with the interest used to finance the maintenance. Then the BIA ran into technical problems blocking its ability to make investments. The program was finally rescued when the tribes and intertribal fish commission agreed on a plan for the commission to contract with BIA to invest the funds and handle the management. The commission estimated the investment income will sustain the program for up to fifteen years. The funding issue was resolved in 2003 and the council took over the BIA's maintenance building near Lone Pine in January 2004.

The commission also handles fisheries enforcement on the river for the BIA under contract and suggested that it also could provide law enforcement on the sites under an addition to the contract. The BIA rejected the suggestion because it lacked money. Instead, the BIA assigned two of its law enforcement officers on a part-time basis, but the fish commission considered that inadequate. Yakama tribal fish and wildlife officers add some law enforcement presence by visiting the sites on the Washington shore. The chairman of the Yakama Tribal Council, Lavina Washines, complained that the BIA and CRITFC officers harass the fishers rather than protecting them. Others see evidence of drug activity and civil disturbances on the sites that could be curtailed with more law enforcement officers. However, despite concerns after a couple of incidents of vandalism when the first sites were new, fishers contacted along the river said they see few problems except for an occasional "rowdy bunch," some Indian, some non-Indian.

Under court order, families still live on the Underwood, Lone Pine, and Cook's Landing sites. Chief Johnny Jackson remains at Underwood and children of David and Myra Sohappy are still at Cook's. The Cascade Locks site also has at least one family in semipermanent residence. The Oatman family home is collapsible, so it could not be designated a permanent residence, explains Emily Oatman. The family—Emily, who is Nez Perce and Umatilla; husband Johnny, who is Nez Perce; and at least some of their three grown children—lives at the site except for a couple of weeks each winter.

Emily Oatman supplements the landscaping by planting a few flowers and arborvitae, watering the grass, and cutting weeds when the maintenance crew fails to do so. Except for the weeds, she thinks the maintenance crews do a good job keeping the site clean. Her only other complaint is the lack of electricity and water hookups at the individual camp sites, with the only lights outdoors and in the rest rooms. The Oatmans have their own generator, as do many of the fishing people camping on a seasonal basis. Across the river at the Fort Raines site, Yakama tribal member Ernie Sutterlict has a similar complaint about the lack of electricity. He uses butane to light his campsite and a five-gallon propane tank to smoke his fish. The fishers have also installed a wood stove in the site's community fireplace to provide heat against the cold winds that frequently whip the Columbia Gorge.

Perhaps the biggest disappointment for the Oatman family is that Indians can no longer make a living as full-time fishers. The Oatman sons, both in their twenties, fish when the season is open and for subsistence but also hold jobs at a Cascade Locks restaurant. Tribal fishers have not been able to make a living for more than thirty years, said Washines, who became chairman of the Yakama Nation Tribal Council in the spring of 2006. "The love of fishing keeps us coming to the water."

Farther up the river, at some of the new sites, fishers from Warm Springs and Yakama said they were pleased with the sites and praised the Corps for its work—although they said it would have been far better to have had them six decades earlier, when they were promised. Virgil Culps, a Warm Springs tribal member who was fishing from the Crow Butte site during a rare spring commercial season, said, "According to the resolutions and agreement I think they've done an excellent job. It's unfortunate it took so long." Culps, a fisher for thirty-five years, said before the treaty site was available there were occasional conflicts with non-Indian fishers at public boat launches. The treaty site eliminated that problem, along with providing better river access and showers for the fishing families. "It [the site] works very well," he said. "I'd say they [the Corps] have done about 90 percent of what they said they would."

At Maryhill, where the treaty site is adjacent to a Washington state park, Virgil Lewis, former vice chairman of the Yakama Tribal Council, also had praise for the site. Lewis, who has been fishing since childhood, said, "Here is a place for our fishermen where they will not be hassled." He and veteran fisher Tony Washines, a former chairman of the Yakama General Council, said the new sites provide needed protection for the fishers' equipment, allowing them to leave nets and boats during the seasons. Washines was chairman of the Yakama Fish and Wildlife Committee during negotiations over the sites after the 1988 legislation. He said he believes the Corps has made an earnest attempt to fulfill its commitment. "The sites have made it possible for a lot of people to engage in their cultural activity," he said.

Residences on the sites remain controversial, supported by some tribal fishers and opposed by others. At the least, they put a strain on sewer and water facilities. When the city of The Dalles expanded its water and sewer systems to serve State Police and transportation buildings at the edge of town, it made it possible to take those systems to the nearby Lone Pine site as part of the refurbishing of the original in-lieu sites. Cook's and Underwood presented more problems. "These are not suitable living sites," Miller said. "We have no ability to improve them." Both are almost entirely rock with little or no soil, making them "impossible for water and sewer facilities."

One place where housing is to be part of the project is Celilo Village. Both the residents of the village and the tribes have long sought to revive the tumbledown enclave that replaced the ancient Indian village at Celilo Falls, the most famous of the fishing places drowned by Columbia River dams. The 1988 legislation included no mention of Celilo. The Corps people in Portland were willing to add restoration of Celilo to the fishing site project but could not do so without authorization from Congress. Nevertheless, they developed a plan for replacing the substandard housing and rebuilding the crumbling water and sewer systems. The proposal got a boost in 2000 when the Northwestern Division engineer, Brig. Gen. Carl Strock, attended a dedication ceremony at the Celilo fishing site across Interstate 84 from Celilo Village. At a feast staged by the villagers after the ceremony, Strock got a look at the derelict buildings and dysfunctional utilities. "Let's fix it," he told Miller. Later that year Congress added three words—"and Celilo Village"—to the original project authorization. The legislation also provided for reviving the Wyam Board, the village's governing council made up of representatives of the fishing tribes and village residents. No appropriation went with the authorization for reconstruction, but the Corps had some money available. It asked the Wyam Board what the first piece of work should be. The response was emphatic: fix the deteriorating longhouse. The Corps had money enough to do the construction but not enough to buy the needed materials. The Confederated Tribes of Warm Springs stepped in, exchanging wood from its tribally owned mills for the needed type of lumber from a private company. "It helps to have your boss support your project," said Miller.

The new longhouse was built on the footprint of the old and with the same design except for a larger and more modern kitchen, where food is prepared for ceremonies such as the first salmon feast. Most of the tribal people seem pleased with the new structure, although one said it seemed smaller than the old longhouse and another that the atmosphere in the new building was different. The longhouse was important "to show that it was not just the impact [of the dams] on the fish but to acknowledge that the fish are fundamental to our beliefs," said Jaime Pinkham, a Nez Perce tribal member and a fish commission administrator. He said the refurbishing of Celilo Village "can be a tremendous step in overcoming the damage to our way of life."

Design work on the village restoration is being completed in 2006 and construction of new water and sewer systems and temporary housing is scheduled for 2007, with the permanent homes to be built in 2008 and 2009. That should complete the Corps' fulfillment of that 1939 promise nearly seventy years after it was made.

However, there may be more. Some say the original agreement did not provide for housing, but more people have begun to acknowledge the inequities that occurred when the dams were built. The corps replaced entire non-Indian towns, including homes, that were flooded. Indians lost not only their places to fish but the places they lived. Only Celilo Village was rebuilt for Indian people.

The Yakama Nation has long pushed for more housing for the displaced river people. After the feast at Celilo Village in 2000, Randy Settler, then a member of the Yakama Tribal Council, took Strock to places the fishing people live: Lone Pine, Celilo, and Cloudville high in the hills above the Columbia on the Washington shore. Cloudville, the village of Yakama elder and longtime council member Louie Cloud, is made up of small houses and shacks occupied by families displaced by dams in the 1950s and 1960s. Residents obtain their water from wells and use propane generators for heat and cooking. There is no electricity. Settler points out the irony of Indians losing their homes to dams that produce billions of kilowatts of electricity yet having no access to that power. Yakama Chairwoman Washines hopes the tour had an effect on the general. She says when all the Indian housing lost to the dams has been replaced at no cost to the tribal people, the Corps will have lived up to its promise.

A by-product of the fishing site construction project has been the success of a tribally owned business, Colville Tribal Services Corp. The company is part of the economic development arm of the Confederated Tribes of the

Colville Reservation in Washington state. In combination with Delbert Wheeler Construction Co., owned by Yakama tribal member Wheeler, it won a competitive bid for the first batch of sites in 1996. Colville did much of the later work, the first by competitive bid and later by negotiated contracts under the Small Business Administration small and diversity program. Most of Colville's subcontractors have been Indian-owned and the projects have hired Indians from the river and elsewhere. "It has worked fairly well," Miller said. "We have been getting fair and reasonable prices. Colville does excellent work." The firm won the Corps award as contractor of the year in the Pacific Northwest. Wheeler has left the construction business and moved into other enterprises.

One paragraph from the late-1999 version of this epilogue could remain almost unchanged: "Meanwhile, as always, other battles continue over issues that will make the fishing sites viable, and some new ones have been added. Most critical of those battles is the regional effort to restore threatened and endangered salmon runs. Arguments go to the purpose of salmon restoration, whether it is to retain remnant runs of genetically pure wild fish or to rebuild abundantly fishable numbers of salmon. The tribes support breaching four Snake River dams, which would return the river to a more nearly natural state to make passage easier for migrating fish. That action also would destroy the power-producing capacity of the dams and end barge traffic on the Snake. The economic interests that pushed for half a century to get the dams built have not lost their political strength—and they adamantly oppose altering the dams. At stake is Lewiston's boast that it is 'Idaho›s only seaport.' The barge companies that transport petroleum products upriver and wheat downriver, the wheat farmers of eastern Oregon and eastern Washington, and the little port cities along the Columbia and Snake rivers all oppose removing the earthen portions of the dams to let the river flow. So do marina operators on the shores of the dam-created lakes and other recreation interests. The states of Oregon, Washington, Idaho, and Montana and Congress, along with several federal agencies, are involved in the controversy. However, unlike the dam-building battles of the 1940s, 1950s, and 1960s, the tribes' voices are being heard in the dam-destroying controversy."

All that remains true, but by 2006, the tribes have found themselves less often fighting alone. To some extent, the river battles have united Indian and sports fishers against lower-river and ocean commercial fishers and other major economic interests on the river—electrical power, barge traffic, and irrigation. At several of the treaty sites native and non-Indian sport fishers share boat ramps and river access. The tribes have been reaching out to work with other interest groups. The Confederated Tribes of the Umatilla Indian Reservation made agreements with irrigators on the Umatilla and Walla Walla rivers that led to hatchery construction, habitat improvement, and more salmon returning to the streams. During the 2006 Memorial Day weekend, in downtown Pendleton, Oregon, non-Indian fishers caught more than 180 fish from a run that was rebuilt from the Umatilla tribal hatchery. The tribe also received a portion of $200 million available under new Washington state water legislation and is using the money for studies and planning. Indian success with hatcheries has helped slow the demise of the salmon.

There is still opposition to Indian fishing and to the Indian sites but the criticism seems have become more muted as tribes gain political sophistication and become larger contributors to their area's economies. The Yakama tribe, for example created its own electric utility that takes power produced on a Yakima [cq] River dam to fuel the tribal lumber mill. The tribe also has a plant that makes juice concentrates and bottles water, selling its products to Costco under contract, and owns a professional basketball team in the Continental Basketball Association. The Umatilla tribes bought the truck stop between their casino and Interstate 84 and the land surrounding the freeway interchange. "We have the vision and staff capability to lay out business parks and money to construct them," said Antone Minthorn, chairman of the Umatilla Board of Trustees.

Minthorn, who also is chairman of the Wyam Board, said one reason tribes are optimistic about restoring the salmon runs is, "We have capability we did not have years ago. Then, no one challenged the dams ... Now the tribes have fisheries biologists, attorneys, analysts. We can go one on one and begin negotiating solutions with the agencies, irrigators, and recreation people. They also respond to CRITFC." He also noted that Upper Columbia River tribes are organizing as the four lower river tribes did in the 1970s, and upper Snake River tribes on the Columbia's major tributary are entering the dispute. They still have a difficult battle. In mid-2006, the government has yet to write a recovery plan for Columbia River and Snake River salmon, but the options the agencies are considering do not include breaching the Snake River dams, which some studies have indicated is the only action that could assure long-term survival of the salmon. Instead, the White House announced it would emphasize reducing the number of fish caught and closing hatcheries that produce fish that compete with the wild runs.

As the population of the Pacific Northwest grew rapidly in the late twentieth century and first few years of the twenty-first, the Indians also found access to some of their other traditional foods affected. Huckleberries are popular with non-Indians too and the berry fields where tribal people have a treaty right to pick are being used by increasing numbers of others, including commercial pickers who have stripped, and sometimes destroyed, bushes. Traditional root food fields have vanished into development or been trampled by increasing crowds in wild areas.

Another contentious issue in the Gorge has changed little since 1999, except to divide tribes. In 1999, the Confederated Tribes of Warm Springs proposed building a casino in Cascade Locks, because the tribe's casino at its Kah-Nee-Ta Resort is far from major traffic routes. Cascade Locks had gone to Congress in the 1960s to keep an Indian fishing site out of the town, but in 1999 the city welcomed the casino plan with enthusiasm. Non-Indian anti-gambling and Columbia Gorge preservation groups that opposed a casino in the Gorge in 1999 continue their efforts to prevent the tribe from building. In addition, other tribes criticize allowing a casino off tribal land. The Confederated Tribes of the Grand Ronde Community, who operate the state's most successful casino on reservation land west of Portland, spent large sums of money in Oregon's 2006 primary election in a failed effort to defeat Gov. Ted Kulongoski, who had agreed to the Cascade Locks casino. The Grand Ronde then offered to finance a casino for Warm Springs if it were built on the Warm Springs Reservation, 100 miles south of I-84 and the river.

Economic and cultural shifts, embodied by the Cascade Locks about-face, are only a part of the ever-changing circumstances surrounding the treaty-fishing sites. There also are changes for many of the people involved in developing the sites and many who supplied information for this book. Many of those who played key roles in the long-running drama did not survive to see the work completed. Among them are Howard Jim, the longtime chief at Celilo Village; Eugene Greene Sr. of Warm Springs, who served as chairman of CRITFC; Frederick Ike Sr., longtime Yakama member of the In-Lieu Site Task Force; and the feisty Myra Sohappy. Two of the federal attorneys who fought the court battles, George Dysart and Sidney I. Lezak, also have died. Others who played parts have moved on to new challenges. Ted Strong relinquished his post as executive director of the Columbia River Inter-Tribal Fish Commission after nearly ten years and returned to the Yakama Reservation as a base for his economic and fisheries consulting business. Strong was replaced by Donald G. Sampson, a fisheries biologist and former chairman of the Umatilla Board of Trustees, who in turn was succeeded by Olney Patt Jr., who had served as chairman of the Warm Springs Tribes. Sampson returned to the Umatilla Reservation and became the tribe's chief operating officer. Randy Settler moved from fishing dissident to Yakama Tribal Council member and chairman of the tribal Fish, Wildlife and Law and Order Committee. He later joined the site maintenance staff and continued fishing. Duane Clark also was elected to the Yakama Council and joined Settler on the fisheries committee. Tribal nemesis Slade Gorton was defeated in his bid for reelection to the Senate in 2000 with the narrow margin supplied largely by a greatly increased turnout of Indian voters. Senator Mark Hatfield retired in 1996 but continued to lend his voice to causes such as the Institute of Tribal Government at Portland State University.

Although people move on to new positions and tribal leadership changes, the tribes' objective remains the same. In the words of Donald Sampson, "Our people's desire is simple—to preserve the fish, to preserve our way of life, now and for future generations." The in-lieu and treaty sites are part of that. To the tribes, completing the sites is in some measure symbolic. It will show that the federal government will keep a promise to the Indians— eventually. The continuing effort also is an indication of the tribes' faith that the salmon will come back. In the spring of 1999, Warm Springs Chief Delvis Heath Sr. urged fellow members of the In-Lieu Site Task Force to keep working. "Maybe there are no fish," he said, "but at least we will have something of the promise. We never got to hear the roar of the (Celilo) falls. The fish will come back some day. We are getting ready."

By 2006 much of the 1939 promise has been fulfilled and the Corps of Engineers is working on the final phase. The promise will be kept even though it is nearly three quarters of a century late.

# ACKNOWLEDGMENTS

Many individuals have contributed to this book. I am especially grateful to the tribal people who shared with me the experiences of their lives. A full list of those who granted interviews is included in the note on sources, but there are several to whom I owe extra thanks for providing access to information or special insights into the Indian people's long struggle to see a promise kept.

Sophie George, a Yakama tribal member whose exquisite bead work has gained national recognition, introduced me to members of her extended family of fishing people and to others of her tribe. She herself provided much valuable information.

Chief Nelson Wallulatum of the Wasco Tribe not only shared his own story, but encouraged others to help me. Jay Minthorn, Umatilla tribal councilman, provided valuable records and access to the In-Lieu Site Task Force. William Yallup Sr., Frederick Ike Sr., and Johnson Meninick voiced insights both as members of affected fishing families and as Yakama tribal leaders.

Cascade Chief Johnny Jackson, Nathan Jim Sr. of Warm Springs, Myra Sohappy of Yakama, and Ted Strong of the Columbia River Inter-Tribal Fish Commission all were especially helpful.

Of those outside the Indian community I owe the greatest thanks to Joyce Justice of the National Archives and Records Administration Pacific Northwest Region in Seattle. She guided my search through massive files of the Bureau of Indian Affairs and land records. George J. Miller of the Corps of Engineers opened the Corps files for research and patiently answered questions. Lynda Walker of the Corps was extremely helpful. Marian Peterson guided me through BIA records in Portland. Laurie Jordan provided me with records of key court decisions compiled by the Columbia River Inter-Tribal Fish Commission and with other information.

U.S. District Court Judge Owen Panner, long-time Warm Springs attorney, graciously searched his old files for valuable information and added much to my understanding in an extended interview.

Portland attorney Gary M. Berne gave me access to the extensive files from his dogged pursuit of justice that confirmed the Sohappys' and Johnny Jackson's right to remain in their homes.

Jeanie Senior provided information, corrections, and photographs. William L. Lang made valuable suggestions in editing this work. Professor Gordon B. Dodds of Portland State University earns my thanks for first suggesting that the in-lieu sites would make a book.

Without the encouragement, patience and computer expertise of John R. Lynch this book would never have been finished.

There are many views of the events recorded in this book. The interpretations here, based on those views, are entirely my own. So are any errors that appear.

# A NOTE ON SOURCES

As is usual with history, documents tell the government's version of the story. And so it is with the in-lieu sites—files of the Army Corps of Engineers and the Bureau of Indian Affairs tell a largely bureaucratic story of a marathon bureaucratic tangle. None of the tribal representatives involved in the beginning of this story are still alive. But the story itself remains alive in the tribal leaders, the families of those early negotiators, and the fishing people whose lives remain affected by the loss of fishing sites.

So this book has two major sources: government files and the memories of people involved. In addition, there were a dozen relevant secondary sources.

Documents, correspondence, and other material of the Bureau of Indian Affairs came from the National Archives and Records Administration Northwest Regional Depository in Seattle, Record Group G, Boxes 114 and 115, Yakima Indian Agency, and Boxes 6, 10, 11, 12, Field Agent, The Dalles, and from the BIA Portland Area Office files entitled In-Lieu Sites, Columbia River Damage to Salmon Fishing through Bonneville Dam, and Celilo and Spearfish, etc.

Corps of Engineers documents came from the files of the Portland District.

Much material was in boxes 1, 4, 5, and 6 of the plaintiff's files in Sohappy v. Hodel in the law offices of Stoll Stoll Berne Lokting & Schlachter PC in Portland.

State involvement was documented in the archives of the states of Washington and Oregon: Washington Department of Fisheries, boxes 9 and 10, and papers of Governor Daniel Evans of Washington, Box 1 Administrative Correspondence; and Governor Douglas McKay of Oregon, Accession number 57-98, Boxes 6 and 10, Oregon Fish Commission.

Other material came from the Columbia River Inter-Tribal Fish Commission, the Yakama Nation Library Bob Pace Collection, and files of the Confederated Tribes of the Umatilla Indian Reservation.

---

*A fully annotated manuscript of this work is available in the Oregon Historical Society Research Library.*

Newspaper accounts, mostly from *The Oregonian* and the *Oregon Journal* in Portland in the 1930s, 1940s, and 1960s provided general information on construction of the dams. *Oregonian* files from 1982 through 1991 were a major source, along with my own contemporary notes and Jeanie Senior's files, on the David Sohappy case.

The following people provided information that ranged from full-scale accounts to bits and facts that filled in the mosaic:

From the Confederated Tribes of the Warm Springs Indian Reservation: Delbert Frank Sr., Eugene Greene Sr., Chief Delvis Heath Sr., Ernest Hunt, Zane Jackson, Nathan Jim Sr., Olney Patt Sr., Ernest Scanawah, Nat Shaw, Dorothy Simtustus, Chief Nelson Wallulatum, Reginald Winishut.

From the Yakama Indian Nation: Virginia Beavert, Duane Clark, Fred Colfax, Rory Snowarrow FlintKnife, Frank Gunnier, Margie Gunnier, Robert Gunnier, Virginia Harrison, Elizabeth Henry, Duane Ike, Frederick Ike Sr., Russell Jim, Richard LaCourse, Agnes Lopez, Jerry Meninick, Johnson Meninick, Mel Sampson, Mamie Jim Smith, Johnson "Chief" Speedis, Walter Speedis, Sylvester Spino, Lillian Tahkeal, Terry Goudy Tecumseh, Lavina Washines, Delbert Wheeler, Merris Whiz, Mildred Whiz, William Yallup Sr.

From the Confederated Tribes of the Umatilla Indian Reservation: Thomas E. Bailor, N. Kathryn Brigham, Percy Brigham, William H. Burke, Alphonse Halfmoon, Mary Lavador, Antone Minthorn, Jay Minthorn, Malissa Minthorn, Art Parr.

From the river: Ed Edmo, Ada Frank, Sophie George, Johnny Jackson, Howard Jim, Karen Jim, Marion Lewis, Margaret Saluskin, Randy Settler, Myra Sohappy, Lonna St. Martin, Chuck Williams.

From the Columbia River Inter-Tribal Fish Commission: Jeff Curtis, Laurie Jordan, Roy Sampsel, Ted Strong, S. Timothy Wapato.

Tribal attorneys and lobbyists: Howard G. Arnett, James Hovis, Charles F. Luce, Owen M. Panner, Mark W.A. Phillips, George Waters, Tim Weaver.

State and federal fisheries officials: Burnie Bohn, Jack Donaldson, Richard T. Pressey, Robert W. Schoning.

Other government officials: Chuck James, Sidney I. Lezak, George J. Miller, Stanley Speaks, Catherine Vandemoer.

Others: Gary M. Berne, Reid Peyton Chambers, Kenneth H. Gardner, Tom Hampson, Joe Mentor Jr., Gladys Seufert.

## DOCUMENTS CITED

**Federal government:**

*Briefing Book on Indian In-Lieu Fishing Sites and Fisheries Law Enforcement on the Columbia River between Bonneville and McNary Dams* (Portland, Columbia River Inter-Tribal Fish Commission, for Senator Daniel J. Evans, 1988).

George W. Gordon, *Report on the subject of fishing privileges etc. guaranteed by treaties to Indians of the Northwest with recommendations in regard thereto*, (U. S. Department of the Interior, Indian Service, Jan. 19, 1889)

House Document 531, Appendix Q, Vol. VII, Flood Control Act, May 17, 1950

Kenneth L. Liscom and Lowell C. Stuehrenburg, "Radio Tracking Studies of 'Upriver Bright' Fall Chinook Salmon between Bonneville and McNary Dams, 1982," (draft) (Seattle, National Oceanic and Atmospheric Administration, March 1983)

Lisa Mighetto, Wesley J. Ebel, *Saving the Salmon, A History of the U.S. Army Corps of Engineers' Efforts to Protect Anadromous Fish on the Columbia and Snake Rivers*, (Seattle, Historical Research Associates, Inc., Sept. 6, 1994).

Public Law 14, Chapter 19, 79th Congress, First Session, 1945

Public Law 82, 84th Congress, Chapter 131, First Session, HR3879, Mar. 2, 1955

Public Law 163, 84th Congress, First Session, July 15, 1955

Public Law 96-561, 96th Congress, Second Session, Dec. 22, 1980

Public Law 97-79, 97th Congress, First Session, Nov. 16, 1981

Portland District, Army Corps of Engineers, *Columbia River Treaty Fishing Access Sites, Final Phase Two Evaluation Report and Finding of No Significant Impact/Environmental Assessment*, April 1995

Select Committee on Indian Affairs, United States Senate, Oversight Hearing on Columbia River Indian Fisheries Management, April 19, 1988, transcript

Edward G. Swindell Jr., *Report on the Source, Nature and Extent of Indian Fishing, Hunting and Miscellaneous Related Rights of Certain Indian Tribes in Washington and Oregon* (Los Angeles, United States Department of the Interior, Office of Indian Affairs, Division of Forestry and Grazing, July 1942)

Leon E. Truesdell, supervisor, *Sixteenth Census of the United States: 1940 Population, Vol. 3 "The Labor Force,"* Part 4: Nebraska-Oregon (Washington, United States Government Printing Office).

United States Civil Rights Commission, *Indian Tribes, A Continuing Quest for Survival,* (Washington, D.C., Commission on Civil Rights, 1981)

**State:**

Status Report, *Columbia River Fish Runs and Fisheries, 1938-1994* (Oregon Department of Fish and Wildlife and Washington Department of Fish and Wildlife, 1995)

**Court cases cited:**

Confederated Tribes of the Umatilla Indian Reservation et al v. Howard Calloway et. al, Civil No. 72-211, (U.S. District Court, Oregon)

Confederated Tribes and Bands v. Baldridge, Civil No. C80-342T (W.D. Wash.)

Maison v. Confederated Tribes of the Umatilla Reservation, 314 F 2nd 169 (1963), Ninth Circuit Court of Appeals

Puget Sound Gillnetters Ass'n v. United States District Court, 573 F. 2nd 1123, 1126 (1978)

Puyallup Tribe v. Dept. of Game of Washington, 391 U.S. 392 (1968) (Puyallup I).

Settler v. Lameer, 507 F. 2nd 231 (Ninth Circuit Court of Appeals 1974)

Seufert Brothers v. U.S. 249 U.S. 194 (1918) 381.

Sohappy v. Hodel, Civil No. 86-715-JU (U. S. District Court, District of Oregon)

Sohappy v. Smith (United States v. Oregon), 302, F Supp., 899 (D.Or. 9)

Tulee v. State of Washington, 315 U.S. 682 (1942)

United States v. David Sohappy, Sr., et al., CR82-51T (U.S. Dist Court, W.D. Wash.)

United States v. Washington, 384 F. Supp. 312 (W.D. Wash. 1974); Civil No. 9213 Phase II (Jan. 16, 1981)

United States v. Winans, 198 U.S. 371 (1905) 199.

U.S. v. 594,464 pounds of salmon, more or less, (Civil; C86-666TB, U.S. District Court, W.D. Wash.) (1986)

Washington et al v. Washington State Passenger Fishing Vessel, 443, U.S. 658 (1979)